EMPLOYMENT TRIBUNAL REMEDIES HANDBOOK

2014-15 Edition

General Editor

James Wynne

Littleton Chambers

Foreword

Judge Brian Doyle

President

Employment Tribunals (England & Wales)

BATH PUBLISHING

First edition

Published April 2014

ISBN 978 0 95677 741 6

Text © Bath Publishing Limited

Typography © Bath Publishing Limited

Bath Publishing Limited
27 Charmouth Road
Bath
BA1 3LJ
Tel: 0870 165 1443

email: info@bathpublishing.co.uk
www.bathpublishing.co.uk

Bath Publishing Limited is a company registered in England: 5209173
Registered Office: As above

FOREWORD

Many Employment Judges will tell you that parties in Employment Tribunal litigation – whether professionally represented or not – often treat the question of remedy as an afterthought or as something that will be dealt with by the Tribunal in due course. My training as a judge has taught me over the last 20 years that one of the first questions to ask a claimant, whether at a case management hearing or at the outset of the final hearing, is what do you seek to achieve if you were to win your case? It is surprising how often a litigant in person or a legally represented party has given relatively little thought and analysis to what their claim is worth or what reductions to their expectations might have to be anticipated. The introduction of early conciliation and of tribunal fees means that such an approach to the valuation of a prospective claim is a luxury that neither prospective party can afford to indulge.

In recent years both standard and bespoke case management orders almost invariably require a claimant to prepare and to serve a statement or schedule of loss and remedy, addressing mitigation of loss as well as the calculation of remedy. In some cases, a counter-schedule might be appropriate or required of the respondent. Employment Judges hope that by this process both parties will give careful consideration to what a claim might be worth, taking account of the various permutations that might arise. The claimant might win on all counts, but what if they only succeed in part of the claim? What heads of loss might arise for consideration by the Tribunal? What are the chances that those heads of loss will be awarded or capped or time limited or excluded altogether? How do you value non-monetary loss, such as loss of a chance or injury to feelings or personal injury? What effect does interest or taxation or recoupment have upon the award? These and many other questions need to be in the forefront of the thinking of the parties and their representatives at the very earliest stages of Employment Tribunal litigation.

In the last couple of years I have been very pleased to be associated (as judicial representative) with the advisory board behind the successful launch by Bath Publishing of its Employment Claims Toolkit. This sophisticated online calculator not only takes the stress out of what are often quite complex calculations, but should give parties, practitioners and judges considerable confidence that they have accounted for all possible heads of loss and remedy and the variables that might inflate or deflate them. However, just as a school student using a calculator also has to understand the basic rules of arithmetic that underpin their calculations, so too does a party using the Toolkit need to understand the basic principles of remedies.

In that context, the publication of the Employment Tribunal Remedies Handbook 2014 is very welcome. Its General Editor, James Wynne, together with the editorial team at Bath Publishing, has added an important resource to the employment law library and one which should be readily accessible to all who use the Employment Tribunal system, whether represented or self-represented.

Judge Brian Doyle

President

Employment Tribunals (England & Wales)

16 April 2014

INTRODUCTION

This handbook, in an A-Z dictionary format, is intended to make the law and practice of tribunal remedies more readily accessible to lawyers, HR professionals, trade union representatives and indeed anyone representing themselves in an employment dispute. The handbook will be relevant throughout the life of every tribunal claim, whether for valuing a claim before proceedings have started, during negotiation and mediation, or identifying the relevant principles at a tribunal hearing.

Each employment right that can be enforced in an employment tribunal is summarised, followed by the principles that will be applied to any remedies. For example, the common claims of unfair dismissal, discrimination and detriment are covered, and also all the numerous less litigated rights such as time off for study and training and the right of a TUPE transferee to be notified of employee liability information. For each such entry the nature of any award is set out, such as the route to calculate a basic award or the principles that will be applied to calculate a compensatory award.

There are also separate entries for each element of a remedy and the principles used in its calculation, such as mitigation, loss of chance, tax and termination payments, grossing up, order of adjustments, recoupment, the definition of a week's pay, and many other elements of a remedy calculation. Each entry is cross-referenced to others, so it is possible to start anywhere in the book when a specific issue arises, not just at the particular right that is being enforced.

The text is supported by worked examples, to show clearly how the law is applied. 40 essential tables are included with up to date information on caps, limitation periods, fees, National Minimum Wage rates and much more, so that the information needed is always to hand.

The book will be republished annually to ensure that the information within it is up to date. A digital version will also be available for use on a computer, tablet and an e-reader.

I would welcome any suggestions for improvement or additions for subsequent editions. Please send any comments to the publishers at info@bathpublishing.co.uk.

James Wynne

Littleton Chambers

April 2014

ALSO AVAILABLE FROM BATH PUBLISHING

Employment Claims Toolkit

The perfect companion to this book, the Employment Claims Toolkit takes all the rules and calculations presented here and puts them into practice by allowing you to create flexible, adjustable, accurate statements of remedy.

Find out more at www.employmentclaimstoolkit.co.uk

Employment Cases Update

The full text of every employment case from the EAT, High Court, Court of Appeal and Supreme Court in a single source and free to view. We have been publishing since 2010 and the site now contains over 1,800 cases with short summaries, keywords and links to other cases cited.

You can also subscribe to our CPD service which transforms your reading into fully accredited CPD for only £75 a year.

Visit www.employmentcasesupdate.co.uk to sign up for our free weekly email or to browse the cases.

CONTENTS

Contents

Contents

Contents

STATUTES

STATUTORY INSTRUMENTS

CASES

ACAS (The Advisory, Conciliation and Arbitration Service)

(see also Adjustments)

An award for compensation can be increased or reduced, by up to 25%, if the employer/employee has unreasonably failed to comply with a relevant code of practice relating to the resolution of disputes (see s207(A) TULRC(A) 1992). A relevant code of practice will have been issued either by ACAS or the Secretary of State under ss199 to 206 TULR(C)A . At present ACAS Code of Practice 1: Disciplinary and Grievance procedures (2009) is the only relevant code of practice.

The full list of tribunal jurisdictions to which s207A applies is detailed in Schedule A2 of TULR(C)A:

- s120 and s127 of the Equality Act 2010 (discrimination etc in work cases);

- s145A TULR(C)A (inducements relating to union membership or activities);

- s145B TULR(C)A (inducements relating to collective bargaining);

- s146 TULR(C)A (detriment in relation to union membership and activities);

- Paragraph 156 of Schedule A1 TULR(C)A (detriment in relation to union recognition rights);

- s23 of the Employment Rights Act 1996 (unauthorised deductions and payments);

- s48 of ERA 1996 (detriment in employment);

- s111 of ERA 1996 (unfair dismissal);

- s163 of ERA 1996 (redundancy payments);

- s24 of the National Minimum Wage Act 1998 (detriment in relation to national minimum wage);

- The Employment Tribunals Extension of Jurisdiction (England and Wales) Order 1994 (SI 1994/1623) (breach of employment contract and termination);

- The Employment Tribunals Extension of Jurisdiction (Scotland) Order 1994 (SI 1994/1624) (corresponding provision for Scotland);

- Regulation 30 of the Working Time Regulations 1998 (SI 1998/1833) (breach of regulations);

- Regulation 32 of the Transnational Information and Consultation of Employees Regulations 1999 (SI 1999/3323) (detriment relating to European Works Councils);

- Regulation 45 of the European Public Limited-Liability Company Regulations 2004 (SI 2004/2326) (detriment in employment);

- Regulation 33 of the Information and Consultation of Employees Regulations 2004 (SI 2004/3426) (detriment in employment);

- Paragraph 8 of the Schedule to the Occupational and Personal Pension Schemes (Consultation by Employers and Miscellaneous Amendment) Regulations 2006 (SI 2006/349) (detriment in employment);

- Regulation 34 of the European Cooperative Society (Involvement of Employees) Regulations 2006 (SI 2006/2059) (detriment in relation to involvement in a European Cooperative Society);

- Regulation 17 of the Cross-border Railway Services (Working Time) Regulations 2008 (SI 2008/1660) (breach of regulations);

- Regulation 9 of the Employment Relations Act 1999 (Blacklists) Regulations 2010 (SI 2010/493) (detriment connected with prohibited list).

Order of Adjustments: Where a compensatory award for unfair dismissal falls to be adjusted for unreasonable failure to comply with a relevant code of practice, the adjustment is applied immediately before any reduction for contributory conduct (s123(6)) or reduction due to the receipt of an enhanced redundancy payment in excess of the basic award (s123(7)) (see s124A(a) and Basic award, Compensatory award, Contributory conduct, Redundancy).

Example 1

An ex-employee is awarded a basic award of £2,000, a compensatory award of £3,000 and damages for breach of contract of £500. The employer is found to have unreasonably failed to comply with a relevant code of practice and an uplift of 25% is applied to the applicable awards. The calculation would be as follows:

The basic award remains as £2,000 because the uplift does not apply to this award.

The compensatory award is now £3,000 x 1.25 = £3,750

The damages for wrongful dismissal are now £500 x 1.25 = £625

Example 2

An ex-employee would be awarded a basic award of £2,000, a compensatory award of £3,000 and damages for breach of contract of £500. However he received an enhanced redundancy payment of £2,500. The employee is found to have unreasonably failed to comply with a relevant code of practice and a deduction of 25% is applied to the applicable awards. The calculation would be as follows:

The basic award is reduced to zero because of the enhanced redundancy payment, but there remains £500 of enhanced redundancy payment to put into the calculation of the compensatory award: £2,500 - £2,000 = £500

The compensatory award is now (£3,000 x 0.75) - £500 = £1,750

The damages for wrongful dismissal are now £500 x 0.75 = £375

Statutory authorities: ERA 1996 s123(6), 123(7) and s124A(a); TULR(C)A Schedule A2

Accelerated payment

(see also Adjustments; Table 23; Table 24)

If an award is made to a claimant to compensate for losses they would have suffered in the future, they are in fact receiving the money before they would have it if they hadn't been dismissed. The idea behind the discount for accelerated payment, therefore, is to take into account any percentage interest that might in fact be earned on this money when it wouldn't ordinarily have been available to the claimant to earn interest.

A discount for accelerated payment can be made on awards for future loss, including the compensatory award and an award for financial losses in a discrimination claim. The reduction will only apply to future losses of course, such as future income and benefits.

No award will need be made if the award for future loss is relatively small, as will often be the case (see *Les Ambassadeurs Club v Bainda* [1982] IRLR 5).

There is no established route to calculate the appropriate reduction. Tribunals sometimes merely apply a single percentage adjustment to

recognise accelerated receipt - however, in *Bentwood Bros (Manchester) Ltd v Shepherd* [2003] IRLR 364 the Court of Appeal overturned a decision to make a single 5% reduction for an award that covered 10 years loss. It will always be necessary for a tribunal to set out the method it has used and its reasons for using it.

A tribunal may choose to use a similar approach to that used (but in the opposite situation) to calculate the interest due on an award paid after the loss has been incurred. Under Regulation 3(1) of The Industrial Tribunal (Interest on awards in Discrimination Cases) Regulations 1996 interest is awarded on financial losses as simple interest accruing from day to day at a specified rate of interest. Interest is calculated from the mid-point date, half way between the act of discrimination and the date of the calculation.

Until 29 July 2013 the interest rate to be applied in England and Wales was that prescribed for the special investment account under rule 27(1) of the Court Funds Rules 1987 which was 0.5%. For claims presented on or after 29 July 2013 the relevant interest rate is that specified in s17 of the Judgments Act 1838 (see The Employment Tribunals (Interest on Awards in Discrimination Cases)(Amendment) Regulations 2013). The interest rate now to be applied is 8% which is in line with Scotland (see Table 23 for a list of interest rates).

Another approach would be to apply half the rate of interest for the whole period of loss.

The accelerated payment calculation should only be applied to the net sum available to the claimant, since it is the net sum that would be available to earn interest.

Where significant sums are awarded for significant periods of time, it may be appropriate to invite a tribunal to use the Ogden tables to calculate a sum suitably discounted for accelerated receipt and contingencies (see Table 24).

Example

If the future sum awarded is £10,000 and a discount percentage of 0.5% is to be applied over a period of 5 years the amount to be awarded will be calculated as follows:

Look down the left hand side of Table 24 and choose a term of 5. Look across to a percentage rate of 0.5. The discount factor is 0.9754. Multiply 10,000 by 0.9754 to get a figure of £9,754.

Adjustments: The discount for accelerated receipt

should be made within the first stage of any calculation, namely calculating the loss suffered by the individual. Any adjustments will be made afterwards (see also *Adjustments*).

Statutory authorities: None

Relevant case law: *Benchmark Dental Laboratories Group v Perfitt* EAT/0304/04; *Bentwood Bros (Manchester) Ltd v Shepherd* [2003] EWCA Civ 380; *Les Ambassadeurs Club v Bainda* [1982] IRLR 5; *York Trailer Co Ltd v Sparkes* [1973] IRLR 348

Accompanied at a disciplinary or grievance hearing, or to a flexible working meeting

A worker has the right to be accompanied at a grievance or disciplinary meeting (s10 and s11 ERelA 1999), at a meeting to discuss their right to flexible working meeting (s14 and s15 FW(PR) Regs 2002) or at a meeting to discuss their right to make a request in relation to study or training (s63D to 63K ERA 1996) (Reg 16 and Reg 17 EST(PR) Regs 2010) and a worker is allowed to have time off to accompany the other worker to the meeting. The worker is allowed to postpone the meeting in certain circumstances.

Remedy: Where a tribunal finds a complaint of a failure to comply well founded, it may make an award of up to 2 weeks pay.

Gross or net: Gross. A week's pay as defined in ss220 to 229 ERA 1996 applies (see *Week's pay*).

Limit on a week's pay: £464 (see Table 1 for historical rates).

Limit on number of weeks: 2

Any maximum or minimum: Maximum = £928; no minimum

Adjustments: None

Tax: The tax treatment relating to non-termination payments is not clear. If the claimant was claiming this head of loss alongside unfair or wrongful dismissal, it is arguable that any award under this head would be included in the compensatory award and therefore taxable under s401. If the claimant's employment has not been terminated however, it could be argued that no tax is payable - the award is not 'earnings', nor is

an award on termination of employment, or change of duties or earnings (see *Tax*).

Recoupment: N/A

Statutory authorities: ERelA 1999 ss10 and 11; ERA 1996 s63D to 63K; EST(PR) Regs 2010 (SI 2010/155) Regs 16 and 17; FW(PR) Regs 2002 (SI 2002/3207) Regs 14 and 15

Actual Notice Period

(see also Damages for wrongful dismissal)

It is important to know the actual notice given to the claimant, differentiated from the statutory or contractual notice period to which an employee would have been entitled, since this is used to calculate the damages to which he might be entitled.

Additional award

(see also Arrears of pay)

An additional award may be made where an employer has failed to comply with an order for reinstatement or re-engagement made under s113 ERA 1996, following a finding of unfair dismissal. See also s166 TULR(C)A 1992.

Remedy: The award differs according to whether there has been partial or total non-compliance. Only where there has been total non-compliance with the order will the additional award be made. In both cases, a separate award of compensation to cover financial losses will be made, subject to a statutory cap (see below).

Partial compliance: An award of compensation will be made, to be paid by the employer to the employee, if and order for reinstatement or re-engagement is made, but though the employee is reinstated or re-engaged, the terms of the order are not fully complied with (s117(1) ERA 1996).

The tribunal will award the amount it thinks fit having regard to the loss sustained by the employee in consequence of the failure to comply with the terms of the order, however there is no power to award an additional award for partial compliance.

Total non-compliance: If an order for reinstatement or re-engagement is made, but the employee is not reinstated or re-engaged, a compensatory award will be made under s124 ERA 1996 and an additional award of compensation of between twenty-six and fifty-two weeks pay will be made (s117(3)).

However, that additional award will not be made if the employer satisfies tribunal that it was not practicable to comply with the order, but the hiring of a permanent replacement will not satisfy this condition unless it was not practicable to arrange for the employee's work to be done without hiring a permanent replacement (s117(4) and s117(7)).

Calculation: Additional award = number of weeks x gross weekly pay

Gross or net: Gross. A week's pay as defined in ss220 to 229 ERA 1996 applies (see *Week's pay*).

Limit on a week's pay: £464 (see Table 1 for historical rates).

Limit on number of weeks: Minimum is 26; maximum is 52

Any maximum or minimum: Minimum depends on employee's gross weekly pay (but see National Minimum Wage); maximum is £24,128

Adjustments: The following applies to compensation (but does not apply to the additional award itself): where the claimant has unreasonably prevented an order for reinstatement or re-engagement from being complied with, and where the tribunal makes an award of compensation for losses suffered (see above) the tribunal will take that conduct into account as a failure on the part of the complainant to mitigate his loss.

Cap: The statutory cap applies to an award under s117(1) and (2) and s123. ERA 1996. The statutory cap is currently the lower of £76,574 or 52 weeks pay (as defined in ss220 to 229 ERA 1996) (see s124 ERA 1996). It should be noted that the cap will be lifted to the extent necessary to compensate for arrears of pay and any additional award:

- in the case of compensation awarded under s117(1) where the order for reinstatement or re-engagement has been partially complied with, the cap can be exceeded to the extent necessary to enable the award fully to reflect the amount specified as payable under s114(2)(a) or s115(2)(d) (see *Arrears of pay*). In other words, the employee is entitled to receive at least their arrears of pay, even if those arrears exceed the cap;

- in the case of an award under s117(3) (i.e. an award where the employer has not complied at all with an order for reinstatement re-engagement at all) the cap may be exceeded to the extent necessary to enable the aggregate of the compensatory and additional awards fully to reflect the amount specified as payable under s114(2)(a) or s115(2)(d) (See *National Westminster Bank Plc v Parry* [2004] EWCA Civ 1563).

This means that

- if the arrears of pay exceed the cap on their own, the individual will receive the total amount of arrears;

- if the arrears of pay do not exceed the cap on their own they will be offset against the compensatory award.

Mitigation: The additional award is not expressly related to an employee's losses, or to mitigation, however a tribunal may well take into account an employee's losses and attempts to mitigate those losses in reaching the amount of the award, particularly perhaps if the statutory cap prevents the employee's losses being fully recovered.

Tax: The additional award is taxable under s401 ITEPA 2003 (see *Tax*) and will fall to be grossed up where is award exceeds the £30,000 limit (see EIM12960, HMRC).

Recoupment: Recoupment does not apply to the additional award but it does apply to any compensation awarded under s123 as a result of non-compliance with s113 and to arrears of pay which may have been ordered by ss114 or 115.

Statutory authorities: ERA 1996 ss113 to 118

Relevant case law: *National Westminster Bank Plc v Parry* [2004] EWCA Civ 1563; *Selfridges Ltd v Malek* [1998] ICR 268

Example 1
Basic award = £3,000

Financial losses = maximum available for this employee (52 weeks) = £25,000

Additional award = £15,000

Arrears of pay = £5,000 (The arrears of pay are included within the compensatory award with the remaining losses capped at £25,000 - £5,000 = £20,000)

Award = £3,000 + £25,000 + £15,000 = £43,000

Example 2

Basic award = £3,000

Financial losses = zero

Statutory cap for this employee is £25,000 (52 weeks pay)

Additional award = zero (reinstatement or re-engagement order was partially complied with)

Arrears of pay = £28,000

Award = £3,000 + £28,000 = £31,000

Example 3

Basic award = £3,000

Financial losses = maximum available for this employee (52 weeks) = £30,000

Additional award = £25,000

Arrears of pay = £60,000

Aggregate of financial losses and additional award = £55,000, which is lower than the arrears of pay (£60,000) so replace the lower figure with £60,000.

Total Award = £3,000 + £60,000 = £63,000

Adjustments and order of adjustments

(see also ACAS Code of Practice; Accelerated payment; Contributory conduct; Interest; *Polkey*; Protected disclosure)

It is important that adjustments are applied to awards in the correct order since the outcome could be very different depending on the order chosen.

For example, looking at a very simple calculation, there are two possible answers to 2 x 3 + 4, depending on whether you do the multiplication first or the addition. If you do the multiplication first, the answer is 10; if you do the addition first, the answer is 14. Strictly mathematically speaking, the answer to the above calculation is 10, because multiplication takes precedence over addition: note 'BIDMAS', the order of operations being Brackets Indices, Division, Multiplication, Addition and Subtraction. However the order of adjustments follow specific legal rules, rather than any mathematical convention.

A demonstration of the importance of the order in which calculations are performed can be seen in *Digital Equipment Co Ltd v Clements* [1997] EWCA Civ 2899; [1998] ICR 258. For Mr Clements it was argued that the redundancy payment of £20,685 should be deducted from the compensatory award of £43,136 leaving a balance of £22,451; that figure should then be reduced by 50% (*Polkey*) giving a compensatory award of £11,275. This would result in the maximum of £11,000 (that being the maximum at the time) being payable. Digital argued that the tribunal should give them full credit for enhanced redundancy payment and first reduce the loss by 50% leaving a compensatory award of £21,568 from which the tribunal should then deduct the £20,685 leaving a balance of £883. The tribunal ruled in favour of the claimant, but the decision was overturned by the EAT and the Court of Appeal, leaving the claimant with £883.

Different adjustments apply to the different types of award - these adjustments, and the correct order in which they should be applied, are listed below.

Adjustments to the compensatory award

1) Calculate the total losses suffered by the claimant

2) A deduction in respect of any amounts received from the employer such as payment in lieu or ex gratia payment which has been made to the employee as compensation for the dismissal (*Digital Equipment Co Ltd v Clements* [1997] EWCA Civ 289. This must exclude any enhanced redundancy payment above the basic award.

3) A deduction of earnings which have mitigated the claimant's loss or a sum which reflects any failure by the claimant's failure to mitigate his/her loss (ERA s123(4)) 1996 (see also *Mitigation*)

4) A '*Polkey*' deduction to reflect the chance that the claimant would have been dismissed in any event and that the employer's procedural errors accordingly made no difference to the outcome (*Polkey v AE Dayton Services Ltd* [1987] IRLR 50 (HL)) (see also *Polkey*)

5) A deduction for accelerated payment of compensation in respect of future loss (*Bentwood Bros (Manchester) Ltd v Shepherd* [2003] EWCA Civ 380) (see also *Accelerated payment*)

6) A percentage increase or reduction up to a maximum of 25% to reflect a failure by the employer or employee to comply with the ACAS disciplinary code (s207A TULR(C)A) (see *ACAS*)

7) From 25 June 2013 - percentage reduction, up to a maximum of 25%, if a protected disclosure was not made in good faith (see also *Protected disclosure*)

8) An extra award for any failure by the employer to provide written particulars of employment (s38 EA 2002) (see also *Written particulars*)

9) A percentage reduction for any contributory conduct on the part of the employee (s123(6) ERA 1996). Please note that this percentage does not have to be same as any deduction for contributory conduct for the basic award (see also *Contributory conduct*)

10) A deduction of any enhanced redundancy payment to the extent that it exceeds the basic award (s123(7) ERA 1996) (see also *Enhanced redundancy*)

11) Interest on past losses, if available (see also *Interest*)

12) Grossing up calculation (see *Grossing up*)

13) Application of statutory cap if relevant (see *Statutory cap*)

Adjustments to the basic award

The basic award can be reduced in the following situations:

- By an amount that the tribunal considers to be just and equitable where the employee has unreasonably refused an offer of reinstatement (s122(1) ERA 1996);

- By an amount to reflect contributory conduct (s122(2) ERA 1996). Note though that s122(2) does not apply in redundancy cases except as provided for in s122(3) (see *Basic award and Basic award, minimum* below). A percentage reduction to reflect contributory conduct does not have to be the same as that for the compensatory award (note the case of *Granchester Construction (Eastern) Ltd v Attrill* UKEAT/0327/12/LA, where a 50% *Polkey* deduction was made to the compensatory award, and both the basic and compensatory awards were also reduced by 10%. The EAT said that 'Whereas it may be appropriate to moderate what would otherwise be the degree of contributory conduct that would reduce an award because there have been matters of conduct taken into account in assessing the chances of a fair dismissal, so that it might be in effect double counting to impose upon the claimant a further reduction

by way of contributory conduct, that reasoning cannot apply to that part of the award to which the *Polkey* principle itself does not apply' [i.e. the basic award];

- By any redundancy payment paid on termination for a genuine redundancy or ordered by the tribunal (but see also *Enhanced redundancy*) (s122(4) ERA 1996. Any excess goes towards reducing the compensatory award (see *Boorman v Allmakes* [1995] IRLR 553);

- By an amount that the tribunal considers to be just and equitable where the claimant has been awarded an amount under a designated dismissal procedures agreement (s122(3A));

- Where the dismissal is unfair by virtue of s104F (blacklists) the basic award will be reduced (or further reduced) by the amount of any basic award paid in respect of the same dismissal under s156 TULR(C)A (minimum basic award in case of dismissal on grounds related to trade union membership or activities).

The basic award cannot be:

- increased or decreased for the failure by the employer/employee to comply with the ACAS Code of Practice (see s124A and s118(1)(b) ERA 1996);

- increased following a failure to provide the employee with a written statement of terms and conditions of employment, as that increase is applied within the compensatory award (s38 EA 2002 and s124A and s118(1)(b) ERA 1996);

- reduced on account of the employee's failure to mitigate their loss;

- reduced where the tribunal considers this to be just and equitable;

- reduced under *Polkey* (unless it is an 'exceptionally rare case where such a (fair) dismissal might have taken place virtually contemporaneously with the unfair dismissal which actually occurred' - see again *Granchester Construction (Eastern) Ltd v Attrill* UKEAT/0327/12/LA, paragraph 19).

Minimum basic award under s120 ERA 1996

If the minimum award of £5,676 has been made because the principal reason for a redundancy dismissal was one of the reasons set out in s120(1) the figure may still be reduced for contributory conduct, but the percentage reduction is applied to the difference between what the claimant would have received under the standard case and the minimum £5,676. For example, if the claimant would only have received £2,000 but does in fact qualify for the minimum £5,676, any contributory conduct will be applied to the difference, i.e. £3,676.

Adjustments to a discriminatory award

1) Possibly contributory conduct (but see *Discrimination* for further information)

2) Failure to comply with the ACAS Code of Practice

3) Interest can be added to the awards for injury to feelings, physical and psychiatric injury, aggravated damages and the award for financial loss (see *Interest*)

4) Where a dismissal is both discriminatory and unfair, the tribunal should make the award for compensation under the discrimination legislation, but may also make a basic award (see *D'Souza v London Borough of Lambeth* [1997] IRLR 677).

Adjustments to damages for wrongful dismissal

Damages for wrongful dismissal can be adjusted in 3 ways:

1) An increase/decrease for the failure by the employer/employee to comply with the ACAS Code of Practice (see s207A and Schedule A2 of TULR(C)A)

2) A deduction for any contingencies and any accelerated payment of damages, which is only likely to arise where the (unexpired) period of notice under the contract is substantial

3) Interest may be awarded from the date of the cause of action to the date of the hearing but only the County Court, High Court and Court of Appeal have jurisdiction to award interest on a breach of contract claim - the ET does not.

Grossing up and the statutory cap

Grossing up is applied after all the adjustments have been applied (see also *Grossing up*).

The statutory cap is applied after the grossing up calculation (see also *Statutory cap*).

Example 1
Awards
Basic award = £3,000

Financial loss = £10,000

Adjustments
Contributory conduct (basic and compensatory awards) = 10%

ACAS uplift = 25%

Calculation
Total award = (£3,000 x 0.9) + (£10,000 x 0.9 x 1.25 but see note below) = £2,700 (basic award) + £11,250 (compensatory award) = £13,950

Note: if the adjustments involve only percentage increases or decreases, i.e without sums being added for written particulars or deducted for redundancy pay, it doesn't actually matter what order the increases/decreases are applied. In the example above, it wouldn't have mattered whether we had calculated the new compensatory award by doing £10,000 x 0.9 x 1.25 or £10,000 x 1.25 x 0.9 - the answer would have been the same.

It is also important to remember that adjustments are **multiplied** cumulatively. In other words, don't add/subtract the adjustment percentages to get the overall change (i.e. an increase of 25% and a decrease of 10% does **not** translate into an increase of 15%). The actual overall increase is 12.5% (because 1.25 x 0.9 = 1.125, where the .125 represents the 12.5%)

Example 2
Awards
Basic award = £3,000

Financial loss = £10,000

Award for lack of written particulars = 2 weeks pay = £600

Credits
Ex gratia payment = £500

Earnings = £750

Adjustments
Contributory conduct (basic and compensatory awards) = 10%

Polkey deduction = 30%

Calculation
Basic award = £3,000 x 0.9 = £2,700 (*Polkey* does not apply to the basic award).

The order of adjustments for the compensatory award must be carefully considered because we have a mixture of multiplication (contributory conduct) and addition/subtraction (lack of written particulars, ex gratia payment and earnings). It is important that the order given on the previous page is followed.

The financial loss has to be first reduced by £500

7

and £750 and then have the *Polkey* deduction applied = (£10,000 - £500 - £750) x 0.7 = £6,125

Next, the failure to provide written particulars has to be added = £6,125 + £600 = £6,725

Then contributory conduct has to be applied = £6,725 x 0.9 = £6,052.50

Total award = £2,700 (basic award) + £6,052.50 (compensatory award) = £8,752.50

Example 3
Awards
Basic award = £3,000

Financial loss = £10,000

Award for lack of written particulars = 2 weeks pay = £600

Credits
Ex gratia payment = £500

Earnings = £750

Redundancy pay paid on termination = £5,000

Adjustments
Contributory conduct (compensatory award only) = 10%

Polkey deduction = 30%

ACAS uplift = 15%

Calculation
First the basic award needs to be reduced by any redundancy pay received. The redundancy pay is greater than the basic award (so it is by definition greater than the statutory redundancy pay) so the basic award is zero. The remainder (£5,000 - £3,000 = £2,000) goes towards reducing the compensatory award, but only at the end of the calculation.

The financial loss has first to be reduced by £500 and £750 and then have the *Polkey* deduction and the ACAS uplift applied = (£10,000 - £500 - £750) x 0.7 x 1.15 = £7,043.75

Next, the failure to provide written particulars has to be added = £7,043.75 + £600 = £7,643.75

Then contributory conduct has to be applied = £7,643.75 x 0.9 = £6,879.38

Finally, the remainder of the redundancy pay should be deducted to the extent of the excess beyond the basic award = £6,879.38 - (£5,000 - £3,000) = £4,879.38

Total Award = £4,879.38

Example 4
This is identical to example 3 apart from the fact that the basic award also has contributory conduct applied to it.

Awards
Basic award = £3,000

Financial loss = £10,000

Award for lack of written particulars = 2 weeks pay = £600

Credits
Ex gratia payment = £500

Earnings = £750

Redundancy pay paid on termination = £5,000

Adjustments
Contributory conduct (basic **and** compensatory awards) = 10%

Polkey deduction = 30%

ACAS uplift = 15%

Calculation
First the basic award needs to be reduced for contributory conduct = £3,000 x 0.9 = £2,700
Next it should be reduced by any redundancy pay received. The redundancy pay is greater than the reduced basic award so the reduced basic award is zero. The remainder (£5,000 - £2,700 = £2,300) goes towards reducing the compensatory award, but only at the end of the calculation.

The financial loss first has to be reduced by £500 and £750 and then have the *Polkey* deduction and the ACAS uplift applied = (£10,000 - £500 - £750) x 0.7 x 1.15 = £7,043.75

Next, the failure to provide written particulars has to be added = £7,043.75 + £600 = £7,643.75

Then contributory conduct has to be applied = £7,643.75 x 0.9 = £6,879.38

Finally, the remainder of the redundancy pay should be deducted to the extent of the excess of the **reduced** basic award = £6,879.38 - £2,300 = £4,579.38

Total Award = £4,579.3

Statutory authorities: EA 2002 s38; ERA 1996 ss118(1)(b), 120, 122(1) & (2), 123(4), (6) & (7) and 124A; The Industrial Tribunals (Interest on Awards in Discrimination Cases) Regulations 1996; TULR(C)A s207A & Schedule A2

Relevant case law: *Bentwood Bros (Manchester) Ltd v Shepherd* [2003] EWCA Civ 380; *Digital Equipment Co Ltd v Clements* [1997] EWCA Civ 2899; *Granchester Construction (Eastern) Ltd v Attrill* UKEAT/0327/12/LA; *Hardie Grant London Ltd v Aspden* [2012] I.C.R. D6 (EAT); *Polkey v AE Dayton Services Ltd* [1987] IRLR 50 (HL)

Adoption leave: see Detriment; Unfair dismissal; Table 40

Age discrimination: see Discrimination

Aggravated damages

Aggravated damages are available in discrimination claims in England and Wales, but not in Scotland (where aggravating factors are taken into account in calculating the award for injury to feelings). Aggravated damages are reserved for outside the ordinary cases, the respondent must have acted in a high-handed, malicious, insulting or oppressive manner in committing the discrimination or in the manner in which the matter was handled, including the conduct of the hearing itself. For example, aggravated damages will not be awarded simply because the employee is upset, distressed or even injured (see *Singh v University Hospital NHS Trust* EAT/1409/01, *Ministry of Defence v Fletcher* [2009] UKEAT/0044/09; *Bungay & Anor v Saini & Ors* UKEAT/0331/10 and *Zaiwalla & Co v Walia* [2002] UKEAT/451/00).

Aggravated damages are a standalone head of compensation in England and Wales and should not be rolled up into the award for injury to feelings.

Remedy: There is no specific calculation but it would appear from the decided cases that £20,000 is the top end of the bracket for aggravated damages. The award is compensatory, not punitive. There is no minimum award.

Adjustments: Interest can be applied (see also *Interest*) but no other adjustments are applicable.

Mitigation: N/A

Tax: The award is likely to be treated in the same way as an award for injury to feelings (see also *Injury to feelings* and *Tax*).

Recoupment: N/A

Relevant case law: *Bungay & Anor v Saini & Ors* (UKEAT/0331/10); *Ministry of Defence v Fletcher* [2009] UKEAT/0044/09; *Singh v University Hospital NHS Trust* EAT/1409/01; *Zaiwalla & Co v Walia* [2002] UKEAT/ 451/00

Ante-natal: see Time off for ante-natal care

Apprentices: see National Minimum Wage

Arrears of pay (reinstatement/re-engagement)

(see also Additional award)

Where a tribunal makes an award for reinstatement or re-engagement, the claimant is entitled to arrears of pay, from the date of dismissal to the date of reinstatement/re-engagement in respect of any benefit that the employee might reasonably be expected to have had but for the dismissal. In the case of *National Westminster Bank Plc v Parry* [2004] EWCA Civ 1563 the court stated: *'Plainly that envisages a sum which will be payable whether or not the order for reinstatement is obeyed.'*

Reinstatement: if the complainant would have benefited from an improvement in his terms and conditions of employment had he not been dismissed, an order for reinstatement shall require him to be treated as if he had benefited from that improvement from the date on which he would have done so but for being dismissed. This could also include accrued holiday pay (s114 ERA 1996).

Re-engagement: again the claimant is entitled to full back pay plus any accrued holiday pay. Arrears are normally calculated on the basis of the claimant's pay prior to dismissal, even if the new job on re-engagement is paid at a lower rate.

Remedy: The award will be the sum of any pay between the date of dismissal and reinstatement/re-engagement. Any payment in lieu, ex gratia payments paid by the employer, and any wages the employee has earned since dismissal should be deducted as well as any other benefits the tribunal thinks appropriate (see s114(4) and s115(3)).

Where an employer reinstates or re-engages an employee but fails fully to comply with the order, the loss suffered by the employee can be compensated for under s117(1), including any arrears of pay.

Where an employer fails to reinstate or re-engage a complainant, the losses suffered, including any unpaid arrears of pay, will fall to be compensated under the compensatory award (see s117(3)(a)).

Gross or net: Calculated on gross pay.

Adjustments: None

Cap: The statutory cap applies to an award under s117(1) and (2) ERA and s123. The statutory cap is currently the lower of £76,574 or 52 weeks pay (as defined in ss220 to 229 ERA 1996) (see s124 ERA 1996). It should be noted that the cap will be lifted to the extent necessary to compensate for arrears of pay and any additional award:

- in the case of compensation awarded under s117(1) where the order for reinstatement or re-engagement has been partially complied with, the cap can be exceeded to the extent necessary to enable the award fully to reflect the amount specified as payable under section 114(2)(a) or section 115(2)(d) (see *Arrears of pay*). In other words, the employee is entitled to receive at least their arrears of pay, even if those arrears exceed the cap.

- in the case of an award under s117(3) (i.e. an award where the employer has not complied at all with an order for reinstatement re-engagement at all) the statutory cap may be exceeded to the extent necessary to enable the aggregate of the compensatory and additional awards fully to reflect the amount specified as payable under section 114(2)(a) or section 115(2)(d) (See *National Westminster Bank Plc v Parry* [2004] EWCA Civ 1563).

This means that

- if the arrears of pay exceed the cap on their own, the individual will receive the total amount of arrears;

- if the arrears of pay do not exceed the cap on their own they will be offset against the compensatory award.

In other words, the arrears of pay award is not freestanding - the arrears of pay, which by itself does not exceed the cap, should not be disregarded when applying the statutory cap (see *National Westminster Bank Plc v Parry* [2004] EWCA Civ 1563).

Mitigation: Any actual mitigation will be taken into account in identifying the loss suffered (s114(4) and s115(3)).

Tax: The arrears of pay sum is compensation for unfair dismissal and so is taxable only under s401 ITEPA 2003. The employer is expected to operate PAYE where the aggregate payments within that section exceed £30,000 (see EIM12960). If, unusually, there is as a matter of fact continuous

employment between the dates of dismissal and reinstatement or re-engagement ordered by the tribunal, any payment for that period is taxable as earnings under Section 62 ITEPA 2003.

Recoupment: Arrears of pay up until the tribunal hearing will form part of the prescribed element for recoupment purposes.

Statutory authorities: ERA 1996 ss114 to 117 and s124

Relevant case law: *National Westminster Bank Plc v Parry* [2004] EWCA Civ 1563

Basic award

(see also Basic award, maximum; Basic award, minimum)

The basic award is a sum awarded to a claimant who has been unfairly dismissed and calculated on the same basis as statutory redundancy pay according to age and number of complete years continuous service.

There are circumstances where a maximum or minimum basic award can be paid - see the separate entries for more details.

Calculation of remedy: The total basic award is calculated as follows:

The employee will receive one and a half weeks gross pay for each year of employment in which they were not below the age of 41, 1 week gross pay for each year of employment in which they were below the age of 41 but not below the age of 22 and half a week's gross pay for each year of employment in which they were below the age of 22. Where an individual's continuous service straddles an age of 41 or 22, the individual only receives the higher rate for the complete years of service that have been worked after that age has been reached. In other words, an employee must reach his 42nd birthday for this year to qualify at the higher rate of 1 ½ weeks.

The maximum amount of a week's gross pay is currently £464. The definition of a week's pay (Now £475) (see *Week's pay*) can be found at ERA 1996 Part XIV Ch II.

The maximum number of years that can be taken into account is 20.

Thus the current maximum basic award is 20 x 1.5 x £464 = £13,920.

Gross or net: Gross. A week's pay as defined in ss220 to 229 ERA 1996 applies (see *Week's pay*).

Limit on a week's pay: Currently £464 (see Table 1 for historical rates).

Limit on number of weeks: The limit depends on the age of the employee during his period of employment, and the maximum is the equivalent of 30 weeks, corresponding to 20 years service all at the age of 41 or greater (1.5 weeks for every year's service).

Any maximum or minimum: Maximum = £13,920; no minimum except in certain circumstances (see *Basic award, minimum* and *Basic award, maximum*).

Adjustments: The basic award can be reduced for contributory conduct (s122(2)) or for unreasonable refusal by the employee to accept an offer of reinstatement (s122(1)). This reduction to a basic award will be the amount the tribunal considers is 'just and equitable' which is broader than the contributory conduct provision for the compensatory award and can take into account conduct which was not known to the employer at the time (see *Optikinetics Ltd v Whooley* EAT/1275/97 and *Parker Foundary Ltd v Slack* [1992] IRLR 11).

The award will not be reduced for contributory conduct in a redundancy dismissal, except where such a dismissal is for one of a number of specified reasons where a minimum basic award must be made, when special statutory rules limit the ability to reduce the basic award (see s122(3) ERA 1996). If the minimum award of £5,676 has been made because the principal reason for a redundancy dismissal was one of the reasons set out in s120(1) the figure may still be reduced for contributory conduct, but the percentage reduction is applied to the difference between what the claimant would have received under the standard case and the minimum £5,676. For example, if the claimant would only have received £2,000 but does in fact qualify for the minimum £5,676, any contributory conduct will be applied to the difference, i.e. £3,676.

The basic award can be reduced by an amount that the tribunal considers to be just and equitable where the claimant has been awarded an amount under a designated dismissal procedures agreement (s122(3A)).

Where the dismissal is unfair by virtue of s104F (blacklists) the basic award will be reduced (or further reduced) by the amount of any basic award paid in respect of the same dismissal under s156 TULR(C)A (minimum basic award in case of dismissal on grounds related to trade union membership or activities).

Any redundancy payment that has been made to the employee must be deducted from the basic award first (see *Allmakes Ltd v Boorman* [1993] UKEAT/695/92). If, on the other hand the tribunal finds that the real reason for dismissal was not redundancy the claimant may be entitled to both payments. So if, for example, the employer mistakenly makes a redundancy payment in circumstances where the dismissal is automatically unfair under TUPE, then the employee will be entitled to recover a basic award despite having received a redundancy payment.

The basic award is not subject to any other adjustments such as for failure to mitigate loss, a failure to comply with a code of practice, or the chance of a future fair dismissal (see *Polkey*).

See also *Basic award, minimum*.

Mitigation: The award cannot be reduced for a failure to mitigate loss.

Tax: The basic award will be taxed under s401 ITEPA 2003 and goes to reduce the tax free amount at termination of £30,000 (see also *Grossing up*).

Recoupment: Recoupment does not apply to the basic award.

Statutory authorities: ERA 1996 ss119 to 122; TULR(C)A 1992 s156

Relevant case law: *Allmakes Ltd v Boorman* [1993] UKEAT/695/92; *Optikinetikcs Ltd v Whooley* EAT/1275/97; *Parker Foundary Ltd v Slack* [1992] IRLR 11

Example 1

An employee was 56 at EDT and had 20 years continuous service, being paid £550 gross per week at an EDT of 10/04/2014. His basic award would be calculated as follows:

Number of years service at or over the age of 41 = 56 - 41 = 15

Each of these years count for 1.5 weeks pay = 15 x 1.5 = 22.5

The other 5 years of service, i.e. 20 - 15, count for 1 week's pay = 5 x 1 = 5

The total number of weeks = 22.5 + 5 = 27.5

The total basic award is then 27.5 x £464 (the maximum gross weekly pay allowed as at 06/04/2014) = £12,760

Example 2

An employee was 35 at EDT and had 15 years continuous service, being paid £330 gross per week at EDT of 01/02/2012. His basic award would be calculated as follows:

Number of years service at or over the age of 22 = 35 - 22 = 13

Each of these years count for 1 week's pay = 13 x 1 = 13

The other 2 years of service, i.e. 15 - 13, count for 0.5 of a week's pay = 2 x 0.5 = 1

The total number of weeks = 13 + 1 = 14

The total basic award is then 14 x £330 = £4,620

Example 3

An employee was 55 at EDT and had 25 years continuous service, being paid £600 per week at EDT of 01/02/2012. His basic award would be calculated as follows:

Number of years service over the age of 41 = 55 - 41 = 14

Each of these years count for 1.5 week's pay = 14 x 1.5 = 21

The other 11 years of service, i.e. 25 - 14, are limited to 6 years, because the maximum number of years is 20. These 6 years each count for 1 week's pay = 6 x 1 = 6

The total number of weeks = 21 + 6 = 27

The total basic award is then 27 x £430 (the weekly limit as at 01/02/2012) = £11,610

See also Statutory redundancy table, Table 37.

Basic award, maximum

(see also Basic award)

The statutory maximum where the reason for dismissal is redundancy but the employee is not entitled to a redundancy payment because they have unreasonably refused an offer of alternative employment, or have had their contract renewed so that there is no dismissal, is 2 weeks gross pay (s121 ERA).

Gross or net: Gross

Limit on a week's pay: £464 (see Table 1 for historical rates).

Limit on number of weeks: 2

Any maximum or minimum: Maximum is £928

Adjustments: Contributory conduct reduction applies (s122 ERA 1996).

Mitigation: The basic award cannot be reduced for failure to mitigate loss.

Tax: The basic award will be taxed under s401 ITEPA 2003 and goes to reduce the tax free amount at termination of £30,000 (see *Grossing up*).

Recoupment: Recoupment does not apply to the basic award.

Statutory authorities: ERA 1996 ss121 and 122

Basic award, minimum

(see also Basic award)

There is a statutory minimum basic award where dismissal is unfair by virtue of

- s100(1)(a) and (b) ERA 1996 (Health and safety cases);

- s101A(d) (employee representative in working time cases);

- s102(1) (trustee of a relevant pension scheme);

- s103 (employee representatives);

- s104F (dismissal where reason relates to union blacklist); or

- s156 of TULR(C)A (union membership).

The minimum is currently £5,676 (s120(1) ERA 1996 and s156 TULR(C)A 1992), except for the s104F (blacklisting) dismissal, where the minimum is £5,000 (s120(1C) ERA 1996). The statutory minimum is ignored if the basic award exceeds this figure when calculated in the normal way.

Adjustments: Contributory conduct reduction applies. However, the percentage reduction is applied only to so much of the basic award as is payable because of s120 (s122(3) ERA 1996) or s156, i.e. the deduction only applies to the difference between what the claimant would have received under the standard case and the minimum £5,676 or £5,000. For example, if the claimant would only have received £2,000 but does in fact qualify for the minimum £5,676, any contributory conduct should be applied to the difference, i.e. £3,676.

Mitigation: The basic award cannot be reduced for failure to mitigate loss.

Tax: The basic award will be taxed under s401 ITEPA 2003 and goes to reduce the tax free amount at termination of £30,000 (see also *Grossing up*).

Recoupment: Recoupment does not apply to the basic award.

Statutory authorities: ERA 1996 ss120 and 122; TULR(C)A 1992 s156

Benefits: see Financial losses

Bonuses

Loss of earnings within an unfair dismissal award can include any commission, bonus or other benefit that the employee reasonably expected to receive had they remained in the employment (s123(2)(b) ERA 1996). The sums do not need to be contractual, provided that the reasonable expectation can be established. The same approach will apply in discrimination awards.

Where the value of a bonus is sought under the unlawful deduction from wages jurisdiction or for breach of contract, specific considerations apply (see *Unlawful deduction from wages*).

Gross or net: Such sums should be paid net of tax and NI and grossed up where appropriate.

Adjustments: Any bonus will be included in the compensatory award and adjusted alongside.

Mitigation: The mitigation rules applicable to the compensatory award apply to bonuses.

Tax: The compensatory award, which includes loss of benefits, is taxable and will fall to be grossed up under s401 if the award overall exceeds £30,000 (see also *Grossing up*).

Recoupment: The recoupment regulations state that 'any amount ordered to be paid and calculated under s123 [of the ERA 1996] in respect of compensation for **loss of wages** for a period before the conclusion of the tribunal proceedings' form part of the prescribed element. It is unclear whether a bonus would be defined as 'wages' but it is likely that any bonus payment awarded would be subject to the recoupment regulations.

Statutory authorities: ERA 1996) s123(2)(b)

Relevant case law: *York Trailer Co Ltd v Sparkes* [1973] IRLR 348

Breach of contract

The Employment Tribunal has a jurisdiction to hear breach of contract claims in certain limited circumstances (Employment Tribunals Extension of Jurisdiction (England and Wales) Order 1994 SI 1994/1623). Claims may be brought by employees where the claim "arises on or is outstanding on" the termination of the employee's employment (Reg 3). A counterclaim (but not a claim) may be brought by an employer similarly where it "arises on or is outstanding on" the termination (Reg 4). Claims on certain contractual terms are excluded by Reg 5, including terms as to living accommodation, intellectual property, an obligation of confidence and a restrictive covenant.

A claim for constructive dismissal will rely on conduct that amounts to a repudiatory breach of contract by the employer, but an unfair dismissal claim will be brought under that jurisdiction without invoking the breach of contract jurisdiction, unless the individual chooses to bring such a claim in addition.

Remedy: The remedy will be damages caused by the breach of contract. Typically such claims are for unpaid notice pay and the value of discretionary bonuses.

Calculation date: see Interest; Week's pay; Table 5

Cap on a week's pay

(see also Week's pay; Table 1)

For several awards, referable to a definition of a "week's pay" in s220-229 ERA 1996, a cap on the gross weekly pay is used in the calculations (see s186 and s227 ERA 1996). The current cap, as at 06/04/2014, is £464. The weekly pay cap applies to the following awards:

- Statutory redundancy pay (s162 ERA 1996);

- Basic award (s119-122 ERA 1996);

- Right to written particulars of employment (s38 EA 2002);

- Right to be accompanied at a disciplinary hearing (s11 ERelA 1999);

- Right to request flexible working (s80I(1)(b) ERA 1996);

- Right to be accompanied at a flexible working meeting (Reg 15 FW(PR) Regs 2002);

- Insolvency provisions (s186 ERA 1996);

- Additional award (s117(3)(b).

The historical weekly pay caps are listed in Table 1.

Cap on wrongful dismissal damages

The cap on wrongful dismissal damages is £25,000 if the claim is brought in the ET (Reg 10 Industrial Tribunals Extension of Jurisdiction (England and Wales) Order 1994). There is no cap if the claim is brought in the County Court or High Court.

Child care costs: see Benefits

Commission: see Bonuses

Company cars: see Benefits

Compensatory award

(see also Adjustments; Immediate loss of earnings: Future loss of earnings; Concurrent unfair and wrongful dismissal; Grossing up; Tax and termination payments; Recoupment; Protected disclosure; Unfair dismissal)

s123 of the ERA 1996 provides that the compensatory award shall be:

'...such amount as the tribunal considers just and equitable in all the circumstances having regard to the loss sustained by the complainant in consequence of the dismissal insofar as that loss is attributable to action taken by the employer'.

Compensation for unfair dismissal should be awarded to 'compensate and compensate fully, but not to award a bonus' according to Sir John Donaldson in *Norton Tool Co Ltd v Tewson* [1973] All ER 183. The object of the compensatory award is to compensate the employee for their financial losses as if they had not been unfairly dismissed - it is not designed to punish the employer for their wrongdoing.

Calculation of remedy: The calculation falls under two headings:

Immediate loss of earnings
This is the loss suffered between the EDT to the date of the remedies hearing. Loss of earnings will be calculated on the basis of net take home pay (that is, after deduction of tax and national insurance). The compensatory award can take into account any pay increase which would have been awarded in the previous employment up to the date of the hearing, including a back-dated pay rise. Conversely, in *Howells School v Gerrard* UKEAT/0079/12/RN, the respondent argued that the loss of earnings should not have been based on the claimant's net earnings at the date of dismissal since the claimant would probably have been paid less than this, if she had not been dismissed, due to the financial constraints on the respondent at the time, and the tribunal agreed.

The employer's liability will normally cease before the date of the remedies hearing either:

i. once the employee has got a new permanent job paying at least as much as the old job as there will no longer be a loss arising from the dismissal; or

ii. on the date at which the claimant should have found an equivalent job .

For claims relating solely to unfair dismissal the period of immediate loss is the number of weeks between the EDT and the remedies hearing, or the date of a new equivalent job, or the date by which the claimant should have found a new job, whichever is the soonest.

If a claim for wrongful dismissal has also been made, the number of weeks for the unfair dismissal immediate loss of earnings should be calculated from the date at which the wrongful dismissal damages period ends through to the date of the hearing, new job or expectation of a new job (see also *Damages for wrongful dismissal*).

Future loss of earnings
An employee may have on-going future losses if by the date of the remedies hearing they have not secured a new job or have obtained a job but with a salary and benefits that is less valuable than their previous employment.

The future loss figure is based on the number of weeks for which it is calculated the particular loss will continue, and it may be that a series of pay rises in the future will reduce the loss suffered in each of those years. The tribunal should take into account the personal characteristics of the employee such as age and health. They also need to take into account contingencies such as whether and for how long the employee would have remained in the original employment, whether there would have been a possibility of promotion and whether the level of earnings would have remained the same. A broad brush approach will be used, with Ogden tables usually used only where there is career long loss, in order to calculate loss based on various statistical contingencies.

[There is a useful website called www.timeanddate.com, which calculates the number of days, weeks or months between two given dates. The calculator will also add a number of days, weeks or months to a fixed date.]

Gross or net: Losses will be calculated on a basis net of tax and NIC, and will be grossed up where appropriate where the employee will pay tax on the sum received (see *Grossing up*).

Limit on a week's pay: There is no limit - the award is based on actual net value of pay and benefits.

Limit on number of weeks: For dismissals occurring after 6 April 2014 the statutory cap (where it applies) is calculated as the lower of £76,574 or 52 week's gross pay (see *Statutory cap*).

Adjustments: (see also *Adjustments, Mitigation, Contributory conduct*)

> *Ex gratia payment:* see *Ex gratia payment*

> *Earnings:* A deduction of earnings which have mitigated the claimant's loss or a sum which reflects any failure by the claimant's failure to mitigate his/her loss.

> *Early payment of compensation:* any compensation paid to the employee before the tribunal hearing should be deducted from the compensatory award (see *Ex gratia payment*).

> *Polkey:* A '*Polkey*' deduction (see also *Polkey*) to represent the chance the claimant may have been fairly dismissed in any event.

> *ACAS:* A percentage increase or reduction up to a maximum of 25% to reflect a failure by the employer or employee to comply with the ACAS disciplinary code of practice (see *ACAS*)

> *Protected disclosure not in good faith:* Deduction, up to a maximum of 25%, if the award is under a s103A claim but the disclosure was not made in good faith (only

for claims brought after 25 June 2013) (see *Protected disclosure*).

> *Written particulars:* An increase for any failure by the employer to provide written particulars of employment (see also *Written particulars*).

> *Contributory conduct:* A percentage reduction for any contributory conduct on the part of the employee (see *Contributory conduct*).

> *Enhanced redundancy:* A deduction of any enhanced redundancy payment to the extent that it exceeds the basic award (see *Enhanced redundancy*).

> *Accelerated payment:* A deduction for accelerated payment of compensation in respect of future loss (see *Accelerated payment*).

> *Interest:* Any interest on the losses suffered (see also *Interest*).

Statutory cap: The cap, currently the lower of £76,574 or 52 week's pay, does not apply in all circumstances. If the reason for dismissal is on the grounds of discrimination (s13, s15, s16, s18, s19, s21, s26, s27 Equality Act 2010), uncapped compensation will be awarded under that statute, and if the dismissal is because of health and safety reasons or whistleblowing by virtue of section 100, 103A (see 105(3) or 105(6A)) the cap will not apply.

The cap is applied **after** the grossing up calculation is applied (see *Hardie Grant London Ltd v Aspden* UKEAT/0242/11/RN).

If an additional award and arrears of pay are being claimed the statutory cap can be exceeded in certain circumstances (see *Arrears of pay* and *Additional award*).

Mitigation: The employee is under a duty to mitigate their loss and a deduction in compensation can be made if they have not fully mitigated their loss.

Tax: If the combined sum of any basic and compensatory award is greater than £30,000 then the excess figure will be subject to tax (see *Grossing up*).

It is important to note that, even if the reason for termination is discriminatory, any award for loss of earnings is taxable under s401 (see *Tax*).

Recoupment: Recoupment will apply to

immediate loss of earnings only (see *Recoupment*). Note that the recoupment regulations do not apply if an award has been made under the Equality Act2010.

Statutory authorities: EA 2010 ss13, 15, 16, 18, 19, 21, 26 and 27; ERA 1996 ss100, 103A, 105(3), 105(6A) and ss123 to 126

Relevant case law: *Hardie Grant London Ltd v Aspden* UKEAT/0242/11/RN; *Norton Tool Co Ltd v Tewson* [1973] 1 All ER 183 [1973] 1 All ER 183

Concurrent unfair and wrongful dismissal

(see also Compensatory award; Unfair dismissal)

It is often the case that unfair and wrongful dismissal are brought concurrently before an ET, for example where an employee has been summarily dismissed for gross misconduct and disputes that his employer was entitled to dismiss him. The wrongful dismissal claim falls within the tribunal's breach of contract jurisdiction which has a separate £25,000 cap.

However, it is important that awards are not double counted. In other words, damages for wrongful dismissal cannot be awarded for the same loss for which compensation for unfair dismissal is also awarded. As a corollary, where an individual's losses may be capped it is possible to take the losses during the notice period out of the (capped) compensatory award to maximise the value of the claims (or to take some of the (capped) wrongful dismissal losses into the compensatory award).

Where losses are compensated for under an award for damages the recoupment regulations will not apply, whereas they will apply to the compensatory award. Also, damages for breach of contract will not be reduced for contributory conduct or '*Polkey*'.

Two matters should be addressed when considering bringing both claims in the tribunal (rather than reserving the breach of contract claim for the High Court/ County Court):

- It is not possible to top up the £25,000 award from a tribunal by bringing a second claim in the civil courts as there will be no remaining cause of action (see *Fraser v HMLAD Ltd* [2006] EWCA Civ 738); and

- Once a breach of contract claim has been started at a tribunal, it is complicated to then withdraw it and bring it instead in the ordinary civil courts, so great care must be taken if that is to be effective.

Calculation

There are two ways in which concurrent claims can be calculated and double counting avoided:

Either:

Calculate the damages for wrongful dismissal and then deduct this figure from the compensation awarded for unfair dismissal

Example

Damages = £5,000
Compensatory award = £6,000

The claimant would receive the damages figure of £5,000 plus (£6,000 - £5,000) = £6,000

Or:

Award the damages and then start the unfair dismissal period from the day after the damages period ended

There are two potential advantages with the second method:

- there is no danger of the recoupment regulations being applied to the damages figure (see *Damages* and *Recoupment*) because the two awards have been calculated completely separately;

- if the compensatory award has to be adjusted, for example for contributory conduct, it is much easier to determine the figure that should be used in the calculation. Damages for wrongful dismissal are not subject to adjustment for contributory conduct or '*Polkey*'.

Continuous employment: see Basic award; Effective date of termination; Qualifying period

Contractual Notice Period

(see also Actual Notice Period; Damages for wrongful dismissal; Effective date of termination)

An employee is entitled to be given notice of his dismissal in accordance with the terms of his contract, unless he has committed gross misconduct in which case dismissal can usually be effected summarily (subject to unfair dismissal and discrimination rights). Where a claimant has been dismissed without the appropriate contractual notice, the claimant is entitled to claim the damages which are equivalent to the wages which he would have earned, between the time of the actual termination and the time at which the contract might lawfully have been terminated (by due notice), together with the value of any contractual fringe benefits which the employee would have received during the same period.

The damages are calculated by reference to the contractual notice period (if there is one) or by the statutory notice period (see *Damages for wrongful dismissal*).

Contributory conduct

(see also Adjustments; Basic award)

A number of awards available to the tribunal may be reduced due to the contributory conduct of the employee. The size of the reduction will be that which the tribunal considers to be just and equitable.

The wording of the test differs between that for the basic award and other awards in that the test for the basic award permits the tribunal to reduce the award where it *"considers that any conduct of the complainant before the dismissal (or, where the dismissal was with notice, before the notice was given) was such as it would be just and equitable to reduce or reduce further the amount of the award to any extent..."*, whereas in the other awards the provision follows the form *"where the tribunal finds that the [act] was to any extent caused or contributed to by any action of the complainant, it shall reduce the amount of the compensatory award by such proportion as it considers just and equitable..."*.

For the basic award (but not other awards),

conduct which was not known to the employer and cannot have caused the dismissal can still be taken into account (see *Optikinetics Ltd v Whooley* [1999] ICR 984 and *Parker Foundary Ltd v Slack* [1992] IRLR 11). Also, for other awards the reduction will be a proportion (which can be expressed as a percentage) – whereas the reduction for the basic award may also be calculated to be a particular sum.

Note that the figure for contributory conduct can be different for the basic award and the compensatory award due to the different method of calculation (see s122(2) and s123(6) ERA 1996). See in particular the cases of *Montracon Ltd v Hardcastle* UKEAT/0307/12/JO; *Optikinetics Ltd v Whooley* [1999] ICR 984; *Compass Group v Baldwin* UKEAT/0447/05/DM; *Rao v CAA* [1994] ICR 495.

Reductions for contributory conduct apply to the following awards:

- Basic award (s122(2) ERA 1996) (but not in redundancy cases unless the reason for selecting the employee for dismissal was one of the those specified in ss100(1)(a) and (b), 101A(d), 102(1) or 103, in which case the contributory conduct reduction applies only to so much of the basic award as is payable because of s120 (see *Basic award, minimum*);

- Compensatory award (s123(6) ERA 1996);

- Award in respect of detriment (s49(5) ERA 1996, s149(6) TULR(C)A 1992 (but see s145E(6)) and Paragraph 159(5) Schedule A1 TULR(C)A 1992;

- Right not to be unjustifiably disciplined (s67(7) TULR(C)A 1992);

- Right not to be expelled or excluded from a union (s176(5) TULR(C)A 1992);

- Part time worker discrimination (Reg 8(13) PTW(PLFT) Regs 2000);

- Reg 7(12) FTE(PLFT) Regs 2002.

Grossing up should take place after all adjustments have been made (see also *Grossing up*).

The statutory cap will be applied after any grossing up has been applied.

Example

Basic award = £4,500

Financial loss = £8,000

Financial loss after contributory fault assessed as

25% on the compensatory award only = £8,000 x 0.75 = £6,000

Award = £4,500 + £6,000 = £10,500

Statutory authorities: ERA 1996 ss49(5), 100(1)(a) and (b), 101A(d), 102(1), 103, 120, 122(2) and 123(6); PTW(PLFT) Regs 2000 Reg 8(13); TULR(C)A 1992 Paragraph 159(5) Schedule A1 and ss67(7), 149(6) and 176(5)

Relevant case law: *Compass Group v Baldwin* UKEAT/0447/05/DM; *Montracon Ltd v Hardcastle* UKEAT/0307/12/JO; *Optikinetics Ltd v Whooley* [1999] ICR 984; *Parker Foundary Ltd v Slack* [1992] IRLR 11; *Rao v CAA* [1994] ICR 495

Costs and wasted costs

The Employment Tribunals (Constitution and Rules of Procedure) Regulations 2013, Schedule 1, Rules 74 to 84 set out the tribunal's approach and powers to award costs incurred by a party to a tribunal claim. Unlike in the ordinary civil courts, the successful party's costs are not as a matter of course borne by the losing party. The costs of one party will only be borne by another party in specified circumstances.

Discretionary orders
By rule 76(1) a tribunal may make a costs order or a preparation time order, and shall consider whether to do so, where it considers that:

   a)   a party (or that party's representative) has acted vexatiously, abusively, disruptively or otherwise unreasonably in either the bringing of the proceedings (or part) or the way that the proceedings (or part) have been conducted; or

   b)   any claim or response had no reasonable prospect of success.

A tribunal may also make a costs order or a preparation time order where a party has been in breach of any order or practice direction or where a hearing has been postponed or adjourned on the application of a party (Rule 76(2)).

In a provision that brings the tribunal regime closer to the costs availability in small claims in the civil courts, by Rule 76(4) where a party has succeeded on a contract claim or counterclaim a tribunal may order the unsuccessful party to pay the tribunal fee paid by the successful party.

A tribunal may make an order that a party pay the expenses incurred by a witness in attending, and this order may be made at the request of the witness (Rule 76(5)).

Mandatory orders
A tribunal must make a costs order against the respondent where at a final hearing for unfair dismissal a claimant has given the respondent 7 days notice that he wishes to be reinstated or re-engaged, but the hearing is postponed or adjourned because the employer has not provided reasonable evidence of the availability of the claimant's job without a special reason (Rule 76(3)).

Where a party has been subject to a deposit order due to a specific allegation or argument in the claim or response having little reasonable prospect of success (of up to £1,000) and the tribunal decides that issue against the paying party for substantially the reasons set out in the deposit order, the paying party is treated as having acted unreasonably in pursuing that allegation, unless he shows the contrary, and the deposit will be paid to the other party (this sum will count towards any other costs award).

Costs orders
Rule 74 defines costs as fees, charges, disbursements or expenses incurred by or on behalf of the receiving party.

Limit: The amount of a costs order where the amount costs is determined by the tribunal under its basic jurisdiction is limited to £20,000. However, the tribunal can order that the amount of costs be determined by way of detailed assessment at the County Court, or by an Employment Judge applying the same principles, (and the equivalent in Scotland), in which case there is no cap on the costs awardable. The limit of £20,000 can also be exceeded if the tribunal orders the losing party to pay back any fee paid by the successful party, or for witness expenses reasonably incurred or if both parties agree to a figure which is higher.

Where the costs are that of a lay representative, the maximum hourly available rate is the figure used for preparation time awards (£34) (Rule 78(2)).

Preparation time orders
Preparation time orders award an amount to a party to reflect their preparation time whilst not represented. A preparation time order and a costs order cannot be awarded in favour of the same party in the same proceedings (Rule 75(3)). The number of hours in respect of which a preparation time order can be made will be determined by the ET according to the actual time spent and the tribunal's own assessment of what

it considers to be a reasonable and proportionate amount of time to spend on such preparatory work (Rule 79).

Hourly rate: the hourly rate is £34.

Calculation: Amount of preparation time order = number of hours assessed by the ET x 33

Wasted costs orders

Wasted costs orders require a party's representative rather than a party itself to pay an amount of costs. A tribunal may make a wasted costs order against a representative in favour of any party ("the receiving party") where that party has either

a) incurred costs as a result of any improper, unreasonable or negligent act or omission on the part of the representative; or

b) incurred costs which, in the light of any such act or omission occurring after they were incurred, the tribunal considers it unreasonable to expect the receiving party to pay.

An award can be made against a representative in favour of his own client.

Allowances

Where a tribunal has made any of the above orders, it may order the paying party to reimburse the Secretary of State for any allowances paid for e.g. witness attendance (see Rule 84).

Ability to pay

In deciding whether to make a costs, preparation time, or wasted costs order, and if so in what amount, the tribunal may have regard to the paying party's (or, where a wasted costs order is made, the representative's) ability to pay (Rule 84).

Time limit

A party may apply for a costs order or preparation time order at any stage up to 28 days from which the judgment finally determining the proceedings in respect of that party was sent to the parties (Rule 77).

Damages for wrongful dismissal

(see also Adjustments; Concurrent unfair and wrongful dismissal)

Damages can be awarded if the employee has been dismissed without the appropriate length of notice.

Calculation of remedy: The damages will cover the lost remuneration and benefits that would have been received during the full notice period.

Damages are only awarded for payments and benefits to which the claimant is contractually entitled. Where the contractual entitlement is discretionary, it can be argued that the failure to give appropriate notice also involves a breach of the duty to exercise the discretion, that the discretion would be exercised genuinely and rationally and that the claimant is entitled to an award to cover the loss of such benefits (see *Cantor Fitzgerald International v Horkulak* [2004] EWCA Civ 1287).

Gross or net: Net

Limit on a week's pay: There is no limit on a week's pay, and the definition of a week's pay does not apply.

Any maximum or minimum: None

Adjustments: Damages can be reduced for mitigation or failure to mitigate, for accelerated payment (see *Accelerated payment*), for failure by the employer/employee to comply with the ACAS code of practice (TULCRA s207A and Schedule A2). Interest may be awarded in the County Court and High Court, but not in the Employment Tribunal.

Cap on award: £25,000 if the claim is brought to the ET, no cap if brought in the County Court or High Court.

Mitigation: The employee is expected to mitigate their loss.

Tax: The award for damages for wrongful dismissal is taxable under s401 ITEPA 2003 and will fall to be grossed up to the extent it causes the £30,000 allowance to be exceeded.

Recoupment: Recoupment does not apply to damages for wrongful dismissal.

Statutory authorities: ERA 1996 s86

Relevant case law: Cantor Fitzgerald

International v Horkulak [2004] EWCA Civ 1287

Damages period: see Damages for wrongful dismissal

Deductions: see Adjustments

Deductions from wages: see Unlawful deductions

Deferred pension

This is the pension entitlement built up by an employee who left employment before normal retirement date (see also *Pension loss*).

Defined benefit: see Pension loss

Defined contribution: see Pension loss

Detriment

There are a large number of employment rights which can themselves be enforced by bringing a direct claim, including the right not to be unfairly dismissed. In addition to this type of right, there are rights protecting employees from suffering detriment because of certain protected behaviour and rights to protection from dismissal because of certain protected behaviour. This section deals with the statutory protections from detriment - some rights apply only to employees, some also apply to the broader class of workers. There also exist protections from dismissal because of certain protected behavior (see *Unfair dismissal*).

An **employee** has the right not to be subjected to any detriment because of him:

- having to attend jury service (s43M ERA 1996);

- acting as a health and safety representative(s44);

- refusing to work on Sundays, if the employee's work is of a particular type (s45);

- being a pension scheme trustee (s46);

- being an employee representative (s47);

- exercising right to time off work for education, study or training (s47A) and s47AA;

- exercising his right to take leave for family or domestic reasons (including ordinary and additional maternity leave, ordinary and additional adoption leave, parental leave, rights during and after parental leave, ordinary and additional paternity leave for birth, ordinary and additional paternity leave for adoption, rights during and after paternity leave) (s47C);

- exercising rights in connection with tax credits (s47D);

- exercising his rights under the flexible working regulations (s47E);

- exercising his rights to request study and training (s47F);

- exercising the right to be accompanied or to accompany someone else to a disciplinary or grievance meeting (ERelAct 1999 s12);

- exercising rights in relation to Part-time Workers (Reg 7(2) PTW(PLFT) Regs 2000.

A **worker** (which includes an employee) has the right not to be subjected to any detriment because of him:

- exercising working time rights (s45A);

- making a protected disclosure (s47B);

- exercising rights in relation to Fixed-term employees (FTE(PLFT) Regs 2002);

- exercising rights related to trade union membership (s146 TULR(C)A 1992); or

- exercising rights related to trade union recognition (Paragraph 156 to Schedule A1 TULR(C)A 1992.

Remedy: If a claim is well founded the tribunal must make a declaration and may make award of such an amount as it considers is just and equitable having regard to:

1) the infringement to which the complaint relates;

2) any loss which is attributable to the act, or failure to act, which infringed the claimant's right (s49(2) ERA 1996, s149(2) and Paragraph 159(2) to Schedule A1, TULR(C)A 1992).

The loss shall be taken to include: any expenses reasonably incurred by the claimant in consequence of the act, or failure to act, to which the complaint relates; and loss of any benefit which the claimant might reasonably be expected to have had but for the act or failure to act (s49(3) ERA 1996, s149(3) and Paragraph 159(3) to Schedule A1, TULR(C)A 1992).

The award may also include compensation for injury to feelings. Where a worker has brought the claim under s45A, 47B or 47D and the detriment is termination of the contract, which is akin to a claim for unfair dismissal of an employee, it is arguable that injury to feelings may be awarded, but only up to the amount of a basic award (see *Injury to feelings*).

In relation to detriment for exercising rights related to trade union membership, in determining the amount of compensation to be awarded no account can be taken of any pressure which was exercised on the employer by calling, organising, procuring or financing a strike or other industrial action, or by threatening to do so, and that question must be determined as if no such pressure had been exercised (s146) TULR(C)A 1992).

Any maximum or minimum:

- For claims under ss43M, 44, 45, 46, 47, 47A, 47C, 47E, and 47F ERA 1996, and for s12 ERelA 1999, the compensation is unlimited;

- For a claim under s 45A ERA 1996, if a worker has brought the claim and detriment is termination of the contract, the cap relevant to being dismissed under s101A (currently none) will apply;

- For a claim under s 47B ERA 1996, if a worker has brought the claim and detriment is termination of the contract, the cap relevant to being dismissed under s103A (currently none) will apply;

- For a claim under s 47D ERA 1996, if a worker has brought the claim and detriment is termination of the contract, the cap relevant to being dismissed under s104B (currently none) will apply.

Adjustments: Contributory conduct (ss49(5) ERA 1996, s149(6) and Paragraph 159(5) to Schedule A1, TULR(C)A 1992) and failure to comply with ACAS code of practice apply (see TULRCA s207A and Schedule A2). Also, for claims brought on or after 29 July 2013, if a protected disclosure has been made but not in good faith, the tribunal can reduce any award by up to 25% (s49(6A) (see *Adjustments*).

Mitigation: The tribunal may reduce the award if the claimant has failed to mitigate their loss (s49(4) ERA 1996, s149(4) and Paragraph 159(4)

to Schedule A1 TULR(C)A 1992).

Tax: The tax treatment will depend on the nature of the loss awarded (see *Tax*).

Recoupment: N/A

Statutory authorities: ERA 1996 ss43M, 44, 45, 46, 47, 47A, 47C, 47E, and 47F; ERelA 1999 s12; TULR(C)A 1992 s149 and Paragraph 159 to Schedule A1

Direct discrimination: see Discrimination

Discrimination

(see also Aggravated damages; Compensatory award; Contributory conduct (discrimination); Exemplary Damages; Financial Loss; Incapacity benefit; Injury to feelings; Physical and psychiatric injury; Sex Equality Clause)

The Equality Act 2010 creates the right not to be discriminated against where the reason for the discrimination is one of a number of protected grounds. The protected grounds are: age; disability; gender reassignment; marriage and civil partnership; pregnancy and maternity; race; religion or belief; sex; and sexual orientation (s4 and ss5 to 12 EA 2010).

Discrimination may take different forms, and the types of conduct prohibited by the Equality Act 2010 are:

- direct discrimination (s13 EA 2010);

- discrimination arising from disability (s15);

- gender reassignment discrimination in cases of absence from work (s16);

- pregnancy and maternity discrimination (s18);

- indirect discrimination (s19);

- failure to comply with the duty to make reasonable adjustments (ss20 and 21);

- harassment (s26); and

- victimisation (s27).

The Equality Act 2010 placed together a number of different strands of discrimination found in SDA 1975 (sex), RRA 1976 (race), DDA 1995 (disability), EE(RB)R 2003 (religion or belief), EE(SO)R 2003 (sexual orientation) and EE(Age)R 2006 (age). Many of the authorities relevant to discrimination under EA 2010 relate to the earlier statutory provisions.

The right to equality of terms, formerly called equal pay, is contained in the EA 2010 (ss64 to 80 and ss127 to 135). The remedies for breach of the right to equality of terms is addressed in the *Sex Equality Clause* entry.

There are other employment rights that protect individuals against less favourable or detrimental treatment on the grounds of the individual having certain characteristics or satisfying certain conditions. These are not strictly speaking prohibitions on 'discrimination', though the prohibitions may take similar forms and the remedies may be calculated in similar ways. For example, the protections against suffering detriment in Part V ERA 1996, the Fixed-Term Employees (Prevention of Less Favourable Treatment) Regulations 2002 and the Part-Time Workers (Prevention of Less Favourable Treatment) Regulations 2000 which both give an employee a right not to be treated 'less favourably' than a comparator employee. Further, the remedy for breach of the right not to be subjected to a detriment under ERA 1996 s47B, and probably other similar protections in Part V ERA 1996 may include not just compensation for financial loss but also an award for injury to feelings.

Remedy:
If a tribunal finds that an employer has discriminated against an employee, there are three types of remedy available (s124 EA 2010). The tribunal may:

a) make a declaration as to the rights of the complainant and the respondent in relation to the matters to which the proceedings relate;

b) order the respondent to pay compensation to the complainant;

c) make a recommendation that the respondent take specified steps for the purpose of obviating or reducing the adverse effect of any matter to which the proceedings relate on the complainant or any other person.

Each of the remedies is discretionary, and though it is highly unusual for a remedy not to be awarded, under previous statutory provisions the motive and intention of the discriminator was relevant to the issue of remedy, in particular the value of any injury to feelings award (though not

to the issue of whether discrimination had occurred) (see *O'Neill v Governors of St Thomas More Roman Catholic Voluntary Aided Upper School* [1997] ICR 33 and *Chief Constable of Manchester v Hope* [1999] ICR 338. It may be that tribunals can apply a similar approach under EA 2010.

Where the tribunal has found indirect discrimination under s19 EA 2010, and where the tribunal is satisfied that the provision, criteria or practice was not applied with the intention of discriminating against the claimant, the tribunal must consider making either a declaration or a recommendation before it awards compensation (see s124(4) and (5) EA 2010).

The remedy most frequently obtained by claimants is compensation and the principles to be applied are outlined below, with detailed analysis set out elsewhere under the specific headings where appropriate.

Failure to comply with recommendation: Where the tribunal has made a recommendation under s124(2)(c) EA 2010, but so far as it relates to the claimant it has without reasonable excuse failed to comply with the recommendation, the tribunal may increase any award for compensation or make an award of compensation where it has not already done so (see s124(7) EA 2010).

Compensation: Any award of compensation will be assessed under the same principles as apply to torts (see s124(6) and s119(2). The central aim in is to put the claimant in the position, so far as is reasonable, but for the tort, thereby compensating him for the losses caused (*Ministry of Defence v Wheeler* [1998] IRLR 23 and *Chagger v Abbey National plc* [2010] IRLR 47). The sum is not determined by what the tribunal considers just and equitable in the circumstances as it would do in an unfair dismissal award (*Hurley v Mustoe (No 2)* [1983] ICR 422), though the two approaches will often generate the same award. One impact is that certain items for which credit must be given by an employee are treated differently under the two awards, such as earnings from a new job during a notice period.

Causation and remoteness limit the damages available to a claimant: only those losses caused by the unlawful act will be recoverable, so for example where an individual would have lost their job at some point in any event, and if the discriminatory dismissal they have suffered has not altered their job prospects, the losses suffered after the date when the individual would anyway have been dismissed have not been caused by the discriminatory dismissal. Further, in the general law of tort losses that are too remote and unforeseeable will not be recoverable. However in *Essa v Laing Ltd* [2004] ICR 746 the Court of Appeal held that this principle does not apply to all statutory torts including discriminatory harassment, such that any loss proved to flow directly from the discriminatory act will be recoverable. It may be that the principle applies to other forms of discrimination.

Awards may be made not just against employers, but also against individual respondents where these have been named (see *Individual respondents*).

Non-financial losses are also recoverable (see *Aggravated damages; Exemplary damages; Injury to feelings; Physical and psychiatric injury*).

The types of financial loss that are recoverable are in general the same as for an unfair dismissal compensatory award, and will include the value of lost earnings and benefits. The calculation of the financial losses the claimant has suffered will also be broadly similar to awards for unfair dismissal (see *Financial loss*).

The central matters the tribunal will need to determine are the 'old job' facts and the 'new job' facts, it will need to compare the financial benefits had the claimant not been treated unlawfully, with the financial benefits the claimant has been able to obtain or will be able to in the future (see *Chagger v Abbey National plc* [2010] IRLR 47). Factors that will be considered include whether the employment would anyway have terminated, whether the individual would have been promoted or received a pay rise, what employment has been or will be obtained, what will the financial rewards be and will these increase to meet the losses currently being suffered at some point in the future.

The tribunal can take into account the chance of the original employment not continuing, and the chance of any particular employment arising in the future (see *Loss of a chance; Polkey*).

Gross or net: Net for the compensatory element.

Limit on a week's pay: There is no limit on a week's pay - the claimant's actual net pay will be used in the calculation of loss.

Limit on number of weeks: There is no statutory limit to the number of weeks loss that can be awarded.

Any maximum or minimum: None

Adjustments:

Contributory conduct: Discrimination is a statutory tort and awards may be reduced for contributory fault, though this is unusual (see *Contributory conduct*).

ACAS: An adjustment for failure by the employer/employee to comply with the ACAS Code of Practice for Grievance and Disciplinary Procedures can also be made (Schedule A2 TULR(C)A).

Failure to comply with recommendation: Where the tribunal has made a recommendation under s124(2)(c) EA 2010, but so far as it relates to the claimant it has without reasonable excuse failed to comply with the recommendation, the tribunal may increase any award for compensation or make an award of compensation where it has not already done so (see s124(7) EA 2010).

Grossing up: where an award will attract a tax liability on the claimant who receives the award, the award will be increased to reflect the net sum the claimant ought to receive. See Grossing up.

Interest: Interest can also be added to the sum awarded (see *Interest*).

Cap: There is no statutory cap on compensation for discrimination.

Mitigation: The claimant is under the usual duty to mitigate their loss (see *Mitigation*).

Tax: s401 ITEPA 2003 will apply to the compensatory element of the award but an award of injury to feelings will generally not be taxed (see in particular *Injury to feelings; Tax and termination payments*).

Recoupment: Recoupment does not apply to compensation for discrimination.

Statutory authorities: Equality Act 2010 ss15 to 27, s119 and s124

Relevant case law: *Carmelli Bakeries Ltd v Benali* UKEAT/0616/12/RN; *Chagger v Abbey National Plc & Anor* [2009] EWCA Civ 1202; *Way & Anor v Crouch* UKEAT/0614/04/CK

Early payment of compensation: see Ex gratia payment

Effective date of termination

(see also Basic award; Cap on a week's pay; Compensatory award; Statutory cap)

The "effective date of termination" (see s97 ERA 1996) or EDT is a statutory concept necessary for the following calculations:

1) identifying the number of years of continuous service necessary to bring a claim (claims of normal unfair dismissal and claims for a redundancy payment can only be brought after 2 years of continuous service (subject to the exceptions listed in s108(3)) (see s108 ERA 1996).

2) determining whether a claim for unfair dismissal has been brought within the time limit (the claim must be presented to the tribunal before the end of the period of three months beginning with the EDT (unless the time limit is extended by the tribunal): for example, if the EDT is 5 July, the claim must be brought by 4 October (see s111 ERA 1996).

3) calculating the basic award, since this is based on the number of continuous years of service (see s119).

The calculation with which we are concerned here is the basic award.

Often, the EDT is the actual date of termination of the employment contract, and there is extensive case law surrounding exactly when the termination of employment takes place, for example where an employee is dismissed during a heated argument but the employer quickly attempts to withdraw the dismissal, or where the dismissal is communicated by a third party and only on a later date communicated directly by the employer. That level of detail is often critical to determine whether a claim has been brought in time, but will rarely be relevant to establishing whether an employee has a particular number of years service, or one more year if the EDT can be pushed to a later date (since the value of a basic award is determined by the number of complete years service whilst within a particular age range, the EDT may be critical to establishing a year's continuity of employment within a higher paying age).

Usually, where notice of termination of employment has been given either by the employee or the employer, the EDT will be the date on which notice expires. If the notice given is greater than that required by s86 ERA 1996, the later date is the EDT.

However, there are two situations where an EDT is 'deemed' to be a particular date other than the date of termination. If the employer gives no notice or the notice given is less than the minimum guaranteed by s86 ERA 1996, the EDT will be the date on which statutory notice would have expired if it had been given (see s97(1) to (3 . If the employee resigns where he is not already under notice, the EDT will be the date the employment terminates, but if that notice period is less than the employer would have had to give the employee under s86 ERA 1996, then the EDT will be the date of the expiry of that notional notice. By s86(6) there is no statutory minimum notice period where either party terminates the contract for repudiatory breach by the other party.

The period of notice begins on the day after the day on which notice was given unless the contract provides otherwise (see *Wang v University Of Keele* [2011] IRLR 542 and *West v Kneels Ltd* [1986] IRLR 430.

Some examples
The claimant is given notice and it is worked out in full
The EDT is the date of expiry of the contractual notice period, or the statutory notice period, whichever is the later (s97(1)(a)).

Contractual notice has been given, the claimant is working during the notice period and then is summarily dismissed before the expiry of the contractual notice period, but after the statutory notice period would have expired
The EDT is the date of dismissal, and not the date when contractual notice would have ended Relevant authorities dealing with a range of such factual circumstances include: *M-Choice UK Ltd v A* UKEAT/0227/11/DA, *Harper v Virgin Net Ltd* [2004] EWCA Civ 271 and *Parker Rhodes Hickmott Solicitors v Harvey* UKEAT/0455/11/SM.

The claimant is summarily dismissed, but the employer was not entitled to do so and the claimant is entitled to statutory notice under s86
The EDT is the date that the statutory notice

would have ended (s97(2) ERA 1996). **Note**: the EDT is only extended by the statutory notice period, not any contractual notice period.

The claimant is summarily dismissed and the employer was entitled to do so due to the conduct of the employee
The EDT is the date on which termination takes effect (s97(1)(b)).

The claimant has been put on garden leave
The EDT is the date the notice period expires.

The claimant is dismissed with a payment in lieu of notice
The contract ends when the PILON clause is successfully put into effect, with the EDT being the date of termination of the contract (see *Societe Generale, London Branch v Geys* [2013] IRLR 122).

The employee resigns in response to a repudiatory breach by the employer
The EDT will normally be the date of expiry of the statutory notice period which the employer would have had to give if they had given the employee notice of termination on the day the employee resigned.

The employer and employee agree on a date when the employment will terminate
The EDT will be the date of the agreed termination, even if the employee had already received notice but then later agreed to an earlier termination date (*Palfrey v Transco Plc* [2004] IRLR 916).

Termination of fixed term contract which is not renewed
The EDT is the last day of the fixed term.

Statutory authorities: ss86, 97, 108 and 119 ERA 1996

Relevant case law: *Gisda Cyf v Barratt* [2010] UKSC 41; *Harper v Virgin Net Ltd* [2004] EWCA Civ 271; *Hawes & Curtis Ltd v Arfan & Anor* UKEAT/0229/12/JOJ; *M-Choice UK Ltd v A* UKEAT/0227/11/DA; *Martin v Yeoman Aggregates Limited* [1983] ICR 314; *Palfrey v Transco Plc* [2004] IRLR 916; *Parker Rhodes Hickmott Solicitors v Harvey* UKEAT/0455/11/SM; *Robinson v Bowskill & Ors Practising as Fairhill Medical Practice* UKEAT/0313/12/JOJ; *Societe Generale, London Branch v Geys* [2013] IRLR 122; *The Governing Body of Wishmorecross School v Balado* UKEAT/0199/11/CEA; *The Secretary of State for Justice v Hibbert* UKEAT/0289/13/GE; *Wang v University Of Keele (Jurisdictional Points : Claim in time and effective date of termination)* [2010] UKEAT/0223/10; *West v Kneels Ltd* [1986]

IRLR 430

Enhanced redundancy: see Redundancy

Enhancement of accrued pension rights: see Pension loss

Equal pay: see Sex Equality Clause

Equality of terms: see Sex Equality Clause

Ex gratia payment

(see also Adjustments; Tax and termination payments)

An employee may receive an ex gratia payment from his employer following his dismissal. There are various reasons why any such payment may be made, and the sum may be viewed as compensation for the losses suffered, advance payment of any liability caused by the dismissal, or as a payment unrelated to the dismissal. An ex gratia payment is made where there is no legal obligation to do so.

The claimant will normally be required to give credit for the ex gratia payment (see *Digital Equipment Co Ltd v Clements (No 2)* [1998] IRLR 134).

The particular reason for the payment dictates how it is factored into the tribunal's calculation of the sum to be paid by the ex-employer. If the payment is taken to reduce the loss suffered by the claimant flowing from the dismissal, credit will be given before the application of any adjustments such as contributory conduct. However if the payment is treated as reducing the ultimate liability of the employer, then the credit will apply to the award before the cap has been imposed. The employee will likely benefit if the former approach is applied, and the employer if the latter approach is applied. Full benefit to the employer will only occur if the award is less than the statutory cap. The following principles apply:

● Payment made under a legal obligation, such as pay in lieu of notice, will be taken to reduce the loss sustained (see *Heggie v Uniroyal Ltd* [1999] IRLR 802);

• Payment of a contractual enhanced redundancy payment is dealt with by s123(7) ERA 1996 (see *Adjustments*);

• Ex gratia payments will usually be taken to reduce the loss suffered (see *Horizon Holiday Ltd v Grassi* [1987] IRLR 371 and *Babcock FATA Ltd v Addison* [1987] IRLR 173);

• Payments made by mistake will usually be taken to reduce the loss suffered (see *Boorman v Allmakes* [1995] IRLR 553);

• Where the payment is expressly made by reference to liability for compensation for an unfair dismissal, it may be set off against any basic award and compensatory award (see *Chelsea Football Club & Athletic Co Ltd v Heath* [1981] IRLR 73.

Where the employee receives an ex gratia payment that he would have received had he not been unfairly dismissed it will not factor into reducing the losses suffered by the claimant (see *Babcock FATA Ltd v Addison* [1987] IRLR 173 and *Roadchef v Hastings* [1988] IRLR 142).

Adjustments: The ex gratia payment, where it is taken to reduce the losses suffered by the claimant, should be deducted before any reduction/increase for contributory conduct, *Polkey*, ACAS, interest and accelerated payment (see *Digital Equipment Co Ltd v Clements (No 2)* [1997] IRLR 140). Credit for the ex gratia payment will be made before the statutory cap is applied (see *McCarthy v British Insulated Callenders Cables Plc* [1985] IRLR 94).

Tax: Assuming that the ex gratia payment has been deducted from the calculation of financial loss, any sums awarded exceeding £30,000 will be taxed under ITEPA 2003 s401. Whether or not the employer should have taxed the ex gratia payment when it was made will depend on the nature of the payment - see HMRC NIM02510 for further information, although this point would not be an issue for the tribunal to decide.

Relevant case law: *Babcock FATA Ltd v Addison* [1987] IRLR 173; *Boorman v Allmakes* [1995] IRLR 553; *Chelsea Football Club & Athletic Co Ltd v Heath* [1981] IRLR 73*Digital Equipment Co Ltd v Clements (No 2)* [1997] IRLR 140; *Heggie v Uniroyal Ltd* [1999] IRLR 802; *Horizon Holiday Ltd v Grassi* [1987] IRLR 371; *McCarthy v British Insulated Callenders Cables Plc* [1985] IRLR 94; *Publicis Consultants UK Ltd v O'Farrell* UKEAT/0430/10; *Roadchef v Hastings* [1988] IRLR 142

Exemplary damages

Exemplary damages are available in discrimination claims but are very rarely awarded. In contrast to the usual awards made by tribunals, exemplary damages are punitive not compensatory. They will only be awarded if compensation is insufficient to meet the justice of the case and if the conduct is either:

• oppressive, arbitrary or unconstitutional action by the agents of government; or

• where the defendant's conduct has been calculated to make a profit which may well exceed the compensation payable to the claimant.

The EAT in *MOD v Fletcher* [2010] IRLR 25.has stated that exemplary cases are reserved for the worst cases of the oppressive use of power by public authorities, where the wrongdoing was *'conscious and contumelious'*.

Remedy: Damages. There is no formulaic calculation.

Any maximum or minimum: None. However, in *MOD v Fletcher*, the EAT held that an award of £50,000 was excessive, it reflected the type of award for false imprisonment, and that had an award been appropriate a sum of £7,500 would have been awarded by the EAT. Such a figure would have reflected the level of award in other torts.

Adjustments: None

Tax: It is unlikely that such an award will be taxable, due to its punitive rather than compensatory nature.

Recoupment: N/A

Relevant case law: *Kuddus v Chief Constable of Leicestershire Constabulary* [2002] 2 AC 122, HL; *London Borough of Hackney v Sivanandan and Ors* [2001] IRLR 740; *MOD v Fletcher* [2010] IRLR 25, UKEAT/0044/09

Expenses

(see also Compensatory award)

Expenses incurred as a result of being unfairly dismissed or discriminated against can be claimed as part of the financial losses suffered. These may include the following costs: looking for alternative work, starting up a new business, extra child or dependant care, accommodation, medical expenses etc. In all cases, the expenses should have been reasonably incurred as a result of the dismissal/discrimination/detriment and the sums claimed should be reasonable.

Fees

(see also Tables 6 to 13)

Fees are payable by those bringing employment tribunal claims and appeals to the EAT from 29 July 2013 (although full and partial remission is available in certain circumstances) - see Tables 6 to 13 for more information.

Final salary pension scheme

(see also Pension loss; Tables 28 to 33)

This is a pension scheme where the value of a person's pension on retirement is calculated by reference to their final salary. Sometimes, the pension may be calculated according to the average of the last few years salary. The value of the pension will also be calculated according to the number of years service, typically entitlement will increase by a particular fraction of final salary for each year of employment. Some pension fractions are more generous than others - a pension fraction of 1/60 is more generous than a pension of 1/80 for example. A person who works for 30 years with a pension fraction of 1/60 will retire on half their final salary, whereas a person with a pension fraction of 1/80 will have to work for 40 years to retire on half their salary.

Financial losses

Financial losses suffered from unfair dismissal and discrimination that an employee can claim will generally include loss of any benefits that have a monetary value as well as loss of actual income. Such benefits could include: bonus; commission; holiday pay for lost holiday leave; stock options and profit related pay; enhanced redundancy pay; company car allowance; accommodation; company loan; food allowance; travel allowance; free telephone; private medical insurance; childcare benefits; share ownership; pensions (see also *Pension loss*).

Calculation: The calculation of the value of lost benefits will often take a broad brush approach

unless, for example with a company car, it can easily be ascertained exactly the value of the benefit the employee has lost.

Bonuses and commission: financial losses can include loss of bonus and commission, and it is not necessary to show that the employee had a contractual right to the bonus or commission: s123(1) of the ERA 1996 states that 'the amount of the compensatory award shall be such amount as the tribunal considers just and equitable in all the circumstances having regard to the loss sustained by the complainant in consequence of the dismissal in so far as that loss is attributable to action taken by the employer.' s123(2) states that the amount may include 'loss of any benefit which he might reasonably be expected to have had but for the dismissal.' The claimant needs to show on the balance of probabilities that he had an expectation of receiving the payment and that that expectation was reasonable. It may be difficult to quantify a bonus where it is discretionary, and tribunals may make an award for the loss of a chance of a particular level of bonus, following from the approach taken in *Allied Maples Group Ltd v Simmons & Simmons* [1995] WLR 1602.

Loss of holiday pay: If the claimant obtains another job with less generous holiday benefits, he may seek compensation for the value of those benefits.

Stock options and profit related pay: Such schemes are common for senior staff and may take a number of forms. The valuation of the lost benefits will depend on the terms of the scheme. One simple way in which to value the lost options is to calculate the value of the shares to the employee at the date of termination, and then to calculate the profit, if any, that the employee might have made if they remained part of the scheme. In addition, if the employee is forced to sell their shares as a result of the dismissal and the share price rises, they may be able to claim the difference in valuation between dismissal and a future date. The valuation of share options can be difficult and tribunals will generally base their assessment on an estimate of what appears just and equitable in the circumstances.

Enhanced Redundancy Payments: Compensation for the loss of any redundancy payment in excess of the statutory redundancy can be claimed (see s123(3), whether contractual or whether the employee would merely have an expectation of such payment. Arguably there is a loss that can be claimed where the employee might have been dismissed as redundant during the period covered by the compensatory award.

Company car: Compensation can only be awarded for the private use of a company car and also any loss of free fuel, insurance etc. Several methods are available to calculate the loss:

• One method that can be used is to consider the AA or RAC estimates for the weekly running costs of a particular car (see http://www.theaa.com/ motoring_advice for more information). Then the cost should be adjusted to take into account the proportion of private use as opposed to business use, and again reduced if the employee had to contribute to the running of the car. If the employer has a different method of valuing the company car benefit, this may be used instead.

• HMRC publish scale charges to be used for company cars (see www.hmrc.gov.uk / payerti/exb/a-z/c/cars-fuel-value.htm). The scale charge is HMRC's method of valuing the company car benefit for tax purposes but this may not be an appropriate way to value the actual benefit lost by the claimant.

• Calculate the cost of buying a car or the hire of a car and claim a proportion of the cost from the employer.

• Cars bought on hire purchase in the employee's name where the employer paid part or all of the repayments. The tribunal could award the employee a proportion of the outstanding amount.

Accommodation: one method to assess the value of free or subsidized accommodation is to find evidence of the open-market value of similar accommodation. Alternatively, if the employee has found somewhere else similar to live, the loss could be calculated as the difference between what he would have been paying to the employer and what he is paying now. If the employee had bought their new accommodation, the loss could be calculated on the basis of a proportion of the interest paid on a mortgage (but not the capital).

Company loans: the value of such a benefit can be calculated as the difference between the cost to the employee whilst still in employment and the comparable market rate.

Free food: the loss may be calculated by finding out the value of the food and drink to which the employee was entitled.

Travel allowances: the loss is the value of the travel allowance.

Telephone: the loss is again the value of the telephone, including line rental and actual call charges.

Medical insurance: this can be calculated by finding out the equivalent cost to the employee of obtaining private medical insurance.

Childcare benefits: the loss can be calculated by working out the cost of equivalent child care that was provided by, or subsidized by, the employer. In the case of a subsidy, the difference between the costs can be claimed.

Pensions: the employee may be able to claim for the value of their lost occupational pension (either defined benefit or defined contribution) as well as loss of enhancement of accrued pension rights. Added to this, they could claim for loss of State Second Pension and NI contributions (see separate entries for *Pension loss, State Second Pension* and *National Insurance Contributions*)

Consequential losses: In *Timbulas v The Construction Workers Guild Ltd* UKEAT/0325/13/GE, the claimant won his claim of unpaid holiday pay and also argued that, because his holiday pay was not paid at the date it should have been, he was unable to take advantage of an offer from his mortgage company to pay off his mortgage without incurring a penalty. In consequence, he paid interest on the outstanding mortgage which would not have been payable if he had paid the mortgage off in full. The ET ruled that interest at 5% above base should be added to the holiday pay award.

Gross or net: Any tax deductible benefits should be calculated net of tax and NI.

Adjustments: Any benefits will be included within the compensatory award and adjusted in the normal way (see *Compensatory award*).

Cap: The loss of benefits will be included in the compensatory award and the statutory cap (where applicable) will be applied to the total.

Mitigation: Normal mitigation expectations apply.

Tax: The compensatory award, including benefits, is taxable above £30,000 and will fall to be grossed up under s401 ITEPA 2003 if the award overall exceeds £30,000 (see also *Grossing up*).

Recoupment: Loss of benefits are not subject to the recoupment regulations. Recoupment applies only to immediate loss of earnings, so loss of benefits during the time between dismissal and the hearing should not be included in the calculation.

Statutory authorities: ERA 1996 s123

Fixed term contract

(see also Damages for wrongful dismissal)

When determining damages for wrongful dismissal, it is important first to identify whether the claimant was employed on a permanent or fixed term contract since the period of loss is calculated depends on the period of notice (see *Damages for wrongful dismissal*).

If the contract is for a fixed term and there is no right to terminate on notice, the earliest date at which the employer can end the contract is at the end of the term. If the contract is terminable by notice, the earliest date at which the contract can be brought to an end is the end of the notice period.

Fixed-term employee protection

An employee working under a fixed-term contract has the right not to be treated by his employer less favourably than the employer treats a comparable permanent employee for the following reasons (see Reg3 FTE(PLFT) Regs 2002 SI 2002/2034):

> • as regards the terms of his contract; or

> • by being subjected to any other detriment by any act, or deliberate failure to act, of his employer.

Particular reference is made in the FTE(PLFT) Regs 2002 to less favourable treatment in relation to qualification for benefits on the basis of periods of service, the opportunity to receive training and the opportunity to secure a permanent position (including being informed of any vacancies).

Less favourable treatment will be permitted where it can be objectively justified (Reg 3(3)(b) and Reg 4).

The employee has a right to written reasons for his treatment from his employer (see Reg 5).

The employee is given the right to not be unfairly dismissed or be subject to detrimental treatment in relation to exercising the rights of a fixed term employee (see Reg 6).

Where an employee has been subject to less favourable treatment under Reg 3 or been subject to detriment under Reg 6, he may bring a complaint to an employment tribunal (see Reg 7).

Remedy: Where a tribunal finds that an employee has been subject to less favourable treatment or detriment as set out above, the tribunal (Reg 7(7)):

> "shall take such of the following steps as it considers just and equitable:

> > (a) making a declaration as to the rights of the complainant and the employer in relation to the matters to which the complaint relates;

> > (b) ordering the employer to pay compensation to the complainant;

> > (c) recommending that the employer take, in all the circumstances of the case, for the purposes of obviating or reducing the adverse effect on the complainant of any matter to which the complaint relates."

There are specific provisions providing for the calculation of compensation awarded under Reg 7 and 7(b) (see Regs 7(8) to (12)):

> • The amount of compensation awarded shall be such as the tribunal considers just and equitable in all the circumstances (this phrase is used in the assessment of the compensatory award for unfair dismissal and similar principles will apply);

> • The tribunal will have regard to the infringement to which the complaint relates

and any loss which is attributable to the infringement;

• The loss will include any expenses reasonably incurred by the claimant as a consequence of the infringement and any loss of any benefit he has suffered as a result;

• Compensation for infringement of the right not to be less favourably treated under Reg 3 will not include an award to injury to feelings (although an award for detriment under Reg 6 may include such an award – see *Detriment* and *Injury to feelings*);

• Where there has been contributory fault by the claimant, the amount of compensation will be reduced by such proportion as the tribunal considers just and equitable having regard to that failing.

Failure to comply with recommendation: Where the tribunal has made a recommendation under Reg 7(c), but the employer has without reasonable excuse failed to comply with the recommendation, the tribunal may increase any award for compensation under Reg 7(7)(b) or make an award of compensation where it has not already done so (see Reg7(13)).

Gross or net: This will depend on whether the sums paid are treated as suppressed wages, an award for discrimination or injury to feelings (see *Tax* below, within this entry). Where a sum is paid to represent a net loss it will be calculated on the net figure, grossed up where appropriate to make the final award. Where the sum is viewed as suppressed wages the award will be calculated on gross earnings, with the employer deducting tax and NI.

Any maximum or minimum: No, the award is unlimited.

Adjustments: A percentage deduction for contributory conduct can be applied (Reg 7(12). Also, if the employer fails to comply with a tribunal's recommendation, the award can be increased to a level that the tribunal considers is just and equitable (Reg 7(13).

Mitigation: The usual rules on mitigation apply.

Tax: Any payment to compensate for an employee's reduced wages or benefits would probably be classed as arrears of pay and taxed under s62 ITEPA 2003 in the normal way (see EIM02550 and EIM02530, HMRC). The tax to be paid should be calculated according to the tax year in which the pay was withheld, not the tax year in which the repayment is made.

However, EIM12965 of the Employment Income Manual states that payments of compensation for discrimination which occurs before termination is not employment income for the purposes of s401 and that they are therefore not taxable. It is arguable that the award for infringement of Reg 3 or Reg 6 FTE would not be subject to tax as they are compensation for discrimination (in its broadest sense).

Injury to feelings awards arising other than from dismissal are not taxable.

Statutory authorities: FTE(PLFT) Regs 2002 (SI 2002/2034) Regs 3, 6 and 7

Flexible working

A qualifying employee may apply to his employer for a change in his terms and conditions of employment (s80F ERA 1996) to enable flexible working.

At the time of writing the Government has confirmed that it plans to extend the right to request flexible working to all employees with 26 weeks service from 2014, not just parents and carers. At the same time, it proposes to permit employees to use their employer's own HR procedures to consider requests rather than the current statutory procedures if the request is considered in a reasonable manner.

Section 80G identifies procedural and substantive rules for how an employer must deal with a request.

Remedy: Where an employee brings a complaint that the employer has failed to comply with the requirements in s80G ERA 1996, or that a decision to reject the application was based on incorrect facts which a tribunal finds to be well founded, the tribunal must make a declaration to that effect, may make an order for reconsideration of the application and may make an order that compensation be paid (s80I ERA 1996).

The amount of compensation is the sum the tribunal considers just and equitable, up to the permitted maximum (s80I(2)).

The maximum award is 8 weeks pay, capped at £464 per week (see Reg 7 FW(ECR) Regs 2002/3236 and s227(za) ERA 1996).

Gross or net: The maximum is calculated according to a week's pay, which is a gross figure. A week's pay as defined in ss220 to 229 ERA 1996 applies (see *Week's pay*).

Limit on a week's pay: £464 (see Table 1 for historical rates).

Limit on number of weeks: 8

Any maximum or minimum: No minimum; maximum is 8 x a week's pay (capped at £464 per week) = £3,712.

Adjustments: None, although any compensation ordered will be the sum which the tribunal considers just and equitable. This will include considerations such as the loss actually suffered and attempts to mitigate.

Mitigation: Within the tribunal's consideration of what sum is just and equitable to award.

Tax: The tax treatment is not clear. To the extent that the sum awarded is compensation for lost earnings, it is likely to be taxed under s62 ITEPA 2003 (see *Tax*).

Recoupment: N/A

Statutory authorities: ERA 1996 s80G to 80I and s220-229 ERA 1996; FW(ECR) Regs 2002/3236

Future loss of earnings

(see also Compensatory award; Financial losses; Mitigation)

Where the remedy available to a claimant includes compensation for losses suffered as a result of the unlawful conduct, the losses may still be continuing at the date of the tribunal hearing. A frequently occurring example is an individual found to have been unfairly dismissed who has not obtained new employment or employment paying as much as the job he held when dismissed. The tribunal must assess the losses that the employee will suffer in the future, and the period over which these will continue.

The tribunal will compare the financial circumstances of the claimant, had the unlawful act not occurred, with the circumstances in which they continue to find themselves. Both require the tribunal to assess uncertain scenarios: would the claimant have remained employed or would he have been dismissed in any event; if so would he have found equivalent employment or would he have suffered the same difficulties as he is currently experiencing, or might he have been promoted and received higher pay; when will the claimant obtain equivalent remuneration, or when ought he to? The tribunal will take into account the personal characteristics of the employee such as age and health.

The tribunal's assessment will be based on findings of fact, and will then go on 'to assess the loss flowing from the dismissal, using its common sense, experience and sense of justice' (see *Software 2000 Ltd v Andrews* [2007] IRLR 568, per Elias P). As HHJ Hand QC said in *Stroud Rugby Football Club v Monkman* UKEAT/0143/13/SM, the assessment of future loss is a '*rough and ready matter. It always has been and it always will be*'.

Garden leave

(see also Effective date of termination; Tax and termination payments)

Garden leave is the practice whereby an employee employed during his notice period, whether notice has been given by the employer or the employee, is instructed not to undertake work for the employer. The motive of the employer will be to deny the employee access to confidential information and prevent him from maintaining client relationships, whilst keeping him bound by the terms of his employment contract including his duties of loyalty that prevent the employee from competing with his employer, until after the notice period has expired.

Gourley principle

(see also Tax and termination payments)

The *Gourley* principle is that damages awarded for loss suffered to the claimant should put him in the same position as he would have been in if he had not suffered the unlawful conduct. Where his remuneration would have been subject to tax and NI, the award will be based on his net loss.

The *Gourley* principle was established in the case of *British Transport Commission v Gourley* [1955] UKHL 4 where a civil engineer was awarded damages by the British Transport Commission in respect of a railway accident. The award included an amount for loss of earnings. The question was whether the amount of damages should be paid to the recipient gross or net of deductions that would have been suffered by the individual had he remained in employment.

The court held that '*the broad general principle which should govern the assessment of damages in cases such as this is that the tribunal should award the injured party such a sum of money as will put him in the same position as he would have been in if he had not sustained the injuries ... to ignore the tax element at the present day would be to act in a manner which is out of touch with reality'.* The significance of the *Gourley* principle is that damages will be calculated on the basis of the loss suffered after tax and NI had been deducted from his earnings.

However, where the claimant will have to pay tax on the award, or where the employer will have to deduct tax and NI, the tribunal must 'gross up' the award to ensure that the claimant's net loss is compensated for by an equivalent net sum (see also *Grossing up*). For example, where an award for unfair dismissal exceeds the tax free £30,000, the tribunal will calculate the net loss suffered by the claimant and increase the sum awarded to reflect any tax that the claimant will have to pay on receipt of the award. The two incidences of tax are set off against each other - see *Parsons v BNM Laboratories Ltd* [1963] 2 All ER 658, and *Shove v Downs Surgical Plc* [1984] 1 All ER 7.

Government Actuary Department

(see also Pension loss; Tables 28 to 34)

The Government Actuary Department has produced guidance on how to calculate pension loss after termination of employment (Compensation for Loss of Pension Rights - Employment Tribunals 3rd Edition, TSO). Tribunals are not obliged to apply the guidance or the tables within but will often at least use them as a guide (see Tables 28 to 34).

Grievance procedure

(see also ACAS; Adjustments)

Employers will often have written procedures for considering grievances raised by employees. The core principles upon which a grievance should be considered have been set out by ACAS in the ACAS Code of Practice 1: Disciplinary and Grievance procedures (2009).This code provides basic practical guidance to employers, employees and their representatives and sets out principles for handling disciplinary and grievance situations in the workplace. The Code is issued under section 199 of the Trade Union and Labour Relations (Consolidation) Act 1992 and came into effect on 6 April 2009 (replacing the code issued in 2004).

In a number of types of tribunal claims, if an employee has unreasonably failed to follow the guidance set out in the code relating to the grievance procedure a tribunal may reduce any award they have made by up to 25 per cent (see *ACAS*).

Gross weekly pay

(see also Week's pay)

This is to be contrasted with Net weekly pay. Gross weekly pay is the total sum payable under the contract of employment before the deduction of tax, NI or pension contributions.

Gross weekly pensionable pay

(see also Pension loss)

The pensionable pay is that part of the employee's salary which will be used to calculate employer and employee pension contributions and may not be the same as their gross weekly pay. If pension loss has to be calculated according to the GAD guidelines, the employee's gross weekly pensionable pay will first have to be ascertained, usually from the pension provider or the employer.

Grossing up

(see also *Gourley* principle; Marginal tax rate; Tax and termination payments)

Awards will be 'grossed up' by a tribunal where the sum to be received by the claimant will be taxed. The purpose is to place in the claimant's hands the sum he would have held had he not been treated unlawfully, i.e. to compensate for the true net loss. Where the award will be taxed by the employer before payment is made to the claimant, such as where the award is for unpaid wages, the tribunal will award the true gross sum. Grossing up therefore applies to awards where s401 ITEPA 2003 operates to tax the sum in the claimant's hands.

Section 401 applies to payments and other benefits which are received directly or indirectly in consideration or in consequence of, or otherwise in connection with:

a) the termination of a person's employment;

b) a change in the duties of a person's employment; or

c) a change in the earnings from a person's employment, by the person, or the person's spouse, blood relative, dependant or personal representatives.

In this case the recipient enjoys a tax free amount of £30,000 in any particular tax year and will then pay tax at their marginal tax rate on sums in excess of this figure.

To avoid disadvantage to the claimant, the tribunal should 'gross up' any award it makes over £30,000. This requires the tribunal to estimate the tax the claimant will have to pay on receipt of the award and add a sum for that tax back on to the award, thus cancelling out the tax burden to the claimant. In other words, where the tribunal has determined the sum a claimant is to be awarded, the tribunal will consider the likely tax consequences and increase the award to ensure that the claimant retains the sum to which the tribunal has determined he is entitled.

Before the £30,000 threshold (see EIM13505) is applied to an award, it is necessary to add together all the payments and benefits within s401 ITEPA 2003 that are made to, or are in respect of, the same person in connection with:

- the same office or employment; and

- different offices or employments with the same employer; and

- different offices or employments with associated employers (see EIM13540).

The threshold is then applied to the total. This ensures that all sums fall within just the one £30,000 threshold.

For example, a director is dismissed from two separate employments with associated employers within the same tax year, receiving payments and benefits worth £25,000 in each case which all fall within s401 ITEPA 2003. He also receives a tribunal award of £40,000 for unfair dismissal. The aggregated total received in connection with the terminated employments is £90,000 and only one £30,000 threshold is available against that total.

The tribunal will gross up the sum in excess of £30,000 taking into account the employee's personal allowance and tax banding (*Shove v Downs Surgical Plc* [1984] 1 All ER 7). This tax rate

that should be applied is called the claimant's marginal tax rate and may be difficult to ascertain. Further, different marginal tax rates may be applied to different elements of the award (see *Yorkshire Housing Ltd v Cuerden* UKEAT/0397/09).

An award for pension loss also falls to be grossed up – see *Yorkshire Housing Ltd v Cuerden* UKEAT/0397/09.

Some heads of loss should not be grossed up - these are ones where

1) the award has been calculated as a gross figure and tax will be deducted either before the claimant receives the payment (for example, accrued holiday pay and the claimant is still employed); or

2) awards which are not taxable (see *Injury to feelings*).

In what order should grossing up be applied?
Calculations should be performed in the following order:

1) Adjustments, including the addition of interest (see *Adjustments*);

2) Grossing up;

3) Statutory cap applied (see *Hardie Grant London Ltd v Aspden* UKEAT/0242/11/RN).

Recoupment: There is no information to explain whether the prescribed element should be calculated before grossing up or after. However, it is likely that the sums involved would render the distinction of no relevance.

Relevant case law: *Hardie Grant London Ltd v Aspden* UKEAT/0242/11/RN; *Shove v Downs Surgical Plc* [1984] 1 All ER 7; *Yorkshire Housing Ltd v Cuerden* UKEAT/0397/09/SM

Examples
All examples assume that the claimant's marginal tax rate is 20% and the maximum statutory cap on an unfair dismissal award as at 6 April 2014, which is £76,574. The calculation for grossing up the award is:

(Grossed up sum) x (1 – marginal tax rate) = true net loss

Therefore:

Grossed up sum = (true net loss) / (1 – marginal tax rate)

Example 1

Basic award = £11,000 (Taxable)

Compensatory award = £70,000 (Taxable)
Tax free element = £30,000

Calculation

Amount of compensation up to the £30,000 tax free element = £30,000 - £11,000 = £19,000

Amount of compensation award that should be taxed = £70,000 - £19,000 = £51,000

The grossed up compensation of £51,000 = £51,000 ÷ 0.8 = £63,750

Total compensation = £19,000 + £63,750 = £82,750

Compensation cap = £76,574

Total award = £11,000 (basic) + £76,574 (statutory cap) = £87,574

Example 2

Basic award = £11,000 (Taxable)

Injury to feelings = £25,000 (Non-taxable)

Compensation for financial loss = £70,000 (Taxable)

Tax free element = £30,000

Calculation

Basic award = £11,000

Amount of compensation up to the £30,000 tax free element = £30,000 - £11,000 = £19,000

Amount of compensation award that should be taxed = £70,000 - £19,000 = £51,000

The grossed up compensation of £51,000 = £51,000 ÷ 0.8 = £63,750

Total compensation = £19,000 + £63,750 = £82,750 (the statutory cap does not apply to awards for discrimination).

Injury to feelings = £25,000 and is not grossed up because it is not taxable.

Total award = £11,000 (basic) + £25,000 (untaxed injury to feelings award) + £82,750 (uncapped compensation) = £118,750

Example 3

Basic award = £11,000 (Taxable)

Detriment award = £25,000 (Taxable)

Compensation award = £10,000 (Taxable)
Tax free element = £30,000

Calculation

Basic award = £11,000

Detriment award = £19,000 plus £6,000, of which £6,000 should be grossed up

Grossed up detriment award = £6,000 ÷ 0.8 = £7,500

Compensation award = £10,000 which will be taxed in full

Grossed up compensation = £10,000 ÷ 0.8 = £12,500

Total award = £11,000 (basic) + £19,000 (untaxed detriment award) + £7,500 (grossed up detriment award) + £12,500 (grossed up compensation) = £50,000

Example 4

Basic award = £11,000 (Taxable)

Compensation award = £40,000 (Taxable)

Tax free element = £30,000

Calculation

Compensation award exceeding the tax free element = £40,000 – (£30,000 - £11,000) = £21,000

Grossed up compensation = £21,000 ÷ 0.8 = £26,250

Total award = £11,000 (basic) + £19,000 (compensation up to tax free limit) + £26,250 (grossed up compensation) = £56,250

Guarantee payment

(see also Week's pay; Table 3)

Employees are entitled to be paid a minimum amount where throughout a day during any part of which an employee would normally be required to work in accordance with his contract of employment the employee is not provided with work by his employer, and the reason is:

a) a diminution in the requirements of the employer's business for work of the kind which the employee is employed to do; or

b) any other occurrence affecting the normal working of the employer's business in relation to work of the kind which the employee is employed to do.

That minimum sum is called a guarantee payment (s28 ERA 1996).

An employee may bring a complaint to a tribunal that his employer has failed to pay the whole or any part of a guarantee payment to which he is entitled (s34 ERA 1996).

Remedy: The remedy is an order from the tribunal that the employer must pay to the employee the amount of guarantee payment that the tribunal has found to be due.

Calculation of remedy: Guarantee pay for a particular day = normal working hours on that day x guaranteed hourly rate, where the guaranteed hourly rate = 1 week's pay ÷ number of normal working hours in a week for that employee when employed under the contract of employment in force on the particular day (s30(1) ERA 1996).

If the number of hours the employee works differs from week to week, the number of normal working hours is calculated by dividing by twelve the total number of the employee's normal working hours during the period of twelve weeks ending with the last complete week before the day in respect of which the guarantee payment is payable. Where the employee has not been employed for a sufficient period to enable the calculation to be made, a number which fairly represents the number of normal working hours in a week will be used (s30(3) and (4) ERA 1996).

Gross or net: Gross. Any guarantee pay either paid by the employer or awarded by the tribunal should be added to other gross pay in that period and PAYE and NI deducted in the normal way.

Limit on guarantee payment: The limit on the guarantee payment for a particular day is £25.00 from 06/04/2014 (s31(1) ERA 1996).

Limit on number of days: A tribunal can order a guarantee payment to be paid for a maximum of 5 days in any 3 month period (s31(2) and (3) ERA 1996).

Any maximum or minimum: No minimum; maximum will be £125.00 in any 3 month period.

Adjustments: None

Mitigation: N/A

Tax: Taxed under s62 ITEPA 2003 (see EIM02550, HMRC)

Recoupment: Any amount found to be due to the employee and ordered to be paid under section 34(3) for a period before the conclusion of the tribunal proceedings will form part of the prescribed element.

Statutory authorities: ERA 1996 ss28 to 35; ITEPA 2003 s62; EP(RJAIS) Regs 1996

Harassment: see Discrimination

Holiday pay

(see also Insolvency; Table 14)

The Working Time Regulations 1998 provide workers with a minimum entitlement to paid leave. The minimum entitlement, subject to certain exclusions, is 5.6 weeks paid holiday per year subject to a cap of 28 days. The 5.6 weeks are made up of four weeks basic annual leave under Reg 13 and 1.6 weeks additional leave under Reg 13(A). 28 days corresponds to 5.6 weeks for a worker working 5 days per week, but if a working week is longer, the statutory minimum remains capped at 28 days even though the full 5.6 weeks of holiday will thereby not be guaranteed. Workers may in addition to the guaranteed minimum holiday be entitled under their contractual terms to enhanced holiday entitlement.

For a typical worker calculating holiday entitlement and the corresponding may be straightforward. Difficulties can arise for example where workers start, or leave, part way through a holiday year, where workers seek to carry over leave from one year to another, or where a worker's working time is non-standard. Special rules apply to calculating statutory holiday entitlement for part time workers, workers working atypical days and hours, and workers absent on sick leave or family related leave.

Holiday claims may arise in a number of circumstances including where: the worker has been denied the right to take holiday; the worker has not been paid for the holiday they have taken; the worker has left their employment without having taken the leave to which they were entitled and seeks pay in lieu of that holiday; or the worker may have been subject to a detriment or dismissed for conduct relating to seeking to take holiday or enforce the right to paid holiday.

Claims for unpaid statutory holiday pay may be made under Reg 30 WTR 1998 and s13 ERA 1996 (see *Revenue and Customs Commissioners v Stringer* [2009] ICR 985). Where the right is contractual, a claim for unpaid holiday pay may be made under s13 ERA 1996. It is also possible to bring such a contractual claim in the ordinary civil courts, or where the contract has been terminated, in the employment tribunal under its limited contractual jurisdiction ETEJ Regs.

The rights not to suffer detriment or be dismissed for seeking to enforce rights to holiday pay flow from s45A, 101A and 104 ERA 1996 (see

Detriment and *Unfair dismissal*).

Remedy: Reg 16(1) WTR 1998 provides that 'A worker is entitled to be paid in respect of any period of annual leave to which he is entitled under regulation 13, at the rate of a week's pay in respect of each week of leave'. A week's pay is calculated according to s221 to 224 ERA 1996 subject to slight technical modifications and the removal of the limit on a week's pay (see *Week's pay*).

Note: the operation of ss221 to 224 often fails to take into account pay a worker would in fact receive during a pay period. The WTR implement EU law and it may well be that ss221 to 224 fail to provide workers with the full entitlement to pay required by EU law (see *British Airways plc v Williams* [2012] IRLR 1014 and *Z.J.R. Lock v British Gas Trading Ltd and Others* [2013] EUECJ C-539/12). A number of cases are progressing through the tribunal system to test whether the current method of calculation is appropriate, or whether some other calculation should be applied.

Where the worker relies not upon the statutory minimum entitlement to holiday, but a contractual term, the calculation of holiday pay will be in accordance with the provisions of the contract.

Gross or net: Any order for the payment of accrued holiday pay should be use gross figures, and the sum will be taxed by the employer.

Adjustments: Accrued holiday pay may be claimed as an unlawful deduction from wages, in which case the ACAS uplift could apply where there has been a failure in any grievance process.

Cap: Accrued holiday pay is not included in the award for financial losses arising from an unfair dismissal, so it falls outside the statutory cap.

Mitigation: N/A

Tax: Tax should be paid either by the employer through the payroll or by the employee under Self-Assessment where this has not been done.

Recoupment: Recoupment will not apply to accrued holiday pay if the employee has been dismissed.

Statutory authorities: ERA 1996 s13; WTR 1998 Regs 13, 14, 16 and 30

Relevant case law: .*British Airways plc v Williams* [2012] IRLR 1014; *Z.J.R. Lock v British Gas Trading Ltd and Others* [2013] EUECJ C-539/12

Housing benefit

(see also Recoupment*)*

In the case of *Savage v Saxena* [1998] UKEAT/605/97 the EAT held that housing benefit the claimant had received since her dismissal should not be deducted from the compensatory award, as it would not be just or equitable to allow a defaulting employer to retain the benefits and to place an unfairly dismissed employee at the disadvantage of possibly having to pay the benefit back once her situation had been reassessed. Housing benefit is not a recoupable benefit so the employer would not have to pay its value to the Secretary of State if were deducted from the claimant's award. If a claimant's entitlement was reassessed and the benefit did not have to be paid back, the claimant would appear to recover from the employer a greater sum than his losses.

Immediate loss of earnings

(see also Compensatory award; Future loss of earnings)

Immediate loss of earnings is the phrase used to describe the loss of earnings up until the tribunal hearing where remedy is determined. It is to be contrasted with future loss of earnings which are those losses suffered after the hearing. Immediate loss of earnings will often be simpler to assess than future loss, as the requirement to predict what will happen in the future is absent.

The tribunal will compare the financial circumstances of the claimant, had the unlawful act not occurred, with the circumstances in which he has found himself. Both require the tribunal to assess uncertain scenarios: would the claimant have remained employed or would he have been dismissed in any event, if so would he have found equivalent employment or would he have suffered the same difficulties as he has experienced, or might he have been promoted and received higher pay; when did the claimant obtained equivalent remuneration, or when ought he to have done so? The tribunal will take into account the personal characteristics of the employee such as age and health.

The tribunal's assessment will be based on findings of fact, and then 'to assess the loss flowing from the dismissal, using its common sense, experience and sense of justice' (see *Software 2000 Ltd v Andrews* [2007] IRLR 568, per Elias P).

Incapacity benefit

(see also Housing benefit; Recoupment)

Incapacity benefit (now Employment and Support Allowance or ESA) may be paid if the individual cannot work because they are ill or disabled.

Damages for wrongful dismissal

Credit must be given for the receipt of state benefits during the damages period. However, some state benefits are excluded. It is not clear whether ESA will always be deducted since it will depend on the facts of the case and how remote or otherwise the benefit is. It could also be argued that state benefits received during the statutory notice period should not be deducted in full (*see Westwood v Secretary of State for Employment* [1984] 1 All ER 874 where the employee was dismissed without the statutory notice period or payment in lieu) because the employee would exhaust their entitlement to state benefits earlier than they would have done if they had been given the statutory notice.

Compensatory award

ESA can be deducted from the compensatory award if, but for the dismissal, the benefit would not have been obtained. *Morgans v Alpha Plus Security Ltd* [2005] UKEAT/0438/04 confirms this position, where the claimant was dismissed and then was unable to work because of his psychological state attributable to the respondent's action in dismissing him. The EAT held that there is no jurisdiction to disregard receipts, or to claim and recover a sum in excess of the actual loss. Where a claimant has suffered a lesser loss, by virtue of his receipt of benefits, which would not have been paid had they remained employed, credit must be given for them.

However, credit need not be given for benefits that are too remote. Often, the decision as to whether the benefits are deductible or not is up for argument.

Relevant case law: *Morgans v Alpha Plus Security Ltd* [2005] UKEAT/0438/04; *Westwood v Secretary of State for Employment* [1984] 1 All ER 874

Income support

(see also Job seekers allowance; Recoupment)

Income Support is paid to those on a low income or none at all, who are working less than 16 hours a week and haven't signed on as unemployed.

Income support is not deducted from an award of compensation but instead is subject to the recoupment regulations (see *Savage v Saxena* [1998] UKEAT/605/97).

If the tribunal is satisfied that in respect of each day falling within the period to which the prescribed element relates the employee has neither received nor claimed jobseeker's allowance or income support the recoupment regulations will not apply.

Statutory cap: If the statutory cap has been applied the prescribed element should be adjusted by the same proportion (see also *Recoupment*).

Statutory authorities: The Employment Protection (Recoupment of jobseekers allowance and income support) Regulations 1996

Relevant case law: *Savage v Saxena* [1998] UKEAT/605/97

Indirect discrimination: see Discrimination

Individual respondents

(see also Discrimination)

An individual employee may be a respondent to a discrimination claim, and it is often the case that claims will be brought against an employer and one or more individual employees responsible for the acts complained of (see s110 EA 2010).

Where a claim against an individual is upheld by the tribunal the tribunal may make individual awards against any particular respondent or make all respondents jointly and severally liable for the award. It is not possible to apportion an award between contributing respondents under the Civil Liability (Contribution) Act 1978 (see *London Bororugh of Hackney v Sivanandan* [2013] EWCA Civ 22).

Industrial action

Sections 237-239 TULR(C)A 1992 make specific provision governing the availability of the right to claim unfair dismissal under s111 ERA 1996 where the dismissal is related to having taken industrial action. Industrial action may take the form of strikes or action less than a strike. Dismissals related to official industrial action, where the action has the support of a trade union's ballot of its members, are treated differently from dismissals related to unofficial industrial action. In general terms, the right to claim unfair dismissal is restricted in some circumstances and a dismissal will be automatically unfair if other conditions are satisfied. The qualifying period and the time limit for bringing certain industrial action unfair dismissal claims are also altered.

Remedy: The unfair dismissal jurisdiction, and the principles that apply to the remedy available, are those for unfair dismissal generally (see *Unfair dismissal*).

Adjustments: The House of Lords in *Crosville Wales Ltd v Tracey* [1997] IRLR 691 held that tribunals should not reduce an award for contributory fault where an employee has been unfairly dismissed for taking industrial action under s238 TULRCA 1992. It is likely that where an employee is dismissed for threatening to take such industrial action a reduction for contributory fault will also be denied (see *Adapters and Eliminators v Paterson* EAT 21 April 1983 unreported). It may be possible to reduce an award for contributory fault where the actions of the employee have gone beyond mere participation in industrial action, for example if the individual has acted in an inflammatory or intimidatory manner. See also *Courtaulds Northern Spinning Ltd v Moosa* [1984] IRLR 43.

Statutory authorities: TULRCA 1992 ss237 to 239

Relevant case law: *Adapters and Eliminators v Paterson* EAT 21 April 1983 unreported; Courtaulds Northern Spinning Ltd v Moosa [1984] IRLR 43; *Crosville Wales Ltd v Tracey* [1997] IRLR 691

Injury to feelings

(see also Discrimination)

Injury to feelings awards compensate for non-economic loss. Injury to feelings awards are available where a tribunal has upheld a complaint of discrimination (see s119(4) EA 2010) or unlawful detriment, but are not available for unfair dismissal (see *Dunnachie v Kingston upon Hull City Council* [2004] IRLR 727).

Subject to the following caveat, such an award is also not available where a worker has suffered the detriment of termination of his or her contract for making a protected disclosure or for reasons related to working time protections (see s49(5A) and (6) ERA 1996), since compensation is limited to that available for unfair dismissal. The caveat is that since both injury to feelings and a basic award compensate for non-economic loss, it would appear that an injury to feelings award may be made, up to the level of an appropriate basic award had in fact the claim been brought as unfair dismissal. This approach would ensure that the availability of an injury to feelings award is not unnecessarily limited where a basic award for equivalent unfair dismissal is not available.

There are other heads of non-economic loss that may be compensated for by a tribunal (see *Aggravated damages; Exemplary damages; Physical and psychiatric injury*).

Remedy: The award of injury to feelings is intended to compensate the claimant for the anger, distress and upset caused by the unlawful treatment they have received, its calculation is not based on any principle of punishment. Tribunals have a broad discretion as to what level of award to make, which can only be overturned on appeal if the figure chosen is obviously wrong, which will only occur very rarely.

General principles

The general principles that apply to assessing an appropriate injury to feelings award have been set out by the EAT in *Prison Service v Johnson* [1997] IRLR 162, para 27:

● Injury to feelings awards are compensatory and should be just to both parties. They should compensate fully without punishing the discriminator. Feelings of indignation at the discriminator's conduct should not be allowed to inflate the award;

● Awards should not be too low, as that would diminish respect for the policy of the anti-discrimination legislation. Society has condemned discrimination and awards must ensure that it is seen to be wrong. On the other hand, awards should be restrained, as excessive awards could be seen as the way to untaxed riches;

• Awards should bear some broad general similarity to the range of awards in personal injury cases – not to any particular type of personal injury but to the whole range of such awards;

• Tribunals should take into account the value in everyday life of the sum they have in mind, by reference to purchasing power or by reference to earnings;

• Tribunals should bear in mind the need for public respect for the level of awards made.

The matters compensated for by an injury to feelings award encompass subjective feelings of upset, frustration, worry, anxiety, mental distress, fear, grief, anguish, humiliation, unhappiness, stress and depression, see *Vento v Chief Constable of West Yorkshire Police (No2)* [2003] IRLR 102.

Bands of compensation

Also in *Vento* the Court of Appeal identified three broad bands of compensation for injury to feelings and gave the following guidance (however, see below for revised figures):

1) The top band should normally be between £15,000 and £25,000. Sums in this range should be awarded in the most serious cases, such as where there has been a lengthy campaign of discriminatory harassment on the ground of sex or race. Only in the most exceptional case should an award of compensation for injury to feelings exceed £25,000;

2) The middle band of between £5,000 and £15,000 should be used for serious cases, which do not merit an award in the highest band;

3) Awards of between £500 and £5,000 are appropriate for less serious cases, such as where the act of discrimination is an isolated or one-off occurrence. In general, awards of less than £500 are to be avoided altogether, as they risk being regarded as so low as not to be a proper recognition of injury to feelings.

Within each band there is considerable flexibility, allowing tribunals to fix what is considered to be fair, reasonable and just compensation in the particular circumstances of the case.

The EAT revisited the exact boundaries of the three bands in *Da'Bell v NSPCC* [2010] IRLR 19 and accepted the arguments of both sides before it

that the EAT should uprate the *Vento* guidelines in line with the RPI as follows:

1) The upper band should be £18,000 to £30,000;

2) The middle band should be £6,000 to £18,000;

3) The lower band should be £600 to £6,000.

The approach taken by the EAT appears to be that the guidelines will be updated every so often, not that the guideline figures should be recalculated by tribunals on an ongoing basis for each discrimination claim before them (see judgment paragraph 46). Nevertheless, since the real value of the award is a factor the tribunal should take into account, it would seem that a tribunal would be entitled to guide itself on the basis of boundaries increased to an updated figure according to RPI. In *Simmons v Castle* [2012] EWCA Civ 1288 the Court of Appeal announced that with effect from 1 April 2013, general damages in tort cases would be increased by 10 per cent on existing levels, and the boundaries updated on that basis would be:

1) The upper band would be £19,800 to £33,000

2) The middle band would be £6,600 to £19,800

3) The lower band would be £660 to £6,600

Other relevant factors

Proof of injury: It is not inevitable that a tribunal will award an injury to feelings award where it is permitted to, though it is very unusual for no such award to be made. It is necessary for the individual to prove the nature of the injury to feelings and its extent, though this could be at its simplest the fact that a claimant has stated he was upset by his dismissal (see *Murray v Powertech (Scotland) Ltd* [1992] IRLR 257 and *Ministry of Defence v Cannock* [1994] ICR 918). The evidence a claimant will want to produce is the material which shows the impact of the discrimination on any subjective feelings of upset, frustration, worry, anxiety, mental distress, fear, grief, anguish, humiliation, unhappiness, stress and depression. For example, this might include evidence about the impact the discrimination has had on relationships with colleagues, friends and family and any particular difficulties caused by the discrimination. Such evidence might include medical evidence, but where the injury to feelings amounts to a mental illness such as depression, the claimant might well consider seeking an award for personal injury in addition to injury to feelings.

Double recovery: Where an individual is awarded sums both for injury to feelings and personal injury (e.g. depression) caused by the discrimination, the injury to feelings and personal injury awards must compensate for different injuries and not overlap. The consequence is that for example where discrimination has caused a period of depression, either the injury to feelings award or the personal injuries award will be less than would be appropriate if only one of the awards had been made.

Claimant's knowledge: It is not necessary for an injury to feelings award to be made that the claimant's injured feelings are caused by his knowledge that he has been discriminated against, contrary to the interpretation given to *Skyrail Oceanic Ltd v Coleman* [1981] IRLR 398. The EAT in *Taylor v XLN Telecom Ltd* [2010] IRLR 49 held that the calculation of the remedy for discrimination is the same as in other torts, and that knowledge of the discriminator's motives was not necessary for recovery of injury to feelings. The EAT nevertheless observed that the distress and humiliation suffered by a claimant will generally be greater where the discrimination has been overt or the claimant appreciates at the time that the motivation was discriminatory.

Separate awards for separate grounds of discrimination: Where an individual has suffered a number of acts of discrimination, some caused by one protected ground, e.g. race, others by another protected ground, e.g. disability, the tribunal should make separate awards for each protected ground, as each is a separate wrong giving a right to damages (see *Al Jumard v Clywd Leisure Ltd* [2008] IRLR 345). However, where the discriminatory acts overlap as they arise from the same set of facts, such as where a dismissal is on grounds of both race and disability, a tribunal will not be expected to separate the injury to feelings and attribute parts to each form of discrimination. This may not necessarily result in an increased award compared to the situation where all the acts of discrimination are caused by one protected characteristic, as the tribunal must always have regard to the proportionality of the overall figure awarded for injury to feelings.

Future contingencies: Where the discriminatory act, such as a dismissal, would have occurred at some point in the future for legitimate reasons in any event, it is not appropriate to reduce the injury to feelings award to reflect that future possibility. The award reflects the injury to feelings caused by the knowledge that the reason for the act was discrimination, which cannot be offset by the fact that a lawful dismissal may have been carried out in any event (see *O'Donoghue v Redcar and Cleveland Borough Council* 2001 IRLR 615).

The severity of the act of discrimination: The *Vento* guideline connect the level of an award to the severity of the discrimination. In *Voith Turbo Ltd v Stowe* [2005] IRLR 228 the EAT observed that a discriminatory dismissal is not to be considered as a one off event, but should fall within the middle *Vento* band. In particularly serious cases of discrimination, an award of aggravated damages may be available (see *Aggravated damages* and *Exemplary damages*).

Adjustments: Interest can be awarded on the sum for injury to feelings (see *Interest*). Reg 6(1)(a) IT(IADC) Regs 1996 provides that the period over which interest accrues begins with the date of the discrimination and ends on the date the tribunal calculates compensation. A *Polkey*-type deduction should not be applied to the award, even if the claimant would have been fairly dismissed at a date soon afterwards (*O'Donoghue v Redcar and Cleveland Borough Council* [2001] IRLR 615).

Tax: It is widely understood that an award for Injury to feelings in a discrimination case is not taxable and so therefore should not be grossed up (see *Walker v Adams* [2001] STC 101, *Orthet Ltd v Vince-Cain (2)* [2004] UKEAT/0801/03 and *Oti-Obihara v Commissioners for HM Revenue & Customs* [2011] IRLR 386). However, the issue is not clear cut as HMRC's Employment Income Manual states awards for discrimination arising out of termination, including injury to feelings, should be taxed under s401 ITEPA. Awards for injury to feelings arising from discrimination that is not connected to dismissal, will not be subject to tax.

Recoupment: N/A

Relevant case law: *A v HM Revenue & Customs* [2009]; *Al Jumard v Clywd Leisure Ltd* [2008] IRLR 345; *Da'Bell v NSPCC* [2009] UKEAT/0227/09; *Dunnachie v Kingston upon Hull City Council* [2004] IRLR 727; *Ministry of Defence v Cannock* [1994] ICR 918; *Murray v Powertech (Scotland) Ltd* [1992] IRLR 257; *O'Donoghue v Redcar and Cleveland Borough Council* [2001] IRLR 615; *Orthet Ltd v Vince-Cain (2)* [2004] UKEAT/0801/03; *Oti-Obihara v Commissioners for HM Revenue & Customs* [2011] IRLR 386; *Prison Service v Johnson* [1997] IRLR 162; *Skyrail Oceanic Ltd v Coleman* [1981] IRLR 398; *Taylor v XLN*

Telecom Ltd [2010] IRLR 49; Vento v Chief Constable of West Yorkshire Police [2002] EWCA Civ 1871; Voith Turbo Ltd v Stowe [2005] IRLR 228; Walker v Adams (SpC344)

Insolvency

The Redundancy Payments Office operates a scheme whereby the National Insurance Fund will make certain payments to ex-employees of an insolvent employer where certain conditions are satisfied (see ss182 to 190 ERA 1996). The ex-employee must make a claim to the Redundancy Payments Office, who may make payments for a limited amount of the debts of the employer to the ex-employee. The debts covered are (s184):

- any arrears of pay in respect of one or more weeks, capped at eight weeks;

- statutory notice pay;

- up to six weeks holiday pay accruing over the twelve months before 'the appropriate date';

- any basic award for compensation for unfair dismissal;

- any reasonable sum by way of reimbursement of the whole or part of any fee or premium paid by an apprentice or articled clerk.

Sections 184(2) to 184(6) define what may amount to arrears of pay (which includes amongst other matters a guarantee payment and a protective award), what amounts to holiday pay and what may amount to 'a reasonable sum'.

The debts must have been due on 'the appropriate date' which is defined in s185, and depending on the nature of the debt may be the date of the formal insolvency of the employer, the date of termination of employment or the date on which the award was made (for example if the debt is the basic award or an unpaid protective award).

Where an individual has applied to the Redundancy Payments Office for payment, but it has not been made, or payment has not been made in full he can make a claim to the employment tribunal (s188 ERA 1996).

Under s124 Pension Schemes Act 1993 there is a comparable scheme for requesting (and enforcing) payment from the National Insurance Fund for unpaid pension contributions

Remedy: Where a tribunal upholds a claim for

payment, the tribunal will make a declaration to that effect stating the amount that ought to be paid to the ex-employee from the National Insurance Fund.

Calculation of remedy
Various limits apply to the entitlement of the ex-employee to be paid certain debts:

- Arrears of pay are limited to 8 weeks, with each week capped at a £464 (or an appropriate proportion of that if the debt arises from part of a week) (ss184 and 186);

- Statutory notice pay is anyway capped at 12 weeks, and each week is capped at £464 (or an appropriate proportion of that if the debt arises from part of a week) (ss184 and 186);

- Holiday pay is limited to six weeks, with each week capped at £464 (or an appropriate proportion of that if the debt arises from part of a week) (ss184 and s186).

Gross or net: Gross. A week's pay as defined in ss220 to 229 ERA 1996 applies (see *Week's pay*).

Limit on a week's pay: £464 (see Table 1 for historical rates).

Limit on number of weeks: See individual limits above.

Any maximum or minimum: Maximum = £3,712 + £5,568 + £13,920 + £2,784 = £25,984; No minimum

Adjustments: None

Mitigation: The nature of the underlying debt will determine whether the duty to mitigate applies. For example, the ex-employee is under a duty to mitigate their loss for failure to pay wages for the length of the statutory notice period, but there is no duty to mitigate loss in relation to a protective award or a basic award. (See *Mitigation* and *Protective award*).

Also, any state benefits that have been received, or could have been claimed, will be deducted (see 'Redundancy & Insolvency: A Guide for Employees' published by The Insolvency Service, paragraph 19).

Tax: Any arrears of pay/protective award and accrued holiday pay will have income tax and national insurance deducted at the basic rate. 'Notional' tax, equivalent to the basic rate, will be deducted from compensation for failure to give statutory notice (this tax is not actually paid to HMRC but may be claimed back by the employee if their total income for the year is less than their personal allowance). The basic award will not be taxed at all unless it exceeds £30,000, which will never happen because of the statutory limit (see paragraphs 19 and 20 of 'Redundancy & Insolvency: A Guide for Employees').

Recoupment: Recoupment does not apply. Any state benefits received will be deducted from the award.

Statutory authorities: ERA 1996 ss182 to 190; Pension Schemes Act 1993 s124; TULR(C)A 1992 s188

Interest

(see also Discrimination; Injury to feelings; Interest on discrimination awards; Interest on unpaid awards; Table 23)

There are two different situations in which interest is available on a tribunal award. First, where a tribunal award has not been paid interest accrues on the unpaid sum (see *Interest on unpaid awards*). Secondly, a tribunal is able to award interest in discrimination claims brought under the EA 2010 as part of its award of compensation, to compensate for the fact that compensation has been awarded after the loss compensated for has been suffered (see *Interest on discrimination awards*).

Interest on discrimination awards

(see also Discrimination; Injury to feelings; Interest on Unpaid Awards; Table 23)

A tribunal is able to award interest on awards of compensation made in discrimination claims brought under s124(2)(b) EA 2010, to compensate for the fact that compensation has been awarded after the loss compensated for has been suffered (see s139 EA 2010, EA 2010 Commencement No 4 etc Order 2010/2317 and IT(IADC) Regs 1996).

The tribunal may award interest to the following types of discrimination award:

- Past financial loss;
- Injury to feelings;
- Aggravated and exemplary damages;
- Physical and psychiatric injury.

Since a tribunal cannot award interest on past loss within a compensatory award for unfair dismissal, where an unfair dismissal is also a

discriminatory dismissal tribunals will often compensate such losses under the discrimination legislation.

Calculation of interest
Interest is calculated as simple interest accruing from day to day (Reg 3(1)).

Interest rate: Until 29 July 2013 the interest rate to be applied in England and Wales was that prescribed for the special investment account under rule 27(1) of the Court Funds Rules 1987. The interest rate until 29 July 2013 was 0.5%. For claims presented on or after 29 July 2013 the relevant interest rate is that specified in s17 of the Judgments Act 1838 (see The Employment Tribunals (Interest on Awards in Discrimination Cases)(Amendment) Regulations 2013). The interest rate now to be applied is 8% which is in line with Scotland (see Table 23 for a list of interest rates).

If the rate of interest changes during the period over which interest is calculated, the tribunal may use such median or average of those rates as seems to it appropriate, in the interests of simplicity (see Reg 3(3)) The Industrial Tribunals (Interest on Awards in Discrimination Cases) Regulations 1996.

Period of calculation, injury to feelings: interest is awarded on injury to feelings awards from the date of the act of discrimination complained of until the date on which the tribunal calculates the compensation (see Reg 6(1)(a)).

Period of calculation, all other sums: Interest is awarded on all sums other than injury to feelings awards from the mid-point of the date of the act of discrimination complained of and the date the tribunal calculates the award (Reg 6(1)(b)). The mid-point date is the date half way through the period between the date of the discrimination complained of and the date the tribunal calculates the award (Reg 4).

Period of calculation, early payment: where payment of any of the sums attracting interest has already been made by the respondent, the date of payment is taken as the date of calculation of the award for those particular sums (Reg 6(2)).

Period of calculation, serious injustice discretion: where a tribunal considers that serious injustice would be caused if interest were to be calculated according to the approaches above, it can calculate interest on such different periods as it considers appropriate (Reg 6(3)). See *Ministry of Defence v Cannock* [1994] IRLR 509, where interest was awarded over a longer period than provided for by the regulations due to the long period since the loss was incurred.

Interest cannot be awarded in respect of future loss or loss arising before the discrimination complained of (Reg 5). This reflects the broad principle behind the award of interest which is that it is compensation to the successful claimant for the loss they have suffered by virtue of not having received payment of the award at the date of the loss suffered.

Calculation
Interest on past loss
Interest runs from the 'mid-point' date to the date of calculation. The mid-point is calculated as the date halfway between the date of the discriminatory act and ending on the calculation date (usually the judgment date). Interest accrues from day to day and is simple rather than compound.

Interest = (number of days from discriminatory act date to calculation date x 1/2 x interest rate x 1/100 x 1/365 x compensatory award (after all adjustments have been made - see *Adjustments*)

Example 1
Compensation award = £20,000

Discriminatory date = 01/04/2009

Calculation date = 05/02/2011

Interest rate = 0.5%

Number of days between discriminatory date and calculation date = 676 inclusive

Interest = 676 x 1/2 x 0.005 x 1/365 x 20,000 = £92.60 (the number of days have been divided by 2 because of the mid-point rule)

Interest on Injury to Feelings
Interest runs from the date of the discriminatory act to the date of calculation. Interest accrues from day to day and is simple rather than compound.

Example 2
Injury to feelings award = £5,000

Discriminatory date = 01/04/2009

Calculation date = 05/02/2011

Interest rate = 0.5%

Number of days = 676 inclusive

Interest = 676 x 0.005 x 1/365 x 5,000 = £46.30

Interest on Physical and Psychiatric Injury and Aggravated Damages
Interest on physical and psychiatric injury runs

from the 'mid-point' date to the date of calculation. The mid-point date is calculated as the date half way between the discriminatory act and ending on the calculation date (usually the judgment date). Interest accrues from day to day and is simple rather than compound.

The calculation works in exactly the same way as that for interest on past loss.

Any maximum or minimum: There is no minimum and in fact interest does not have to be awarded if the tribunal considers it would be unjust to do so (Reg 2). The maximum would be determined by the interest rate in force during the relevant period.

Adjustments: Interest is calculated after the final adjustments have been made to the award and after enhanced redundancy has been deducted (see *Adjustments*).

Tax: Interest is awarded on the net loss suffered by the individual, see *Bentwood Bros (Manchester) Ltd v Shepherd* [2003] IRLR 364. Any grossing up, if required, will apply after interest has been calculated (see *Grossing up*).

Recoupment: The recoupment regulations do not apply to discrimination claims and hence they will not apply to any interest awarded.

Statutory authorities: Court Funds Rules 1987 r 27(1); Judgments Act 1838 s17; The Employment Tribunals (Interest on Awards in Discrimination Cases)(Amendment) Regulations 2013; The Employment Tribunals (Interest on Awards in Discrimination Cases) Regulations 1996 s3(3)

Interest on unpaid compensation

If the employer fails to pay the compensation that has been awarded to the claimant within a certain prescribed time period, interest will accrue to the award.

Until 29 July 2013, interest on unpaid compensation awards in non-discriminatory cases did not start to accrue until 42 days after judgment had been given. However, for any claims received by the ET from 29 July 2003, interest will start accruing from the date of the judgment but no interest will be payable if the award is paid within 14 days of the judgment. This brings interest on non-discriminatory awards into line with interest in discriminatory cases (see Employment Tribunals (Interest) Order

(Amendment) Order 2013 Art 3).

Interest will accrue on unpaid sums but any sums withheld on account of the recoupment regulations will not accrue interest.

Interim relief

Where a claim for unfair dismissal is brought, and where it is alleged that the reason or principal reason for the dismissal was for one of a number of protected reasons, the claimant may claim interim relief. Specific procedural rules apply, including that the claim must be brought within seven days of the effective date of termination (see s161 to 163 TULR(C)A 1992 and s128 to 129 ERA 1996). The protected reasons are:

- Relating to enforcement of rights given to shop and betting shop workers, s100(1)(a) and (b) (see s128(1)(a)(i));

- Relating to acting as a representative under the WTR 1998, s101A(d) (see s128(1)(a)(i));

- Relating to performing the functions of a pensions trustee, s102(1) (see s128(1)(a)(i));

- Performing the functions of an employee representative, 103 (see s128(1)(a)(i));

- Making a protected disclosure, 103A (see s128(1)(a)(i));

- Relating to action over trade union recognition, para 161(2) Sch 1A TULR(C)A 1992 (see s128(1)(a)(ii));

- Relating to blacklisting, s104F(1) (see s128(1)(b));

- Membership of a trade union, participating in its activities, or making use of trade union services, s152(1)(a) , (b) and (c) TULR(C)A 1992 (see s161(1) TULR(C)A 1992);

- Refusing to accept an offer to give up membership or collective bargaining rights, s152(bb) TULR(C)A 1992 (see s161(1) TULR(C)A 1992).

Remedy: If at the hearing of an application for interim relief it appears to the tribunal that the claim for unfair dismissal is likely to succeed, the tribunal will announce its findings and explain to the parties its powers and how it can exercise them. If the employer is willing, pending the final determination of the unfair dismissal complaint, the tribunal can order that the employee be reinstated or re-engaged. Otherwise, the tribunal will make an order that the contract of

employment is continued. Such an order has the effect that until the unfair dismissal complaint is determined, the contract of employment is continued for the purposes of pay, seniority, pension rights and similar matters, and for continuity of employment.

Either party may apply to the tribunal for the revocation or variation of such an order on the grounds that there has been a relevant change in circumstances (see s165 TULR(C)A 1992 and s131 ERA 1992).

If a claimant makes a complaint, and the tribunal finds, that the employer has failed to comply with an order for reinstatement or re-engagement, the tribunal will make an order for the continuation of the contract of employment and such compensation as it considers just and equitable in all the circumstances having regard to the infringement of the order and the loss suffered as a consequence. If a claimant makes a complaint, and the tribunal finds, that the employer has failed to comply with an order for the continuation of the contract of employment, it will make an order for such compensation as it considers just and equitable in all the circumstances having regard to the infringement of the order and the loss suffered as a consequence (see s166 TULR(C)A or s132 ERA 1996).

Gross or net: The award of any unpaid salary will be made gross under the continuing contract of employment and subject to PAYE.

Cap: There is no statutory cap, and this award falls outside the compensatory award (see s166 TULR(C)A 1992 and s132 ERA 196).

Statutory authorities: ERA 1996 ss128 to 132; TULR(C)A 1992 ss161 to 166

Itemized pay statement

An employee has the right to be given by his employer, at or before the time at which any payment of wages or salary is made to him, a written itemised pay statement (s8 ERA 1996).

Calculation: Where the tribunal finds that an itemized pay statements has not been given to the employee and further that any unnotified deductions have been made from the pay of the employee during the period of thirteen weeks immediately preceding the date of the application for the reference (whether or not the deductions were made in breach of the contract of employment), the tribunal may order the employer to pay the employee a sum not exceeding the aggregate of the unnotified deductions so made (s12(4) ERA 1996).

Gross or net: Gross

Limit on a week's pay: None

Limit on number of weeks: 13

Any maximum or minimum: None

Adjustments: N/A

Tax: The employer will deduct tax and national insurance as normal if the employee is still employed. However, if the employee is no longer in employment, the employee will be responsible for declaring this income on their self-assessment.

Statutory authorities: ERA 1996 ss8 and 12(4)

Job seekers allowance

(see also Recoupment)

There are 2 types of job seekers allowance:

- Contribution based, where the claimant has paid enough national insurance contributions during their employment

- Income based, where the claimant has not paid enough national contributions as an employee but was on a low wage

Receipt of job seeker's allowance should be treated in 2 different ways, depending on whether the claim is for damages for wrongful dismissal or compensation for unfair dismissal.

Damages
Credit should be given for any job seekers allowance received during the damages period and during the statutory notice period. However, as with other state benefits, it could be argued that full credit should not be given if the employee did not receive their statutory notice period or payment in lieu, because they would exhaust their entitlement to state benefits sooner than they would have done if they had received their statutory notice.

Compensatory award
Job seekers allowance is not deducted from the compensatory award but is instead subject to the recoupment regulations (see *Recoupment*).

Adjustments: See *Recoupment* (Prescribed element)

Cap: See *Recoupment* (Prescribed element)

Recoupment: Only for compensation for unfair dismissal. Recoupment does not apply to wrongful dismissal.

Statutory authorities: The Employment Protection (Recoupment of Jobseeker's Allowance and Income Support) Regulations 1996

Leave for family and domestic reasons, maternity, paternity, adoption; see Detriment; Parental leave; Time off

Limitation period

This is the maximum period allowed between the act complained of and when the claim should be lodged at the ET (see Table 26).

Loss of chance

Once a tribunal has upheld a complaint of unlawful treatment such as discrimination or unfair dismissal, it is necessary for it to assess the remedy available to the claimant. Where the remedy includes an award to compensate for financial loss, it will be necessary to identify the sums the claimant would have received had the unlawful conduct not taken place. For a dismissal, in a straightforward case this will be the salary that would have been earned by the claimant.

In assessing the loss suffered by the tribunal will take into account the chance of events having occurred following the unlawful act, and determine the award on the basis of the loss of that chance. For example, if there was a 25 per cent chance that an individual would have been dismissed fairly in any event six months after their unlawful dismissal, the tribunal will calculate the losses suffered after that date as 75 per cent of salary etc that would have been earned had the individual remained in employment after that event. Another example would be an individual who had say a 50 per cent chance of being promoted shortly after their unlawful dismissal, where the tribunal could award future losses based on 50 per cent of the increased salary to reflect the chance of it having been obtained (see *O'Donoghue v Redcar and Cleveland Borough Council* [2001] IRLR 615 and *Ministry of Defence v Wheeler* [1998] IRLR 23).

Where the chance of a future event is very high, or very low, the tribunal may well treat the chance as 100 per cent or zero per cent, as appropriate. There is no guideline cut off for such marginal chances.

The approach of a *Polkey* reduction is an example of the approach in the unfair dismissal context (see *Polkey*), but in considering the future actions of the employer the tribunal will take account of the actions of a reasonable employer (see *Abbey National v Formso* [1999] ICR 222). In discrimination cases the tribunal will seek to determine the future conduct of the actual employer. It will require evidence to demonstrate the chances of future events occurring (see *Wardle v Credit Agricole Corporate & Investment Bank* [2011] IRLR 604 and *Chagger v Abbey National plc & Anor* [2010] IRLR 47). Statistical evidence may well be relevant and admissible (see *Vento v Chief Constable of West Yorkshire Police* [2003] ICR 318).

Marginal tax rate

(see also Grossing up)

The marginal tax rate is the rate that should be applied to a claimant's award when grossing up the award (see *Grossing up*). When deciding on the marginal tax rate, account should be taken of the claimant's personal tax free allowance (which can be found from their tax code at the date of dismissal), earnings already earned in that tax year (including since dismissal), the relevant tax thresholds (see Tax tables 15 and 16) and any other income the claimant may earn in the remainder of that tax year.

Different marginal tax rates may apply to different elements of the award (see *Yorkshire Housing Ltd v Cuerden* [2010] UKEAT/0397/09)

For example, if the employee earned £15,000 gross and their tax code was 800L at the date of dismissal, the first £8,000 would be tax free, leaving them having to pay tax (@20%) on the balance (£7,000). If in addition, their fully taxable tribunal award is £50,000, they would have to pay tax @20% on the first £25,010 (£32,010, which is the 20% threshold for the year 2013 to 2014) - £7,000) and 40% on the balance of £24,990. So the first element would need to be grossed up by 20% and the second element by 40%.

Maternity Equality Clause

Women on maternity leave must receive any increases in pay due to them at the time they would have received them, had they not been on leave and their pay, when they return, must reflect the increases they would have had, had they not been absent. The Maternity Equality Clause (s73 EA 2010) modifies the woman's contract so that her maternity related pay is increased in line with any actual increase in pay, or any increase that she would have been paid had she not been on maternity leave.

The tribunal has jurisdiction to determine a complaint relating to breach of an equality clause under s127 EA 2010.

Remedy: Arrears of up to 6 years actual pay may be ordered (s132 EA 2010).

Gross or net: Gross

Limit on a week's pay: None

Limit on number of years: 6

Any maximum or minimum: None

Tax: Taxable under s62 ITEPA 2003.

Statutory authorities: EA 2010 ss73, 127 and 132

Maternity: see Detriment; Maternity Equality Clause; Unfair dismissal; Table 40

Maximum compensatory award: see Statutory cap

Minimum wage: see National Minimum Wage

Misconduct: see Contributory conduct

Mitigation

It is a fundamental principle that any claimant will be expected to mitigate the losses they suffer as a result of an unlawful act by giving credit, for example for earnings in a new job (mitigation in fact), and that the tribunal will not make an award to cover losses that could reasonably have been avoided (mitigation in law). For example, an unfairly dismissed employee is expected to search for other work, and will not recover losses beyond a date by which the tribunal concludes the individual ought reasonably to have been able to find new employment at a similar rate of pay. Such an individual may be awarded the difference between the salary of a lower paid new job, and their previous salary, for a period until the tribunal concludes they could reasonably have found similarly well paid work.

The claimant is expected to minimise the losses suffered as a consequence of the unlawful act. The burden of proving a failure to mitigate is on the respondent (*Fyfe v Scientific Furnishing Ltd* [1989] IRLR 331). The tribunal will ask itself:

1) what steps should the claimant have taken to mitigate his or her losses; and

2) from what date would an alternative income have been obtained?

The duty arises only after dismissal, so a failure to take up an alternative job offer made before that date will not constitute a failure to mitigate. It may be reasonable to attempt to mitigate loss by setting up a new business or becoming self-employed (see *Gardiner-Hill v Roland Berger Technics Ltd* [1982] IRLR 498) or by retraining (see *Sealy v Avon Aluminium Co Ltd* UKEAT/515/78, *Holroyd v Gravure Cylinders Ltd* [1984] IRLR 259 and *Orthet Ltd v Vince-Cain* [2004] IRLR 857).

Mitigation and "good industrial relations practice": an unfairly dismissed employee will not need to give credit for earnings received from a new job during the notice period where good industrial relations practice would have required payment in lieu of notice to the employee (see *Norton Tool Co Ltd v Tewson* [1973] All ER 183 and *Voith Turbo Ltd v Stowe* [2005] IRLR 228). However, the principle does not apply to constructive dismissal (*Stuart Peters Ltd v Bell* [2009] IRLR 941).

Mitigation and receipt of pension: In *Knapton v ECC Card Clothing Ltd* [2006] IRLR 756 the EAT held that credit does not need to be given for the early receipt of pension following dismissal, as it is deferred wages not a sum analogous to incapacity benefit which would be brought into account. However, if an individual is dismissed after the date when the pension can be drawn and there is no reduction in the value of the pension by being drawn at dismissal, it may be that a failure to draw the pension would be seen as a failure to mitigate a loss, and a sum for which the ex-employer should receive credit.

Money purchase: see Pension loss

National Insurance Contributions

An unemployed person may receive Class 1 National Insurance credits to fill any gaps in their national insurance contributions (these contributions are automatically made if the person claims JSA). However, s7(1) of The Social Security (Unemployment, Sickness and Invalidity Benefit) Regulations 1983 SI 1983/1598 states that if the person has received compensation for unfair dismissal, they are not entitled to receive national insurance contributions for the same period. If the person is unemployed for a long time, this could affect their entitlement to a state pension and other state benefits. The loss of NI contributions can therefore be claimed from the employer as a head of loss. The amount of compensation is fixed by reference to the weekly Class 3 NIC rate (see Table 20).

Remedy: Compensation per week = weekly Class 3 NIC rate (see Table 20).

Limit on a week's pay: The class 3 rate

Limit on number of weeks: None

Any maximum or minimum: None

Adjustments: Loss of NIC will form part of the compensatory award or damages and thus will be adjusted along with these awards.

Recoupment: Recoupment does not apply to this head of loss.

Statutory authorities: Social Security (Unemployment, Sickness and Invalidity Benefit) Regulations 1983 (SI 1983/1598) Reg7(1)

National Minimum Wage

(see also Unlawful deductions from wages; Table 39)

A broad range of workers are entitled to receive the national minimum wage. The rate depends upon the age of the worker, and whether they qualify for an apprentice rate or if an agricultural worker, the agricultural minimum wage (see Table 39). Calculating the pay received for the purposes of assessing whether the national minimum wage has been paid may in some cases be complex. An employer must keep sufficient records to show that workers who qualify have been paid the national minimum wage (Reg 38(1) NMWR and s9 and s31 NMWA), and a worker is entitled to inspect the records (s10 NMWA 1998).

There are four main routes by which an individual may enforce NMW rights:

1) A worker may bring a claim to the ET for unlawful deductions from wages (s17 NMWR 1998) (see *Unlawful deductions from wages*);

2) It is automatically unfair to dismiss a worker because he has asserted his right to the NMW or might qualify for the NMW (s104A ERA 1996) (see *Unfair dismissal*);

3) Under section 23(1) NMWA 1998, a worker has the right not to be subjected to any detriment by any act or failure to act for specified reasons relating to the NMW (see *Detriment*);

4) A worker may bring a claim to the ET that his or her employer has refused access to records in accordance with s10 NMWA 1998 (s11 NMWA 1998).

Remedy for refusal to permit access to records
Where a tribunal finds a complaint under s11 well founded, it will make a declaration to that effect and will make an award of 80 times the hourly minimum wage in force at the date when the award is made (s11(2) NMWA 1998).

Gross or net: Gross

Tax: It is likely that this award will not be subject to tax, and should be characterised as a punishment or fine, not earnings or a payment connected to termination.

Statutory authorities: NMWA 1998 ss10 and 11

Net weekly pay

(see also *Gourley* Principle; Gross weekly pay; Week's pay)

This is the figure used to calculate the actual net loss to the claimant in a number of awards. This will often be the gross weekly pay less tax and NI, and may also be less employer's pension contributions and other benefits if the value of the loss of those benefits is calculated separately, which is often the approach used. Some awards are calculated on gross weekly pay, for example where an employer is ordered to pay unpaid remuneration (where tax will be deducted at source upon payment in the usual way). The following awards use net weekly pay as the basis of the loss:

- Compensatory award;

- Damages for wrongful dismissal;

- Financial losses suffered as a result of unlawful discrimination.

Non-recoupable state benefits

(see also Recoupment)

The state benefits of job seekers allowance and income support, income-related employment support allowance and universal credit are subject to recoupment under the Employment Protection (Recoupment of Jobseeker's Allowance and Income Support) Regulations 1996 (SI 1996/2349). The Regulations provide that, where a monetary award is made by the tribunal, it must identify any part of that award that constitutes the prescribed element (past loss of earnings) and the period to which it relates.

Other benefits, benefits awarded outside of the 'prescribed period', or benefits received in relation to awards that do not fall within the recoupment provisions are non-recoupable benefits.

Normal retirement date

(see also Pension loss; Tables 35 and 36)

There is no longer a normal retirement age as between employers and their employees (see Employment Equality (Repeal of Retirement Age Provisions) Regulations 2011/1069). Any dismissal on grounds of age will be discriminatory, subject to any justification, and so far as unfair dismissal is concerned the usual protections, regardless of age, will apply. However, pension scheme rules may specify a normal age at which employees are able to begin to receive a pension, and some schemes may make provision for earlier receipt of benefits.

Normal working hours: see Week's pay

Notice Pay

(see also Breach of contract; Contractual notice period; Effective date of termination; Garden leave; Statutory notice period; Table 38)

If an employee gives or is given notice of termination of their employment, they will usually be entitled to their normal pay during this period of notice. Four general approaches can be taken to whether the individual works their notice period and how they are paid:

1) The employee works their notice and gets paid their normal wage;

2) The employee is placed on garden leave, in which case they do not actually work during their notice but the employment contract is still in force and they get paid as normal;

3) The employee does not work their notice period, the contract is terminated earlier, and instead receives a payment equivalent to what would have been earned during this period (payment in lieu of notice or PILON);

4) The employee does not work during the notice period, and does not get paid all or some of their normal wage for the notice period In case 4, the employee may be entitled to compensation.

In the fourth example, the employee may be entitled to compensation for breach of the obligation to be paid under the contract.

Occupational pension scheme: see Pension loss

Order of adjustments: see Adjustments

Overtime: see Compensatory award; Holiday pay; Week's pay

Parental leave

(see also Detriment)

An employee may present a complaint to an employment tribunal that his employer:

a) has unreasonably postponed a period of parental leave requested by the employee; or

b) has prevented or attempted to prevent the employee from taking parental leave (s80 ERA 1996).

Remedy: By s80(4) ERA 1996 the amount of compensation shall be such as the tribunal considers just and equitable in all the circumstances having regard to:

a) the employer's behaviour; and

b) any loss sustained by the employee which is attributable to the matters complained of.

Gross or net: Whether this is paid gross or net will depend on whether payment amounts to earnings or some other loss.

Limit on a week's pay: None

Limit on number of weeks: No, except in relation to the amount of leave the employee is entitled to by statute.

Any maximum or minimum: None

Adjustments: None

Tax: The tax treatment of any award is unclear. To the extent that the sum awarded is compensation for lost earnings, it is likely to be taxed under s62 ITEPA 2003 (see *Tax*).

Recoupment: N/A

Statutory authorities: ERA 1996 s80

Part-time worker protection

A worker working part has time the right not to be treated by his employer less favourably than the employer treats a comparable permanent employee, on the ground that the worker is a part time worker: either as regards the terms of his contract; or by being subjected to any other detriment by any act, or deliberate failure to act, of his employer. Less favourable treatment will be permitted where it can be objectively justified. In assessing whether a part time worker has been less favourably treated, the tribunal will apply the pro rata principle unless that is inappropriate (reg 5 PTW(PLFT) Regs 2000).

A worker has the right to request written reasons for any treatment which he or she considers might infringe the Reg 5 right, and is entitled to be provided with such a statement within 21 days of the request (Reg 6(1)).

Reg 7 establishes automatic unfair dismissal and detriment protections for the actions of individuals related to exercising and enforcing the Reg 5 and 6 rights (see *Unfair dismissal* and *Detriment*).

A worker may present a complaint to the tribunal that a right conferred on him or her by Reg 5 has been infringed (Reg 8(1)).

Remedy: Where a tribunal upholds a complaint that a worker has been subject to less favourable treatment, the tribunal may take any of the following steps as it considers just and equitable (Reg 8(7)):

- make a declaration as to the rights of the complainant and the employer in relation to the complaint;

- order the employer to pay compensation to the complainant;

- make a recommendation that the employer take certain steps to obviate or reduce any relevant adverse effect.

Where compensation is awarded the amount will be that which the tribunal considers just and equitable in all the circumstances (this phrase is used in the assessment of the compensatory award for unfair dismissal and similar principles will apply). The tribunal will have regard to the infringement and any loss which is attributable to it. Losses suffered by the complainant will be taken to include any expenses reasonably incurred as a consequence of the infringement and the loss of any benefit he has suffered but for the infringement (see Regs 8(9) and (10)). The common law principles of mitigation apply and the tribunal may reduce any award for contributory fault (Reg 8(13)).

There is no right to compensation for injury to feelings where there has been infringement of the right not to be less favourably treated under Reg 5 (however, an award for detriment under Reg 7 may include such an award. See Detriment, and Injury to feelings).

If an employer fails, without reasonable justification, to comply with a recommendation (see above), the tribunal may make an award of compensation if it has not already done so, or increase an award of compensation it has already made (Reg 8(14)).

Gross or net: This will depend on whether the sums paid are treated as suppressed wages, an award for discrimination or injury to feelings (see *Tax*, below within this entry). Where a sum is paid to represent a net loss it will be calculated on the net figure, grossed up where appropriate to make the final award. Where the sum is viewed as suppressed wages the award will be calculated on gross earnings, with the employer deducting tax and NI.

Any maximum or minimum: No, there is no statutory cap.

Adjustments: A percentage deduction for contributory conduct can be applied (Reg 8(13)). Also, if the employer fails to comply with a tribunal's recommendation, any award may be increased (Reg 8(14)).

Mitigation: The usual principles of mitigation apply.

Tax: Any payment to compensate for an employee's reduced wages or benefits would probably be classed as arrears of pay and taxed under s62 ITEPA 2003 in the normal way (see EIM02550 and EIM02530, HMRC). The tax to be paid should be calculated according to the tax year in which the pay was withheld, not the tax year in which the repayment is made.

However, EIM12965 of the Employment Income Manual states that payments of compensation for discrimination which occurs before termination is not employment income for the purposes of s401 and that they are therefore not taxable. It is arguable that the award for infringement of Reg 5 would not be subject to tax as it would be compensation for discrimination (in its broadest sense).

Statutory authorities: PTW(PLFT) Regs 2000 Regs 5 to 8

Paternity leave: see Detriment; SPP table; Unfair dismissal

Payment in lieu of notice: see Compensatory award; Effective date of termination; Notice pay; Tax and termination payments

Penalty for leaving pension scheme early: see Pension loss

Pension loss

(see also Tables 28 to 34)

Awards for financial loss may include the value of pension loss (see *Copson v Eversure Accessories Ltd* [1974] IRLR 247 and *Ministry of Defence v Mutton* [1996] ICR 590). The nature of the loss and the route to calculate it will depend on the duration of the loss and the nature of the scheme. Schemes can usefully be divided into defined benefit schemes such as final salary schemes, and defined contribution (or money purchase) schemes, and within those employees may be required to contribute part of their salary, or the scheme may be non-contributory. The benefit available on retirement will depend on the terms of the scheme. Various state pensions exist, including the basic state pension, a graduated retirement benefit, the State Earnings Related Pension Scheme and the state second pension. Where the value of such a state scheme will be impacted by the unlawful conduct for which the tribunal makes an award, this impact will need to be taken into account in establishing the pension loss.

Official guidance has been produced for the calculation of pension loss. Currently it is the 2003 edition of "Compensation for Loss of Pension Rights: Employment Tribunals" (available from the Tribunal Service at this link: http://www.employmenttribunals.gov.uk/Documents/Publications/LossOfPensionRights.pdf).

Tribunals do not need to follow this guidance, though they must explain the route by which the loss has been calculated (*Orthet Ltd v Vince-Cain* [2004] IRLR 857 and *Bingham v Hobourn Engineering Ltd* [1992] IRLR 298). In some cases where significant value attaches to the method of calculation, it may be appropriate to use expert actuarial evidence (*Port of Tilbury (London) Ltd v Birch* [2005] IRLR 92).

Defined contribution scheme

Calculation of the loss suffered where there is a defined contribution scheme should be relatively straightforward, since the loss is the value of the contributions which have not been paid as a result of the unlawful act, subject to the usual principles of mitigation etc. The tribunal may factor in losses (or benefits) arising from the money not having been paid into a fund at the relevant times, and any penalty for leaving the scheme early.

Defined benefit pension scheme

The losses arising where there has been a defined benefit scheme can usefully be divided into past loss and future loss.

Past loss arises at dismissal, and includes the value of the existing pension rights that would have been enhanced had the individual remained in employment. If the individual is able to transfer the value of their pension to a new fund there will be no loss of enhancement of accrued pension if the valuation takes into account any projected increases in salary (*Freemans plc v Flynn* [1984] IRLR 486 and *Yeats v Fairey Winches Ltd* [1974] IRLR 362).

Future loss includes losses suffered from dismissal until the remedies hearing and from the remedies hearing into the future. Where the period of future loss is short, perhaps less than 2 to 5 years, the tribunal may award the value of the lost contributions. The basis for such an award will be that an equivalent defined benefit pension will be (or has been) entered into at the end of that period. However where the period of loss is substantial a more sophisticated approach will be required (*Clancy v Cannock Chase Technical College* [2001] IRLR 331).

The tribunal will take into account the chance of withdrawal from the pension scheme (*Manpower Services Ltd v Hearne* [1982] IRLR 281), and the value to the claimant of accelerated receipt. Employers might argue that, and a tribunal should assess whether, an employer's defined benefit scheme would continue to be provided (*Glen Dimplex UK Ltd v Burrows* EAT/0265/03).

The guidance (see above) suggests two possible approaches for calculating pension loss for defined benefit schemes; the simplified approach and the substantial approach. In the simplified approach the tribunal assumes that the employee will have found a comparable job within a reasonably short period either with a similar pension or a higher salary to compensate for the loss of pension. In the substantial loss approach the tribunal looks at longer periods of loss potentially up to retirement. The Ogden tables are used to calculate career long loss of pension and earnings following personal injury claims, and could be used to calculate pension loss for employment claims if the tribunal takes the view that would be appropriate.

Both simplified and substantial approaches use tables from the GAD guidelines (see Tables 28 to 34). The tables provide the multiplying factor to be applied in the calculation, depending on factors such as age at EDT, sex and normal retirement age.

Pension loss under the simplified approach
Immediate loss
Pension loss up the hearing = gross weekly pensionable pay x percentage contributed by employer (typically 15% for a contributory scheme, 20% for non-contributory) x multiplying factor (from the GAD tables) x number of weeks from EDT to hearing x (1 - (withdrawal %/100))

The withdrawal factor is a percentage representing the likelihood that the claimant might have withdrawn from the scheme before the hearing.

Future loss
Pension loss up from hearing onwards = gross weekly pensionable pay x percentage contributed by employer (typically 15% for a contributory scheme, 20% for non-contributory) x multiplying factor (from the GAD tables) x number of weeks of future loss x (1 - (accelerated payment %/100))

The accelerated payment percentage represents a deduction because the claimant would be receiving the pension before the normal date.

Loss of enhancement already accrued
With defined benefit schemes, the loss of enhancement of accrued pension rights may also need to be considered. This takes into account the loss suffered because the claimant's salary has not increased because they are no longer in employment. The value of the deferred pension should be obtained from the pension scheme provider and any percentage deduction representing the probability of the claimant

leaving the scheme before their normal retirement date should be determined. The type of pension scheme, whether it is a public or private scheme, must also be determined.

Loss of enhancement of pension rights = deferred pension x multiplying factor from tables 4.1 to 4.4 x (1 - (withdrawal factor %/100)).

The withdrawal factor represents the probability of the claimant losing his job before normal retirement date, for reasons other than dismissal or discrimination.

Example 1
The claimant is male aged 47 at dismissal in a public sector pension scheme, with a normal retirement age of 65.

Gross annual salary/pensionable salary = £50,000

Deferred pension = £15,000

Withdrawal factor estimated to be 35%

Employer contribution = 12%

Weeks from EDT to hearing = 16

Number of weeks of future loss = 26

> *Loss of enhancement of accrued pension rights* = 15,000 x 3.32 (from table 4.2) x 0.65 (which is 1 - 35%) = £32,370
>
> *Loss of pension from EDT to hearing* = 16 x 50,000 ÷ 52 x 0.12 x 1.06 (from table 7.1) = £1,956.92
>
> *Loss of future pension* = 26 x 50,000 ÷ 52 x 0.12 x 1.06 (from table 7.1) = £3,180.00
>
> **Total loss of pension** = £37,506.92

Pension loss under the substantial approach
This approach is made up of three calculations, A, B and C, which are combined to find the loss of pension rights.

Loss of pension rights is = A - B - C where:

> **Calculation A** is the value of prospective final salary rights up to normal retirement age in the former employment (if she or he had not been dismissed).
>
> **Calculation B** is the value of accrued final salary pension rights to date of dismissal from the former employment.
>
> **Calculation C** is the value of prospective final salary rights to normal retirement age in the new employment.

The substantial loss approach automatically includes the loss of enhancement of accrued pension rights at the date of dismissal the loss of pension rights from the date of dismissal to the date of hearing as well as the loss of future pension rights from the date of the hearing.

The calculations depend on certain pieces of information and it might be helpful to find out first the age at dismissal, age at date of new job, gender, whether a member of a private or public pension scheme and normal retirement date.

Calculation A = Pension fraction in former job (for example 1/60: meaning that 1/60 of the final salary is accrued for every year worked) x (Number of years service in former job + Number of years from dismissal to retirement) x Gross Pensionable Salary at dismissal x Multiplying factor from tables 5.1 to 5.4 (depending on sex and type of scheme) x (1 - withdrawal factor*)

(Note: the withdrawal factor is the probability, expressed as a decimal, that the claimant will leave the job before normal retirement age. For example, if the probability of leaving is 0.6, the figure to input at * above is 0.4).

Calculation B = Pension fraction in former job x Number of years service in former job x Gross Pensionable Salary at dismissal x Multiplying Factor from table 6.1 to 6.4 x (1 - withdrawal factor)

Calculation C = Pension fraction in new job (if any) x Number of years from new job start date to normal retirement in new job x Gross pensionable salary in new job x Multiplying Factor from table 5.1 to 5.4 x (1 - Withdrawal factor from the new job) (note that this may be different from the withdrawal factor in the old job)

Then Pension loss = A - B - C

If the applicant loses a job with a final salary pension scheme and obtains one with a money purchase scheme or signs up to a stakeholder pension, the loss here is calculated as only A minus B. However, credit will need to be given for the value of the future pension rights to be earned in new employment.

Example 2
The claimant is female and was aged 56 at dismissal (normal retirement at 65) having worked for 20 years and was a member of a private sector pension scheme which offered 1/40th of a year's salary for every year worked.

Gross annual salary/pensionable salary = £50,000

Deferred pension = £15,000

Withdrawal factor in old job estimated to be 35%

Withdrawal factor in new job estimated to be 20%

New job: employed at age 57, now member of public sector pension scheme, salary £50,000 but pension is 1/60th of final salary for each year worked, normal retirement age 65.

> *Calculation A* = 1/40 x 29 x 50,000 x 13.58 (from table 5.3) x 0.65 = £319,978
>
> *Calculation B* = 1/40 x 20 x 50,000 x 11.75 (from table 6.3) x 0.65 = £190,937.50
>
> *Calculation C* = 1/60 x 8 x 50,000 x 17.48 (from table 5.4) x 0.8 = £93,226.67
>
> **Total loss of pension** = £319,978 - £190,937.50 - £93,226.67 = £35,813.83

What happens if the pension tables don't list the exact normal retirement age?
The pension tables only list multiplying factors for retirement ages of 55, 60 and 65. However, in a particular case it may be appropriate to use a retirement age of say 62. In this case it will be necessary to interpolate between 2 values. Taking a look at example 1 again, in which the loss of enhancement was calculated, the factor used for age 47 and retirement at age 65 was 3.32. Using the guidance from the Ogden tables the following calculations could be used:

1) A retirement age of 62 falls between 60 and 65. In our case the person is 15 years from retirement so, assuming the same number of years to retirement, work out the ages of people who would retire at 60 and 65. They would be 45 and 50 respectively.

2) Look up from table 4.2 the factors for retirement at age 60 (age at dismissal being 45) and at age 65 (age at dismissal being 50). They are 3.33 and 2.90 respectively.

3) Work out the difference between the retirement age of the claimant and age 60 (which is 2) and between 65 (which is 3).

4) Multiply the factor applying to the younger retirement age (3.33) by 3 and the factor applying to the older retirement age (2.90) by 2 and add them together to get 3.33 x 3 + 2.90 x 2 = 15.79

5) Finally, divide by the difference between 65 and 60 to get 15.79 ÷ 5 = 3.16

3.16 is the factor to be applied

What happens if the anticipated retirement age is say 67?
The tables only go as far as age 65 but anticipated retirement ages could well exceed this. In this situation it will be necessary to extrapolate the table i.e. stretch them out to include figures beyond 65. This will provide only a rough estimate, and will be less sound than the route to choose a figure between a higher and a lower number. In cases where large sums turn on the exact calculation, it may be that actuarial advice should be sought.

Relevant case law: Yorkshire Housing v Cuerden UKEAT/0397/09/SM

Perks: see Benefits

Permanent employment: see Damages for wrongful dismissal

Physical and psychiatric injury

(see also Discrimination; Interest)

Claimants can claim damages for personal injury caused by unlawful discriminatory acts including detriment for whistleblowing (see *Sheriff v Klyne (Lowestoft) Ltd* [1999] IRLR 481 and *Virgo Fidelis Senior School v Boyle* [2004] IRLR 268). However, it is not always easy to identify where injury to feelings ends and physical and psychiatric injury starts and there could be a risk of double counting. Medical evidence will be as critical to any claim for personal injury in the tribunal as it is in a County/High Court.

Remedy: When it comes to the assessment of damages in relation to a proven psychiatric injury, tribunals are "obliged to approach the assessment of damages for psychiatric injury on the same basis as a common law court in an ordinary action for personal injuries." (*HM Prison Service v Salmon* [2001] IRLR 425).

The Judicial Studies Board has published guidelines for the assessment of general damages in personal injury cases. According to the JSB, the following factors need to be taken into account when valuing claims of psychiatric injury:

a) the injured person's ability to cope with life and work;

b) the effect on the injured person's relationships with family, friends and those with whom he comes into contact;

c) the extent to which treatment would be successful;

d) future vulnerability;

e) prognosis;

f) whether medical help has been sought;

g) whether the injury results from sexual and/or physical abuse and/or breach of trust; and if so, the nature of the relationship between victim and abuser, the nature of the abuse, its duration and the symptoms caused by it.

There are 4 categories of award:

a) Minor awards of between £1,000 and £3,875 can be made where the claimant has suffered temporary symptoms that have adversely affected daily activities;

b) Moderate awards of between £3,875 and £12,500 can be made in cases where, while the claimant has suffered problems as a result of the discrimination, significant improvement has been made by the date of the hearing and the prognosis is good;

c) Moderately severe cases can lead to awards of between £12,500 and £36,000. Moderately severe cases include those where there is work-related stress resulting in a permanent or long-standing disability preventing a return to comparable employment, but the prognosis is more optimistic than in the severe category cases;

d) Severe cases are defined as those where the claimant has serious problems in relation to their ability to cope with life and work; the effect on their relationships with other people; the extent to which treatment would be useful; and their future vulnerability, and the prognosis is poor. Awards of between £36,000 and £72,000 may be appropriate in these circumstances.

Any maximum or minimum: Only so far as the guidelines have suggested.

Adjustments: The award can be adjusted to allow for the extent to which the act of discrimination caused the illness. So, if it is found that the discriminatory act caused the illness to the extent of 30%, the award will be reduced by 70%.

Injury to feelings and physical and psychiatric injury are distinct heads of loss, but care should be taken that no double counting has taken place. Either one could be reduced if this is the case.

Interest: Interest could also be awarded (see *Interest*).

Mitigation: N/A

Tax: Awards for injury to feelings are exempted from tax under s401 ITEPA 2003 (see *Tax*).

Recoupment: N/A

Relevant case law: *HM Prison Service v Salmon* [2001] IRLR 425; *Sheriff v Klyne (Lowestoft) Ltd* [1999] IRLR 481; *Virgo Fidelis Senior School v Boyle* [2004] IRLR 268

Polkey

(see also Adjustments)

A '*Polkey*' deduction is the phrase used in unfair dismissal cases to describe the reduction in any award for future loss to reflect the chance that the individual would have been dismissed fairly in any event (*Polkey v AE Dayton Services Ltd* [1987] IRLR 50 (HL)). This may take the form of a percentage reduction, or it may take the form of a tribunal making a finding that the individual would have been dismissed fairly after a further period of employment (for example a period in which a fair procedure would have been completed).

This adjustment is only applicable to the compensatory award, not the basic award (apart from in very limited circumstances where such a (fair) dismissal might have taken place virtually contemporaneously with the unfair dismissal which actually occurred, presumably applying s122(2) ERA 1996 - see *Granchester Construction (Eastern) Ltd v Attrill* UKEAT/0327/12/LA paragraph 19. A similar approach to a *Polkey* deduction is taken in discrimination cases where the tribunal will assess the chance that a particular future loss has been suffered (see *Loss of chance*).

Pregnancy: see Discrimination; Time off for ante-natal care

Prescribed element: see Recoupment

Prescribed period: see Recoupment

Presidential guidance on remedy

Appendix 1 reproduces paragraphs 1 to 25 of the Presidential Guidance on Remedy issued on 14 March 2014. This sets out in easily readable form the tribunal's procedure and expectations for dealing with remedy. The tribunal will expect parties to comply with the guidance.

Profit related bonus: see Benefits; Bonuses

Protected act: see Discrimination

Protected disclosure

(see also Detriment; Unfair dismissal)

Where an employee has suffered a detriment, which might be the dismissal of the employee, for making a protected disclosure or for another reason, the tribunal may award financial compensation.

The right to bring a claim for detriment is established by s47B ERA 1992, and the right to not be unfairly dismissed for the sole or principal reason of making a protected disclosure is established by s103A ERA 1996.

For detriment (not dismissal) the tribunal must award such an amount as it considers is just and equitable having regard to:

1) the infringement to which the complaint relates;

2) any loss which is attributable to the act, or failure to act, which infringed the claimant's right (s49(2) ERA 1996).

If the employee has been dismissed, awards can

be made for unfair dismissal (see *Additional award; Basic award; Compensatory award; Unfair dismissal*)

Remedy: For detriment (not dismissal) the loss shall be taken to include: any expenses reasonably incurred by the claimant in consequence of the act, or failure to act, to which the complaint relates; and loss of any benefit which the claimant might reasonably be expected to have had but for the act or failure to act (s49(3) ERA 1996).

Gross or net: If the claimant has been dismissed, see the individual awards for unfair dismissal. Otherwise, it will be a figure that the tribunal considers just and equitable (see *Detriment*).

Any maximum or minimum: The award is unlimited unless the detriment is termination of the contract of a worker when any compensation must not exceed the compensation that would be payable if the worker had been an employee and had been dismissed for making a protected disclosure (there is currently no limit to financial losses) (s49(6) ERA 1996).

Adjustments: If the tribunal considers that the act or failure to act was caused or contributed to by action of the claimant, it may reduce the award if it thinks that it would be just and equitable to do so (ss49(4) and (5) ERA 1996).

The tribunal can also reduce the award of compensation by up to 25% if they find that any disclosure occurring after 25 June 2013 was not made in good faith.

Cap: The statutory cap on unfair dismissal does not apply if the employee has been dismissed as a result of making the protected disclosure.

Mitigation: The tribunal may reduce the amount if it considers that the claimant has failed to mitigate his/her loss.

Tax: The award will be taxable under s401 ITEPA 2003 if the employee has been dismissed, although the tax treatment is unclear in the case of an employee who receives a payment because of suffering detriment but is still employed (see *Detriment; Tax and termination payments*).

Recoupment: Recoupment will only apply to unfair dismissal awards.

Statutory authorities: ERA 1996 ss49 and 103A

Protective award

Where an employer is proposing to dismiss as redundant 20 or more employees at one establishment within a period of 90 days or less, the employer shall consult about the dismissals all the persons who are appropriate representatives of any of the employees who may be affected by the proposed dismissals or may be affected by measures taken in connection with those dismissals (s188 and s188A TULR(C)A 1992).

The consultation shall begin in good time and in any event:

a) where the employer is proposing to dismiss 100 or more employees, at least 45 days; and

b) otherwise, at least 30 days,

before the first of the dismissals takes effect.

Note that, for dismissals before 6 April 2013, the number of days referred to in a) above was 90, not 45.

Where it is alleged that an employer has failed to comply with the consultation requirements the appropriate representatives, or in some limited situations an affected employee, may bring a complaint to a tribunal who, if the complaint is well founded, shall make a declaration to that effect and may make a 'protective award' covering the employees affected by the failure.

The protective award is remuneration for the 'protected period', of up to 90 days.

If the employer is insolvent, the employees may make a claim to the National Insurance Fund for payment of some (or in some cases all) of this award (see *Insolvency*).

Remedy (1): Under TULR(C)A 1992 s189(3) , (4) and s190 the tribunal may make an award of up to 90 days pay, with the length of the period determined by what is just and equitable in all the circumstances having regard to the seriousness of the employer's failure to comply with TULR(C)A 1992 s188. The award is calculated as starting on the day the first dismissals took effect. The award will identify the description of employees to whom it applies, who will be those employees whose representative has not been consulted properly.

The rate of remuneration payable is a week's pay for each week of the protected period; and remuneration in respect of a period less than one week shall be calculated by reducing proportionally the amount of a week's pay (s190(2)).

A day's pay is found by dividing the employee's actual gross weekly pay by 7.

Remedy (2): If the employer fails to comply with s190 by not paying an employee within the description the amount due under the award, the employee may bring a complaint to the tribunal who may order the employer to pay the amount of remuneration due (s192(1) and (3)).

Gross or net: Gross. A week's pay as defined in ss220 to 229 ERA 1996 applies (see *Week's pay*). Part weeks are to be calculated pro rata. Only the basic pay should be taken into account and not any discretionary bonus (see *Canadian Imperial Bank of Commerce v Beck* UKEAT/0141/10/RN).

Limit on a week's pay: None. The limit on a week's pay does not apply.

Limit on number of days: 90. The principles for determining the length of a protective award are set out in *Susie Radin Ltd v GMB & Ors* [2004] ICR 893. The award is designed to be punitive, not to compensate the employee for losses suffered, with the calculation starting at 90 days where there has been no consultation and being reduced to reflect the seriousness of the breach and any mitigating factors. It is important to remember that, even if the consultation period is only 30 days, the starting point and maximum protected period is still 90 days.

An employee will be entitled to payment of the protective award from the date the protected period begins but will cease being entitled at the date he is fairly dismissed, unreasonably terminates his contract of employment or unreasonably refuses an offer of employment during the protected period (see s191 TULR(C)A 1992).

Any maximum or minimum: None

Adjustments: None

Cap: There is no cap on the award.

Mitigation: N/A, as the award is a sanction for breach, not compensation for losses suffered.

Tax: The award will be taxable under s401 ITEPA 2003 if the employee is no longer in employment (EIM02550, HMRC). Also, see *Mintec Ltd v Inland Revenue* [2001] STC 101 (see *Tax*).

Recoupment: Yes, the prescribed element being any amount ordered to be paid to the employee in respect of so much of the relevant protected period as falls before the date of the conclusion of the tribunal proceedings (see Table 27).

Statutory authorities: ITEPA 2003 s401; The Employment Protection (Recoupment of Jobseeker's Allowance and Income Support) Regulations 1996; TULR(C)A 1992 ss189 and 190

Relevant case law: *Canadian Imperial Bank of Commerce v Beck* UKEAT/0141/10/RN; *Mintec Ltd v Inland Revenue* [2001] STC 101; *Susie Radin Ltd v GMB & Ors* [2004] ICR 893

Example

The claimant's gross weekly pay is £500 (which has been calculated in accordance with ss220 to 229 ERA as above) and is awarded 80 days protective award.

A day's pay = 500/7 = £71.43 (note: the weekly pay must be divided by 7, not the number of days per week actually worked)

Thus the protective award = £71.43 x 80 = £5,714.40

Qualifying period

(see also Effective date of termination)

This is the length of continuous employment (see s211 ERA 1996) that must have been worked by the claimant before a tribunal will consider any particular complaint. Different qualifying periods apply for different types of claim (see Table 26).

The employee's continuous employment begins with the day on which the employee starts work, and ends with the day by reference to which the length of the employee's period of continuous employment is to be ascertained for the purposes of the provision.

But, if an employee's period of continuous employment includes one or more periods which (by virtue of section 215, 216 or 217) while not counting in computing the length of the period do not break continuity of employment, the beginning of the period shall be treated as postponed by the number of days falling within that intervening period, or the aggregate number of days falling within those periods, calculated in accordance with the section in question.

Rate of pay: see Week's pay

Recoupment

(see also Non-recoupable state benefits)

A number of awards made by tribunals are subject to recoupment, whereby the state recovers from the respondent the value of certain state benefits paid to the claimant. This involves the tribunal identifying a part of the award that corresponds to a period of loss during which the claimant was in receipt of job seeker's allowance, income-related employment support allowance, income support or universal credit. The respondent is required to not pay the claimant the sum the tribunal identifies, but to wait until the DWP recoups from them any benefits paid, with the remainder then being paid to the claimant by the respondent. The principles to be applied are contained in the Employment Protection (Recoupment of Jobseeker's Allowance and Income Support) Regulations 1996 (SI 1996/2349).

The types of award which may be covered by the prescribed element (see below) are listed in Table 27, the most common awards being for unfair dismissal, failure to make a guarantee payment, failure to pay during a period of maternity or medical suspension and protective awards (see Column 1 to the Schedule to the regulations, and Reg 3(1)(a)).

The recoupment regulations do not apply if the claimant has not claimed the relevant benefits, or if the award is compensation for discrimination statutes or for dismissal by reason of redundancy. Nor do the recoupment regulations apply to settlements – this may create an incentive to settle where, because the Secretary of State will not recoup the benefits paid, a smaller sum paid by the respondent that would be awarded by the tribunal would result in a higher sum received by the claimant.

Required information
The tribunal must in its judgment identify four items of information that will then be provided to the DWP: the amount of any 'prescribed element', the prescribed period, the total amount of the award and the balance. In essence this will define the sum within any award from which the state may seek recoupment. No greater sum will be recouped, and the respondent will be ordered by the tribunal to pay the remainder to the claimant.

Prescribed element
The prescribed element is that part of the award which is held back from the claimant until the value of any state benefits subject to the recoupment procedures is known. It is defined in Reg 3(1)(a) and Column 3 to Schedule 1, and is that part of the monetary award attributable to loss of wages or arrears of pay or losses due to the claimant (including a protective award) for the period before the conclusion of the tribunal proceedings, or if it covers a protective award or award for failure to inform or consult under TUPE, up to the final day of the period covered by that protective award. The prescribed element does not include the figure that may have been awarded for loss of statutory rights, right to written particulars or the loss of benefits or pension.

The prescribed element will also be reduced in line with any deduction for contributory fault that may have been made to the compensatory award. Further, the prescribed element will be reduced by the same proportion as the compensatory award when applying the statutory cap. For example, if the compensatory award has been reduced from £85,082.22 to the cap of £76,574 (that is, by 10%), the prescribed element will also be reduced by 10% (see Reg 4(2)).

Prescribed period
The prescribed period is identified in column 3 to the Schedule to the regulations. For straightforward unfair dismissal claims the prescribed period is the period between the EDT and the date of the remedy hearing (or the date at which the tribunal sent the remedy judgment to the parties). For concurrent wrongful and unfair dismissal claims, since recoupment does not apply to the award for breach of contract, the prescribed period is the period between the end of the period over which damages have been awarded and the date of the hearing (or the date at which the parties were sent the remedy judgment).

Total award
This is the total of all the awards that have been made by the tribunal

Balance
This is the difference between the total and the prescribed element and must be paid to the claimant.

Once the actual state benefits that are subject to recoupment are known, the DWP will claim this figure from the prescribed element retained by the respondent and any remaining monies must be paid by the employer to the employee.

Statutory authorities: Employment Protection

(Recoupment of Jobseeker's Allowance and Income Support) Regulations 1996

Example 1 (where the statutory cap is not applicable)

Basic award = £500

Immediate loss of earnings = £2,000

Future loss of earnings = £700

Loss of statutory rights = £200

Contributory conduct of 20% applies to compensatory award only

Calculation

Prescribed element applies only to the immediate loss of earnings, i.e. £2,000

But this amount has been reduced by 20% and is now 2,000 x 0.8 = £1,600

Total award = 500 + 1,600 + 700 + 200 = £3,000

Prescribed element is therefore £1,600 which should be held back from the claimant.

Balance payable immediately to claimant = 500 + 700 + 200 = £1,400, the other £1,600 being payable if the DWP do not serve a recoupment notice on the employer. If they do, and the value of the state benefits received by the claimant is, say, £500, the employer must pay £500 to the DWP and the remaining £1,100 to the claimant.

Example 2 (where adjustments have to be made for the statutory cap)

Basic award = £11,000

Compensatory award = £100,000, of which immediate loss = £30,000 and future loss is £70,000

Loss of statutory rights = £200

Contributory conduct of 20% applies to compensatory award only

Calculation

First, the basic award remains intact.

Secondly, the compensatory award AND the loss of statutory rights should be reduced for contributory conduct = (£100,000 + £200) x 0.8 = £80,160

Thirdly, a grossing up calculation needs to be performed:

Gross up £11,000 + £80,160 - £30,000 = £61,160

Grossing up £61,160 at, say, 20% = 61,160 ÷ 0.8 = £76,450

The compensatory award is now the remainder of £30,000 - £11,000 = £19,000 plus the grossed up figure of £76,450 which comes to £95,450. This

will be capped at £76,574.

Before the contributory conduct and the cap, the compensatory award was £100,200, and after these adjustments the award was £76,574 and we need to calculate the proportion by which the compensatory award has been reduced as a result. The calculation is (100,200 – 76,574) x 100/100,200 = 24% approximately.

So, the prescribed element of £30,000 (i.e. the immediate loss) should be reduced by 24%. Therefore the prescribed element = 30,000 (immediate loss) x 0.76 = £22,800.

Redundancy

An employee with two years service is entitled to be paid a redundancy payment if he or she is dismissed by reason of redundancy, or eligible by reason of being laid off or kept on short-time, see s135 ERA 1996. An employee may also be entitled to an enhanced redundancy payment by virtue of an express, incorporated or implied term of their contract of employment.

Statutory redundancy pay (see also *Basic award*)
If an employee has been dismissed by reason of redundancy and has not been paid the statutory redundancy to which they are due, s163 ERA 1996 permits the employee to bring a claim to the tribunal, which may order the employer to pay such amount as it thinks appropriate to compensate the worker for any financial loss arising from this non-payment (s163(5)). However, the claimant is not entitled to receive both a redundancy payment and a basic award, and any redundancy pay already paid will reduce the basic award accordingly. If redundancy was not the real reason for dismissal, the redundancy payment will not be set off against any basic award (*Boorman v Allmakes Ltd* [1995] IRLR 553).

Calculation: The redundancy payment is calculated according to the employee's length of service, age and gross weekly pay (up to the specified limit) (s162 ERA 1996). The calculation is identical to that for working out the basic award.

The employee will receive one and a half weeks gross pay for each year of employment in which they were not below the age of 41, 1 week gross pay for each year of employment in which they were at some point below the age of 41 but not below the age of 22 and half a weeks gross pay for each year of employment in which they were at any point below the age of 22. The maximum number of reckonable years is 20.

Limit on a week's pay: £464. A week's pay as defined in ss220 to 229 ERA 1996 applies (see *Week's pay* and Table 1 for historical rates).

Limit on the number of weeks: 30

Adjustments: The ACAS uplift applies (Schedule A2 TULR(C)A). However, the 2009 ACAS Code of Practice states that that guidance does not apply to redundancy dismissals so it could be argued that nor does the ACAS adjustment. The redundancy payment can also be reduced (or in certain circumstances withheld completely), for example if the employee commits an act of misconduct, leaves before the redundancy notice period has expired or the employee had taken part in a strike and refused to comply with a notice of extension served by the employer (see ss140 to 143 ERA 1996).

Mitigation: N/A

Tax: Any redundancy pay will be taxed under s401 ITEPA 2003 and therefore be counted towards the £30,000, tax free allowance.

Recoupment: N/A

Enhanced redundancy payment (awarded at tribunal)

An employee entitled to an enhanced redundancy payment may claim this from the tribunal.

Remedy: Any amount that the employee would have been entitled to over and above the statutory redundancy payment can be claimed.

Adjustments: Any enhanced redundancy payment will be part of the compensatory award and adjusted accordingly.

Cap: The statutory cap will apply to the whole of the compensatory award which includes any enhanced redundancy payment.

Tax: The enhanced redundancy payment, if awarded, will form part of the compensatory award and will be taxed under s401 ITEPA 2003 and therefore be counted towards the £30,000, tax free allowance.

Recoupment: Recoupment does not apply to any enhanced redundancy pay awarded.

Statutory authorities: ERA 1996 ss155, 162 and 163

Enhanced redundancy payment (paid on termination of employment)

The employee is not permitted to receive both a statutory redundancy payment and a basic award. The basic award will be reduced by the equivalent of the statutory redundancy payment made

(s122(4) ERA 1996), and any enhanced redundancy payment that has been paid in excess of the statutory redundancy figure will go towards reducing the compensatory award (s123(7) ERA 1996). Note that the employer will enjoy the full benefit of any enhanced redundancy paid. In other words, any adjustments, such as contributory conduct, are made before the enhanced redundancy payment is taken off the compensatory award but interest will apply after the enhanced redundancy payment. The statutory cap is applied after the enhanced redundancy payment has been taken into account. It is important that the order is complied with, as in the following example:

Example 1

Compensatory award before adjustments = £50,000

After contributory conduct @ 10% has been applied, compensatory award = £45,000

Enhanced redundancy payment of £25,000 reduces the compensatory award to £20,000

Example 2 (where the redundancy pay received reduces the tax free sum available for other awards)

Redundancy payment received (tax free) = £5,000

The tax free sum available after the redundancy payment has been made is £30,000 - £5,000 = £25,000

Basic award = £11,000

Compensatory award = £40,000

The amount that should be grossed up = £11,000 + £40,000 - £25,000 = £26,000.

Statutory authorities: ERA 1996 ss122(4) and 123(7)

Re-engagement: see Additional award; Unfair dismissal

Reinstatement: see Additional award; Unfair dismissal

Retirement: see Normal retirement age; Pension loss; Tables 35 and 36

SERPS: see State Second Pension (S2P)

Settlement agreements

(see also Tax and termination payments)

Employment may be terminated by mutual agreement, as may tribunal proceedings. Tribunal claims may be settled through early conciliation through ACAS, after the proceedings have begun through a COT3 by ACAS, by agreement between the parties or in the form of a tribunal order dismissing the proceedings upon agreement having been reached between the parties. Agreement between the parties may be reached by a number of routes both informal and formal including mediation, with some cases being mediated by tribunal judges under the official judicial mediation schemes.

Formalities

Where the agreement between the parties is reached other than by use of a COT3 form, any agreement by an individual that they will not bring any of a number of employment rights will be ineffective unless certain formalities have been undertaken (see for example s203 ERA 1996 and s144 and 147 EA 2010). For the compromise of a claim to be valid:

- The contract must be in writing

- The contract must relate to a particular complaint

- The individual must, before entering into the contract, have received advice from an independent legal advisor about its terms and effect

- On the date of giving the advice there must have been in force insurance or an indemnity against losses arising from giving the advice

- The contract must identify the advisor

- The contract must state that bullet points 3 and 4 above have been complied with.

Contractual entitlements

Where a settlement agreement makes payment for contractual payments that have already crystallised, it may well be that such sums would be taxable as earnings rather than under s401 ITEPA 2003 (see EIM12856).

Legal expenses

The employer may agree to pay legal costs incurred by the employee. Such a payment may be within s401 ITEPA 2003 since it is made in connection with the termination (see EIM13010) but may not be charged (see *Tax and termination payments*).

What tax rate should be used when deducting tax?

PAYE74015 explains the different rules when deducting tax.

Termination payment made on or before date of P45

If the termination payment is paid on or before the P45 is issued, tax and NI will be deducted from any taxable termination payment through the normal payroll using the employee's tax code at that date.

Termination payment made after the date of P45

Prior to 6 April 2011, any taxable termination payment made after the P45 was issued was taxed by the employer at the basic rate. For employees who paid tax at a higher rate this regime gave them a cash flow advantage in that any further tax to be paid via their self-assessment would not be due for several months. This changed from 6 April 2011 such that any taxable termination payments made after the P45 was issued should have tax deducted using the tax code 0T (effectively ignoring any personal tax allowance) and on a non-cumulative basis (which treats each pay period as a separate tax period). This can mean that the employee pays too much tax initially and would have to claim it back from HMRC on their self-assessment.

Sometimes payments paid in instalments may benefit the cash flow for both parties. Each tranche of the termination payment will be taxable independently on the above 0T basis, on the date of entitlement.

For monthly paid employees (using 2013/2014 tax bands)

Only the first £2,667 (i.e. 1/12 x £32,010) of the settlement payment will be charged at basic rate of 20%;

The next £9,832 (i.e. 1/12 x £117,990 (£150,000 - £32,010) will be charged to tax at the higher rate of 40%; and

Any remaining balance of the termination payment will be taxed at 45%.

Example

A termination payment of £75,000 is paid to an employee on 01/05/2013 after his P45 has been issued. £55,000 of this payment is taxable. He will pay:

20% of £2,667 = £533.40, plus

40% of £9,832 = £3,932.80, plus

45% of (55,000 − 2,667 − 9,832) = 45% of 42,501 = £19,125.45

So his total tax liability, which is payable immediately by the employer, is £23,591.65.

If the employee had received his payment prior to 6 April 2011, his immediate tax liability would have been 20% of £55,000 = £11,000.

Sex discrimination: see Discrimination

Sex Equality Clause

A 'sex equality clause' is implied into every contract of employment, if one is not already present (s66 EA 2010). The effect of a sex equality clause is that any term of an individual's contract of employment, if it is less favourable to him or her than the same term is to a comparable employee of the opposite sex, will be modified so as to not be less favourable. A comparable employee will be of the opposite sex, and the work they are employed to do will be equal (s64 and 65 EA 2010).

This applies to all the parts of the contract including:

- wages and salaries;
- non-discretionary bonuses;
- holiday pay;
- sick pay;
- overtime;
- shift payments;
- occupational pension benefits; and
- non-monetary terms such as holiday or other leave entitlements or access to sports and social benefits.

An employee may bring a claim to the tribunal for breach of his/her sex equality clause under s132 EA 2010.

Remedy: If a tribunal finds that there has been a breach of the sex equality clause it may make a declaration as to the rights of the parties (for example, stating what pay or rate of pay the individual is entitled to). The tribunal may also order an award of arrears of pay or damages (s132 EA 2010).

A limit is imposed on the period over which arrears of pay may be claimed (see s132(4)). In the standard case arrears over the preceding 6 years may be awarded, but where the breach of the clause has been concealed or the individual had an incapacity at the date of the breach, and the claim was presented within 6 years of the date the claimant knew of the claim or was capable of bringing the claim, arrears may be claimed from the date the arrears first occurred (s132(3) EA 2010).

Gross or net: Gross (but then taxed by the employer in the normal way through the payroll).

Limit on a week's pay: None

Limit on number of years: Normally 6.

Adjustments: Interest can be awarded for arrears of pay and will be calculated according to the mid-point rule (see *Interest*).

Any maximum or minimum: None

Tax: Awards (or settlements) in respect of claims under the Equal Pay Act 1970 (now EA 2010 Part V, Ch 3) are arrears of pay and therefore should be taxed under s62 ITEPA 2003 (see EIM02530 HMRC). The tax liability arises in the year of entitlement not in the year of eventual payment. It is unclear whether any interest would also be taxed.

Statutory authorities: EA 2010 ss66 and 132; The Employment Tribunals (Interest on Awards in Discrimination Cases) Regulations 1996)

Share options: see Benefits

Short time working: see Guarantee payment; Week's pay

Sickness: see Holiday pay

Simplified approach: see Pension loss

Social security benefits: see Income support; Job seekers allowance; Non-recoupable state benefits; Recoupment

State pension

This is the pension based on previous NI contributions paid (see Tables 35 and 36 for state pension ages for men and women). Claimants are not expected to give credit for any state pension benefits received when a tribunal assesses losses suffered by a claimant.

State Second Pension (S2P)

The State Second Pension, or S2P, (formerly SERPS) is additional to the basic State Pension and is based on the level of National Insurance contributions paid. To lift the burden of paying additional state pension to every worker, the government previously allowed pension savers to 'contract out' of the state second pension. This meant that people who contracted out paid less National Insurance and therefore didn't get the additional state pension, the money saved in National Insurance being put into a workplace or private pension instead.

For any employee who is not a member of an occupational scheme or is a member of an occupational pension scheme which was not contracted out of S2P (circumstances which applied to about three-quarters of the private sector working population in 2003, but to only a small proportion of public sector workers) there is a potential future loss of rights in relation to S2P if an employee is dismissed and does not obtain another job immediately.

Until 2004, this loss of S2P was calculated with reference to a table of factors which was produced when the third edition of 'Compensation for Loss of Pension Rights - Employment Tribunals' was published in 2003. However, the factors are only applicable to the year 2003/2004 and have not been updated. Thus for dismissals after 2004, there is no approved method for calculating the loss of S2P unless actuarial advice is sought. For this reason, the table of factors has not been reproduced.

Contracting out of money purchase pension schemes was abolished in 2012. Both the state second pension and contracting out of defined benefit pension schemes will end when the new flat-rate pension comes into force in 2016.

Statutory cap

(see also Additional award; Arrears; Compensatory award; Discrimination; Recoupment; Table 1)

A statutory cap applies to a compensatory award under s117(1) and (2) ERA and s123. For dismissals with an EDT before 29 July 2013 the statutory cap is as detailed in Table 1. For dismissals with an EDT on or after 29 July 2013 the statutory cap is currently the lower of £76,574 or 52 weeks gross pay (as defined in ss220 to 229 ERA 1996) (see s124 ERA 1996). Because the definition of a week's pay does not cover all pay or valuable benefits received, an employee may not be compensated for an entire year's losses. However the cap applies to 52 weeks gross pay, which effectively means that a claimant could be awarded up to 15 to 16 months net pay, assuming a combined tax/NI rate of 30%.

There are three situations in which the cap does not apply:

- If the reason for dismissal was discriminatory, the financial losses will be awarded under the discrimination legislation where there is no cap;

- If the employee is regarded as unfairly dismissed by virtue of section 100 or 105(3) (Health and Safety cases), 103A or 105(6A) (Whistleblowing);

- If an award under s117 would otherwise not fully reflect the amount of arrears payable to the employee (see also *Arrears of pay*).

The cap is applied after all the adjustments such as contributory conduct and *Polkey* have been applied. It is also applied after any grossing up calculation has been done. Table 1 lists the historical statutory caps.

Example
Basic award = £11,000

Compensatory award after all adjustments (see *Adjustments*) = £90,000

Grossing up calculation (assuming marginal tax rate of 25%)

Gross up £11,000 + £90,000 - £30,000 = £71,000

Grossed up compensatory award of £71,000 = 71,000 ÷ 0.75 = £94,666.67

Compensatory award now = £19,000 + £94,666.67 = £113,666.67

Statutory cap = £76,574

Total award = £11,000 + £76,574 = £87,574

Note: the grossing up should be done **before** the cap is applied.

Statutory authorities: ERA 1996 ss117(1) & (2), 100, 103A, 105(3), 105(6A), 123 and 124

Statutory notice period

(see also Contractual notice period; Effective date of termination; Table 37)

Section 86 ERA 1996) provides for minimum notice of termination to be given by the parties to the contract of employment. Under normal circumstances, an employee with more than one month continuous service is entitled to one week's notice, and having completed two years service is entitled to two weeks, with the number of weeks increasing by one each year until a maximum of twelve weeks notice. The notice an employee must give an employer, having completed one month's service, is one week (see Table 37).

By s86(6) no notice need be given by either party where the other has so seriously breached the contract as to be regarded as having repudiated the contract, in which case the other party may accept the breach and terminate the contract without notice.

The parties to an employment contract may agree to a longer, contractual notice period. The parties may also waive their right to notice on any occasion or accept payment in lieu of notice (see s86(3)).

Statutory redundancy: see Redundancy

Statutory rights

One of the heads of loss for which a tribunal may award compensation is the value of accrued statutory rights that have been lost: where an employee begins a new job following the termination of their employment, they will need to accrue two years continuous service before they will have acquired the right to claim unfair dismissal or a statutory redundancy payment, and may have lost the right to a lengthy statutory notice period if they have been employed for several years. The sum awarded is usually between £250 and £350, and is not generally governed by the personal circumstances of the employee such as would increase or decrease the actual value of the loss.

Remedy: There is no particular figure that should be awarded, but it is usually around £250 to £350.

Any maximum or minimum: None

Adjustments: The award is part of the compensatory award and will be adjusted accordingly (see *Hope v Jordan Engineering Ltd* [2008] UKEAT/0545/07).

Cap: The award is part of the compensatory award (see *Statutory cap*).

Tax: The award is part of the compensatory award and will be subject to the grossing up calculation, if appropriate, in the normal way.

Recoupment: Recoupment will not apply to this head of loss.

Relevant case law: Hope v Jordan Engineering Ltd [2008] UKEAT/0545/07

Substantial loss approach: see Pension loss

Summary dismissal: see Effective date of termination; Notice pay; Notice period

Suspension

Part VII ERA 1996 provides the express right for an employee to be paid whilst suspended for particular reasons:

1) An employee who is suspended from work by his employer on medical grounds is entitled to be paid by his employer remuneration while he is so suspended for a period not exceeding twenty-six weeks (s64(1) ERA 1996);

2) An employee who is suspended from work on maternity grounds is entitled to be paid remuneration by her employer while she is so suspended (s68(1) ERA 1996). Suspension on maternity grounds in effect means suspension on grounds that a woman is pregnant, has recently given birth or is breastfeeding;

3) However, the employee has a right to be offered suitable alternative work, where it exists, before being suspended from

work on maternity grounds (s67(1) ERA 1996);

4) Related rights to remuneration or alternative work apply to agency workers, see s68A to 68D ERA 1996.

A common thread between these rights is that the suspension must be required by other legislative provisions, generally regarding the health and safety of workers (see s64(2) to (4) and 66).

An employee may bring a claim that his or her employer has not paid them the remuneration to which they are entitled (see s70 ERA 1996). A similar right exists for agency workers, regarding their maternity suspension rights (see s70A ERA 1996).

Remedy: Where the tribunal finds that the employee or agency worker has not been paid the remuneration to which he or she was entitled, the tribunal will order the employer (or agency) to pay the individual the amount of remuneration which it finds is due to him or her (ss70(3 and 70A(3) ERA 1996). Remuneration is calculated according to the definition of a week's pay (see *Week's pay*) in s220 to s229 (see s69), save that the limit on a week's pay does not apply.

Where a tribunal finds that suitable alternative work has not been provided to an employee or agency worker, the tribunal may make an award of compensation (see s70(6) and (7) and s70A(6) and (7) ERA 1996). The amount of the compensation is that which the tribunal considers just and equitable in all the circumstances having regard to

a) the infringement of the employee's right under section 67 by the failure on the part of the employer to which the complaint relates; and

b) any loss sustained by the employee which is attributable to that failure.

It is likely that an award for injury to feelings can be made where there has been a failure to provide suitable alternative work, since the statutory wording for calculating the loss is that used in the detriment provisions (s49 ERA 1996) and the protection of a woman who may be suspended on maternity grounds may be seen to be akin to the protection provided by discrimination legislation.

Gross or net: The award for lost remuneration will be calculated gross, as the definition of a week's pay in ss220 to 229 ERA 1996 applies (see *Week's*

pay).

The award for a failure to provide suitable alternative work will be based on net losses, and also any injury to feelings award.

Limit on a week's pay: None

Limit on number of weeks: 26 weeks remuneration for suspension on medical grounds (see s64(1); otherwise unlimited

Any maximum or minimum: None, other than the maximum award will be 26 weeks actual gross pay where the award is for remuneration for suspension on medical grounds (see s64(1)).

Adjustments: None

Tax: To the extent that the sum awarded is compensation for lost earnings, it is likely to be taxed under s62 ITEPA 2003 (*Tax and termination payments* and EIM02550).

Recoupment: Recoupment applies to awards made in respect of a failure to pay remuneration (see Schedule to The Employment Protection (Recoupment of Jobseeker's Allowance and Income Support) Regulations 1996).

Statutory authorities: ERA 1996 ss64(1), 67(1) and s68(1); Schedule to The Employment Protection (Recoupment of Jobseeker's Allowance and Income Support) Regulations 1996

Tax and termination payments

(see also *Gourley* principle; Grossing up; Injury to feelings)

Specific tax regimes apply to income and benefits derived from employment (s62 ITEPA 2003), and to payments made in connection with employment (s401 to 416 ITEPA 2003). Where a tribunal makes a monetary award it will take into account how that sum will be treated for tax: the award may amount to an order that the employer pay salary, the award may be for a sum due in connection with employment, an award may fall outside the tax regimes, or fall within an exception or allowance. Where tax will be paid by the claimant on the sum he receives, the tribunal will gross up the award to ensure that the sum after tax is appropriate.

The tax regimes apply to a variety of sums including earnings, ex gratia payments, sums paid under settlement agreements and tribunal awards. The tax treatment of any sum will depend on the nature of the underlying sum, and the circumstances of its payment. Essentially, any sum will be taxed under the applicable employment provisions (see further below) - if none of them apply then the sum may be taxed as being paid in connection with termination. If none of the foregoing regimes apply, the payment will not be subject to tax.

By way of example:

- Earnings and benefits will be taxed (and have NIC deducted) by the employer under the applicable tax code;

- An award by a tribunal that an employer pay unlawfully deducted wages, will be calculated gross, and the employer will pay the sum (and deduct tax on it) as he does wages;

- Sums paid under a termination agreement between employer and employee, providing for sums owing under the contract that are earnings, will be taxed by the employer under the applicable tax code;

- Sums paid under a termination agreement between employer and employee, which do not amount to sums owing under the contract that are earnings, such as an enhanced redundancy payment, may fall within the regime for payments made in connection with termination. A £30,000 allowance applies to such sums;

- An award by a tribunal for losses arising from unfair dismissal, including the failure to pay an enhanced redundancy payment, will be treated as a payment made in connection termination, where the £30,000 allowance applies.

Some sums do not fall easily within easily identifiable categories, for example: punitive awards such as a protective award, injury to feelings, an award for discrimination occurring independently of termination, and payments in lieu of notice.

The applicable principles are dealt with below.

Identifying the applicable tax regime

The starting point is to ascertain whether the payment could be classed as earnings, in which case tax and employee and employer NI will be payable under s62 ITEPA 2003, or as a taxable benefit under Part 3 Chapters 2 to 11 ITEPA 2003.

If the payment does not fall under the category of earnings, the next consideration is whether it is a payment in consideration of a restrictive covenant, in which case it is fully taxable (s225

ITEPA 2003).

If neither of the first two conditions apply, the next question is whether the payment is in respect of an employer-financed retirement benefit, taxable under Part 6 Chapter 2 of ITEPA 2003.

If the answer to all the previous questions is in the negative, and the payment is 'received directly or indirectly in consideration of or in consequence of or otherwise in connection with the termination of employment', it will be taxed under Part 6 Chapter 3 of ITEPA. A tax free allowance of £30,000 applies to such payments.

Any payments which fall under s401 ITEPA 2003 are also exempt from National Insurance completely, even if they exceed £30,000 (s401 and 403 ITEPA 2003).

If none of the above apply, the compensation is unconnected with the employment or its termination and is therefore outside the scope of income tax and NIC. For example, payments or awards for damages for breach of contract prior to termination do not fall within the above provisions, neither do awards for injury to feelings from discrimination unconnected with termination.

Fully taxable and subject to NI deductions

- Earnings from employment;

- Arrears of pay;

- Accrued holiday pay;

- Payments made in consideration of restrictive covenants (s225 ITEPA 2003), unless the specific consideration is attached to the restatement of existing covenants or an agreement to discontinue proceedings (see *Appellent v Inspector of Taxes* [2001] STC (SCD) 21;

- Payment in respect of a non-approved retirement benefit;

- Contractual PILONs;

- Implied contractual right to a PILON;

- Contractual termination payments;

- Contractual benefits in kind;

- Payments during garden leave;

- Payments to an employee suspended from work on medical grounds under Sections 64 and 70(3) ERA 1996 (EIM02550, HMRC);

- Maternity suspension payments under Sections 68 and 70(3) ERA 1996 (EIM02550, HMRC);

- Payments under Sections 51(3)(b) or 63(4) ERA 1996 for infringing the employee's rights to time off for public duties under Section 50 or Trade Union duties or activities under Sections 61 and 62 respectively (EIM02550, HMRC);

- Payments under the Sex Discrimination Acts, the Equal Pay Act 1970 (see EIM02530), the Wages Act 1986, the Trade Union and Labour Relations (Consolidation) Act 1992 and the National Minimum Wage Act 1998 for wrongfully depressing the employee's remuneration in the employment (EIM02550, HMRC).

Payments which are fully taxable by the employer before payment to the individual should not be grossed up by the tribunal.

Payments in lieu of notice (PILONS)

Payments made in exercise of contractual PILONs are fully taxable as earnings; they will not be taxed or qualify for any exemptions in s401-416 ITEPA 2003. Similarly, if there is an implied contractual right to a PILON, or where there is a discretion to make a PILON (see *EMI Group Electronics Ltd v Coldicott* [1999] IRLR 630), such a payment will be fully taxable. It is possible for an employer to terminate an employment contract without notice, and not exercise a PILON, so that the sums are not taxed as earnings (see *Cerberus Software v Rowley* [2001] IRLR 160). The factors that HMRC will take into account in such a situation have been set out in Tax Bulletin 63 (February 2003), and include whether there has been a reduction for mitigation, whether all salary and benefits are compensated for, and that the payment takes into account appropriate tax treatments for termination payments.

Termination payments

Where a payment made on termination, in a settlement agreement or in the form of a tribunal award falls within Part 6 Chapter 3 of ITEPA, that particular regime will apply. This includes a £30,000 allowance, so for example in a straightforward unfair dismissal award made by a tribunal the first £30,000 will be exempt from tax, and any award above this will be grossed up by the tribunal to ensure the individual retains the value of his net loss.

Payments and other benefits that fall within this regime include:

- Non-contractual benefits in kind;

- Statutory, non-contractual and contractual redundancy payments, provided that they are genuinely on account of redundancy (see *Mairs v Haughey* [1994] 1 AC 303);

- Basic award;

- Awards for financial loss whether for unfair dismissal or as a result of discrimination;

- Damages for wrongful dismissal;

- An additional award;

- An award for employer failing to provide a statement of written particulars (see EIM12960);

- Protective awards.

Payments in excess of the £30,000 tax free allowance should be grossed up to ensure the employee receives the sum that has been awarded.

Exempt from taxation

Certain payments are exempted from taxation under s401 ITEPA 2003 and will therefore not be taxed at all. Payments include:

- payment made by reason of the death of an employee or on account of an injury to, or disability of, the employee;

- payment of legal expenses and either the sum is awarded by the tribunal or is paid under a settlement agreement and is paid to the individual's layer (Enactment of Extra-Statutory Concessions Order 2011 SI 2011/1037, Article 10);

- certain costs in connection with counselling, outplacement and retraining courses (s310 and 311 ITEPA 2003);

- foreign service exemption - full and partial exemptions apply to payments made in respect of foreign service, where an employee was both non-resident and non-ordinarily resident in the UK (s413 ITEPA 2003).

Payments which are exempt from tax should not be grossed up.

Specific categories of award
Unlawful deduction from wages

A tribunal ought to award payment for unlawful deduction from wages under s13 ERA 1996 gross, with the employer deducting tax and NIC at source, as such payments fall within s62 ITEPA 2003.

Reinstatement or re-engagement

Where a tribunal has made an award for lost salary between the date of dismissal and the reinstatement or re-engagement, that sum is not taxed as earnings under s62 ITEPA 2003 but will fall within s401 (*Wilson v Clayton* [2005] IRLR 108). Such sums will be calculated on a net basis and grossed up where appropriate (see EIM 12960).

Discrimination not involving termination

According to HMRC in EIM12965 and *Yorkshire Housing Ltd v Cuerden* UKEAT/0397/09, compensation payments made for discrimination that does not cause termination will not be subject to tax. This would include any financial and non-financial losses such as an award for injury to feelings. Such an award should be calculated on a net basis, and there will not be a need to gross up.

Discrimination involving termination

Awards made in connection with termination arising from discrimination will be taxable under s401 ITEPA 2003 (*Walker v Adams* [2001] STC 101, *Orthet v Vince Cain* [2004] IRLR 857 and *Oti-Obihara v Commissioners for HM Revenue & Customs* [2011] IRLR 386).

Equality clauses

Where an award is made for breach of an equality clause, the award will be subject to tax on the basis of the tax due in the year the sum ought to have been paid (EIM02530). The award should be calculated on a gross basis, with the employer operating an appropriate special PAYE procedure.

Injury to feelings

An injury to feelings award made in relation to discrimination that does not amount to termination will not be subject to tax (EIM12965 and *Yorkshire Housing Ltd v Cuerden* UKEAT/0397/09). However, there is uncertainty regarding injury to feelings awards arising from a discriminatory termination and whether they fall within s401 ITEPA 2003. HMRC take the view that such injury to feelings awards are subject to tax (EIM12965), however a number of tribunals have applied the contrary approach (see *Walker v Adams* [2001] STC 101, *Orthet v Vince Cain* [2004] IRLR 857 and *Oti-Obihara v Commissioners for HM Revenue & Customs* [2011] IRLR 386). There is an argument that s406 ITEPA 2003 which applies to payments made on account of injury, which is not expressly restricted to actual personal injury, might therefore include mere injury to feelings. It is the experience of the authors that employment tribunals tend to regard all injury to feelings awards as not subject to tax and so do not gross up such awards.

Protective awards and TUPE consultation

Though protective awards are calculated by reference to pay over a protected period, such sums are not paid by reference to the individual acting as an employee, but under statute (and as punishment for breach of a statutory obligation) (see *Mintec Ltd v Inland Revenue* [2001] STC 101). They therefore fall under s401 rather than s62 ITEPA 2003.

The logic applied in *Mintec* might suggest that where an award has been made for failure to inform and consult under TUPE, which is unconnected to any termination, the award would not be subject to tax at all. Where an individual in receipt of such an award has been subject to a transfer, it might be argued that the transfer, for the purposes of the tax regime, did amount to a termination (see *Kuehne & Nagel Drinks Logistics Ltd, Scott & Joyce v HMRC* [2009] UKFTT 379 (TC)). That argument would not however apply to an individual affected by the transfer, whose representatives were not appropriately consulted, but who did not themselves transfer.

Payments unrelated to termination

Where an award is made for breach of a statutory right, for example if the employer has not complied with the right of an employee to be accompanied at a disciplinary hearing, this is unrelated to the individual's termination and may well not be earnings. There is no official guidance on how such sums should be treated. However, the logic in *Mintec Ltd v Inland Revenue* [2001] STC 101, that such sums are not paid by reference to the individual acting as an employee but under statute (and as punishment for breach of a statutory obligation), could apply. Such payments may well not be subject to tax and should not be grossed up.

Time off for ante-natal care

An employee who has an appointment for the purpose of receiving ante-natal care is entitled to be permitted by her employer to take time off during the employee's working hours in order to enable her to keep the appointment (s55 ERA 1996).

The employee is entitled to be paid at their "appropriate hourly rate" for their period of absence. Unless the employee works a varying number of working hours, the appropriate hourly rate is one week's pay divided by the normal working hours in a week when the time off was taken. For employees whose hours of work vary over a week or longer period, the appropriate hourly rate is obtained by dividing one week's pay by the average number of hours worked over the previous twelve weeks, or where the employee has not been employed for twelve weeks, a number which fairly represents the number of normal working hours in a week (see s56(2), (3) and (4)).

A week's pay will be calculated in accordance with s220 to s229 ERA 1996 (see *Week's pay*).

Any contractual remuneration paid to an employee in respect of such a period of time off goes towards discharging the liability under s56 (see s56(5) and (6)).

An employee may bring a complaint to a tribunal that her employer has unreasonably refused to permit her to take the time off under s55, or has failed to pay the sums due under s56 (see s57(1) ERA 1996).

Equivalent rights to time off and remuneration for the period of absence are given to agency workers, with the remuneration to be paid by the agency (see s57ZA to 57ZD).

Remedy: Where a tribunal finds a complaint well founded, it will make a declaration to that effect (s57(3).

Further, if the tribunal has found that the employer has unreasonably refused to permit the employee to take time off, the tribunal will also order the employer to pay to the employee an amount equal to the remuneration to which she would have been entitled under s56 if the employer had not refused (s57(4).

Also, if the tribunal finds that the employer has failed to pay the employee the whole or part of any amount to which she is entitled under s56, the tribunal will also order the employer to pay to the employee the amount she is owed (s57(5)).

For employees working fixed number of hours per week
Sum to which the employee is entitled = (gross weekly pay) x 1/(number of normal working hours in a week) x (number of hours absent) (s56(2) ERA 1996)

For employees with varying number of hours worked per week
Sum to which the employee is entitled = gross weekly pay x 12/(number of normal hours worked in the last 12 weeks ending with the last complete week before the day on which the time off is taken) x (number of hours absent) (s56(3) ERA 1996)

For employees with varying number of hours worked per week and who have worked for less than 12 weeks
Sum to which the employee is entitled = (gross weekly pay) x 1/(number of normal hours which fairly represents the number of normal working hours in a week) x (number of hours absent) (s56(3) and (4) ERA 1996)

Gross or net: The sum for unpaid earnings will be calculated gross and paid through payroll as with ordinary remuneration.

Any maximum or minimum: None

Adjustments: The claimant will have to give credit for any amount paid towards the entitlement under the contract.

Mitigation: N/A

Tax: The tax treatment is not clear. To the extent that the sum awarded is compensation for lost earnings for work done, it is likely to be taxed under s62 ITEPA 2003 (see *Tax*).

Recoupment: N/A

Statutory authorities: ERA 1996 ss55, 56 and s57ZA to 57ZD

Time off for dependants

An employee is entitled to be permitted by his employer to take a reasonable amount of time off during the employee's working hours in order to care for or sort out issues in relation to a dependant (s57A ERA 1996). The definition of a dependant includes amongst others a spouse, a civil partner, a child and a parent.

An employee may bring a complaint to a tribunal that his employer has unreasonably refused to permit him to take this time off (s57B ERA 1996).

Remedy: Where the tribunal finds such a complaint well founded it will make a declaration to that effect (s57B(3)(a). It may also make an award of compensation to be paid by the employer (s57B(3)(b) and (4).

The amount of compensation will be that which it considers just and equitable in all the circumstances having regard to-

a) the employer's default in refusing to permit time off to be taken by the employee; and

b) any loss sustained by the employee as a result.

Any maximum or minimum: There is no statutory limit to the compensation.

Adjustments: N/A

Mitigation: It is likely that the principle of mitigation would be applied in an appropriate case. However this would most likely operate to restrict the losses that would be compensated for where it would have been reasonable for the employee to have incurred a lower level of losses than were in fact incurred, for example where the alternative care was unreasonably expensive and reasonably avoidable.

Tax: The tax treatment is not clear. To the extent that the sum awarded is compensation for lost earnings for work done, it is likely to be taxed under s62 ITEPA 2003 (*Tax and termination payments* and EIM02550).

Recoupment: N/A

Statutory authorities: ERA 1996 s57A and 57B

Time off for employee representatives

An employee representative for the purposes of collective consultation or TUPE consultation is entitled to take reasonable time off during the employee's working hours to perform his functions as such an employee representative, or candidate in an election for such a role, or in order to undergo training to perform such functions (s61 ERA 1996).

The employee is entitled to be paid at their "appropriate hourly rate" for their period of absence. Unless the employee works a varying number of working hours, the appropriate hourly rate is one week's pay divided by the normal working hours in a week when the time off was taken. For employees whose hours of work vary over a week or longer period, the appropriate hourly rate is obtained by dividing one week's pay by the average number of hours worked over the previous twelve weeks, or where the employee has not been employed for twelve weeks, a number which fairly represents the number of

normal working hours in a week. (s62 ERA 1996).

A week's pay will be calculated in accordance with s220 to s229 ERA 1996 (see *Week's pay*).

Any contractual remuneration paid to an employee in respect of such a period of time off goes towards discharging the liability under s62 (see s62(5) and (6)).

An employee may bring a complaint to a tribunal that his or her employer has unreasonably refused to permit him or her to take the time off under s61, or has failed to pay the sums due under s62 (see s63(1) ERA 1996).

Remedy: Where a tribunal finds a complaint well founded, it will make a declaration to that effect (s63(3) ERA 1996).

Further, if the tribunal has found that the employer has unreasonably refused to permit the employee to take time off, the tribunal will also order the employer to pay to the employee an amount equal to the remuneration to which he or she would have been entitled under s62 if the employer had not refused (s63(4) ERA 1996)).

Also, if the tribunal finds that the employer has failed to pay the employee the whole or part of any amount to which he or she is entitled under s62, the tribunal will also order the employer to pay to the employee the amount he or she is owed (s63(5) ERA 1996).

For employees working fixed number of hours per week
Sum to which the employee is entitled = (gross weekly pay) x 1/(number of normal working hours in a week) x (number of hours absent) (s62(2) ERA 1996

For employees with varying number of hours worked per week
Sum to which the employee is entitled = gross weekly pay x 12/(number of normal hours worked in the last 12 weeks ending with the last complete week before the day on which the time off is taken) x (number of hours absent) (s62(3)(a) ERA 1996)

For employees with varying number of hours worked per week and who have worked for less than 12 weeks
Sum to which the employee is entitled = (gross weekly pay) x 1/(number of normal hours which fairly represents the number of normal working hours in a week) x (number of hours absent) (s62(3) and (4) ERA 1996)

Gross or net: The sum will be calculated gross and paid through payroll as with ordinary remuneration.

Any maximum or minimum: None

Adjustments: The claimant will have to give credit for any amount paid towards the entitlement under the contract.

Mitigation: N/A

Tax: Taxable under s62 ITEPA 2003 (see EIM02550).

Recoupment: N/A

Statutory authorities: ERA 1996 ss61 to 63

Time off for employee representatives (ICE)

An employee representative who is a negotiating representative or an information and consultation representative within the Information and Consultation of Employees Regulations 2004 is entitled to take reasonable time off during the employee's working hours to perform his functions as such a representative (Reg 27 ICE Regs 2004).

The employee is entitled to be paid at their "appropriate hourly rate" for their period of absence. Unless the employee works a varying number of working hours, the appropriate hourly rate is one week's pay divided by the normal working hours in a week when the time off was taken. For employees whose hours of work vary over a week or longer period, the appropriate hourly rate is obtained by dividing one week's pay by the average number of hours worked over the previous twelve weeks, or where the employee has not been employed for twelve weeks, a number which fairly represents the number of normal working hours in a week (see Reg 28(3), (4) and (5)).

A week's pay will be calculated in accordance with s220 to s229 ERA 1996 (see *Week's pay*) (Reg 28(2)).

Any contractual remuneration paid to an employee in respect of such a period of time off goes towards discharging the liability under Reg 28 (see Reg 28(6) and (7)).

An employee may bring a complaint to a tribunal that his or her employer has unreasonably refused to permit him or her to take the time off under Reg 27, or has failed to pay the sums due under Reg 28 (See Reg 29 ICE 2004).

Remedy: Where a tribunal finds a complaint well founded, it will make a declaration to that effect (Reg 29(3)).

Further, if the tribunal has found that the employer has unreasonably refused to permit the employee to take time off, the tribunal will also order the employer to pay to the employee an amount equal to the remuneration to which he or she would have been entitled under Reg 28 if the employer had not refused (Reg 29(4)).

Also, if the tribunal finds that the employer has failed to pay the employee the whole or part of any amount to which he or she is entitled under Reg 28, the tribunal will also order the employer to pay to the employee the amount he or she is owed (Reg 29(5).

For employees working fixed number of hours per week
Sum to which the employee is entitled = (gross weekly pay) x 1/(number of normal working hours in a week) x (number of hours absent) (Reg 28(3) ICE 2004))

For employees with varying number of hours worked per week
Sum to which the employee is entitled = gross weekly pay x 12/(number of normal hours worked in the last 12 weeks ending with the last complete week before the day on which the time off is taken) x (number of hours absent)

For employees with varying number of hours worked per week and who have worked for less than 12 weeks
Sum to which the employee is entitled = (gross weekly pay) x 1/(number of normal hours which fairly represents the number of normal working hours in a week) x (number of hours absent) (Reg 28(4) and (5) ICE 2004)

Gross or net: Gross. A week's pay as defined in ss220 to 229 ERA 1996 applies (see *Week's pay*) (Reg 28(2))

Limit on a week's pay: None. The calculation is based on actual gross weekly pay.

Limit on number of weeks: None

Any maximum or minimum: None

Adjustments: None

Mitigation: N/A

Tax: The tax treatment is not clear. To the extent that the sum awarded is compensation for lost earnings for work done, it is likely to be taxed under s62 ITEPA 2003 (*Tax and termination payments* and EIM02550).

Recoupment: N/A

Statutory authorities: ICE 2004 (SI 2004/3426) Regs 27 and 29

Time off for employee representatives (OPPS)

A "consulted representative" within the Occupational and Personal Pension Schemes (Consultation by Employers and Miscellaneous Amendment) Regulations 2006 is entitled to take reasonable time off during the employee's working hours to perform his functions as such a representative (Sch para 2 OPPS 2006). A "consulted representative" is an employee who is a trade union representative, appointed representative, elected representative or one identified in an appropriate agreement (Reg 12(2)(a) and (3) and Reg 13(2) of OPPS Regs 2006).

The employee is entitled to be paid at their "appropriate hourly rate" for their period of absence. Unless the employee works a varying number of working hours, the appropriate hourly rate is one week's pay divided by the normal working hours in a week when the time off was taken. For employees whose hours of work vary over a week or longer period, the appropriate hourly rate is obtained by dividing one week's pay by the average number of hours worked over the previous twelve weeks, or where the employee has not been employed for twelve weeks, a number which fairly represents the number of normal working hours in a week (see Sch para 3 (3), (4) and (5)).

A week's pay will be calculated in accordance with s220 to s229 ERA 1996 (see *Week's pay*) (Sch para 3(2)).

Any contractual remuneration paid to an employee in respect of such a period of time off goes towards discharging the liability under Sch para 3 (see Sch para 3(6) and (7)).

An employee may bring a complaint to a tribunal that his or her employer has unreasonably refused to permit him or her to take the time off under Sch para 2, or has failed to pay the sums due under Sch para 3 (see Sch para 4 OPPS 2006).

Remedy: Where a tribunal finds a complaint well founded, it will make a declaration to that effect (Sch para 4(3)) OPPS 2006).

Further, if the tribunal has found that the employer has unreasonably refused to permit the employee to take time off, the tribunal will also order the employer to pay to the employee an amount equal to the remuneration to which he or she would have been entitled under Sch para 3 if the employer had not refused (Sch para 4(4)).

Also, if the tribunal finds that the employer has failed to pay the employee the whole or part of any amount to which he or she is entitled under Reg 28, the tribunal will also order the employer to pay to the employee the amount he or she is owed (Sch para 4(5)).

For employees working fixed number of hours per week

Sum to which the employee is entitled = (gross weekly pay) x 1/(number of normal working hours in a week) x (number of hours absent) (Sch para 3(3) OPPS 2006)

For employees with varying number of hours worked per week

Sum to which the employee is entitled = gross weekly pay x 12/(number of normal hours worked in the last 12 weeks ending with the last complete week before the day on which the time off is taken) x (number of hours absent) (Sch para 3(4) OPPS 2006)

For employees with varying number of hours worked per week and who have worked for less than 12 weeks

Sum to which the employee is entitled = (gross weekly pay) x 1/(number of normal hours which fairly represents the number of normal working hours in a week) x (number of hours absent) (Sch para 3(4) and (5) OPPS)and (5))

Gross or net: Gross. A week's pay as defined in ss220 to 229 ERA 1996 applies (see *Week's pay*).

Limit on a week's pay: None. The calculation is based on actual gross weekly pay.

Limit on number of weeks: None

Any maximum or minimum: None

Adjustments: None

Mitigation: N/A

Tax: The tax treatment is not clear. To the extent that the sum awarded is compensation for lost earnings for work done, it is likely to be taxed under s62 ITEPA 2003 (*Tax and termination payments* and EIM02550).

Recoupment: N/A

Statutory authorities: OPPS 2006 (SI 2006/349) Regs 12, 13 and Schedule paragraphs 2 to 4

Time off for members of a European Works Council

An employee who is:

a)   a member of a special negotiating body;

b)   a member of a European Works Council;

c)   an information and consultation representative; or

d)   a candidate in an election in which any person elected will, on being elected, be such a member or representative,

is entitled to take reasonable time off during the employee's working hours to perform his functions as such a representative (Reg 25 TICE 1999).

An employee who is-

a)   a member of a special negotiating body;

b)   a member of a European Works Council;

is entitled to take reasonable time off during the employee's working hours to undertake the training permitted by Reg 19B (Reg 25(1A) TICE Regs 1999).

The employee is entitled to be paid at their "appropriate hourly rate" for their period of absence. Unless the employee works a varying number of working hours, the appropriate hourly rate is one week's pay divided by the normal working hours in a week when the time off was taken. For employees whose hours of work vary over a week or longer period, the appropriate hourly rate is obtained by dividing one week's pay by the average number of hours worked over the previous twelve weeks, or where the employee has not been employed for twelve weeks, a number which fairly represents the number of normal working hours in a week (see Reg 26 (3), (4) and (5)).

A week's pay will be calculated in accordance with s220 to s229 ERA 1996 (see *Week's pay*) (Reg 26(2)).

Any contractual remuneration paid to an employee in respect of such a period of time off goes towards discharging the liability under Reg 26 (see Reg 26(6) and (7)).

An employee may bring a complaint to a tribunal that his or her employer has unreasonably refused to permit him or her to take the time off under Reg 25, or has failed to pay the sums due under Reg 26 (see Reg 27 TICE 1999).

Remedy: Where a tribunal finds a complaint well founded, it will make a declaration to that effect (Reg 27(3)).

Further, if the tribunal has found that the employer has unreasonably refused to permit the employee to take time off, the tribunal will also order the employer to pay to the employee an amount equal to the remuneration to which he or she would have been entitled under Reg 26 if the employer had not refused (Reg 27(4)).

Also, if the tribunal finds that the employer has failed to pay the employee the whole or part of any amount to which he or she is entitled under Reg 26, the tribunal will also order the employer to pay to the employee the amount he or she is owed (Reg 27(5)).

For employees working a fixed number of hours per week

Sum to which the employee is entitled = (gross weekly pay) x 1/(number of normal working hours in a week) x (number of hours absent) (Reg 26(3) TICE 1999)

For employees with varying number of hours worked per week

Sum to which the employee is entitled = gross weekly pay x 12/(number of normal hours worked in the last 12 weeks ending with the last complete week before the day on which the time off is taken) x (number of hours absent) (Reg 26(4) TICE 1999)

For employees with varying number of hours worked per week and who have worked for less than 12 weeks

Sum to which the employee is entitled = (gross weekly pay) x 1/(number of normal hours which fairly represents the number of normal working hours in a week) x (number of hours absent) (Reg 26(4) and (5) TICE 1999)

Gross or net: Gross. A week's pay as defined in ss220 to 229 ERA 1996 applies (see *Week's pay*).

Limit on a week's pay: None. The calculation is based on actual gross weekly pay.

Limit on number of weeks: None

Any maximum or minimum: None

Adjustments: None

Mitigation: N/A

Tax: The tax treatment is not clear. To the extent

that the sum awarded is compensation for lost earnings for work done, it is likely to be taxed under s62 ITEPA 2003 (see *Tax* and EIM02550).

Recoupment: N/A

Statutory authorities: TICE 1999 (SI 1999/3323) Regs 19B, 25 to 27

Time off for pension scheme trustees

An employee who is the trustee of his employer's pension scheme is permitted to take time off to perform the duties of a trustee and undergo relevant training. The amount of time off is that which is reasonable in all the circumstances having regard to how much time is required to be taken off and the effect of the employee's absence on the running of the employer's business (s58 ERA 1996).

The employee must be paid by his or her employer for the time taken off under section 58 (s59). Where the employee's remuneration would not have varied with the amount of work done during the period of absence, the employee should be paid as if he or she had worked for the whole of that time (s59(2)). However where the employee's remuneration would have varied with the amount of work done, he or she should be paid their average hourly earnings for the period (s59(3) and (4)).

Any contractual remuneration paid to an employee in respect of such a period of time off goes towards discharging the liability under Reg 26 (see s59(5) and (6)).

An employee may bring a complaint to a tribunal that his or her employer has unreasonably refused to permit him or her to take the time off under s58, or has failed to pay the sums due under s59 (see s60 ERA 1996).

Remedy: Where the tribunal finds such a complaint well founded it will make a declaration to that effect (s60(3)(a). It may also make an award of compensation to be paid by the employer (s60(3)(b) and (4)).

The amount of compensation will be that which it considers just and equitable in all the circumstances having regard to:

a) the employer's default in refusing to permit the employee to take time off; and

b) any loss sustained by the employee as a result.

Gross or net: Payment under s60(5): gross but taxable as normal under PAYE; Payment under s60(4): N/A

Limit on a week's pay: None. For payment under s60(5) the calculation is based on actual weekly pay.

Any maximum or minimum: There is no statutory limit to the award.

Mitigation: It is likely that the principle of mitigation would be applied in an appropriate case. However this would most likely operate to restrict the losses that would be compensated for where it would have been reasonable for the employee to have incurred a lower level of losses than were in fact incurred, for example where the expenses incurred in making alternative arrangements were unreasonably expensive and reasonably avoidable.

Tax: The tax treatment is not clear. To the extent that the sum awarded is compensation for lost earnings for work done, it is likely to be taxed under s62 ITEPA 2003 (*Tax and termination payments* and EIM02550).

Statutory authorities: ERA 1996 ss58 to 60

Time off for public duties

An employee who holds any of a number of specified public offices is entitled to take time off during his or her working hours for the purpose of performing specified duties. The duties that fall within the right depend on the office held. Offices include Justice of the Peace, and members of statutory tribunals, independent monitoring boards and visiting committees of a prison, a relevant health or education body, the Environment Agency, the Scottish Environment Protection Agency and Scottish Water. Duties for which an individual is entitled to time off include meetings and discharging the functions of the body (see s50(1) to (3) and (5) to 9B ERA 1996).

The amount of time off permitted is that which is reasonable in all the circumstances having regard to how much time is required to be taken off, how much time off the individual has taken off for trade union duties and activities and the effect of the employee's absence on the running of the employer's business (s50(4) ERA 1996).

An employee may bring a complaint to a tribunal that his or her employer has unreasonably refused to permit him or her to take the time off under s50 (s51).

Remedy: Where the tribunal finds such a complaint well founded it will make a declaration to that effect (s51(3)(a)). It may also make an award of compensation to be paid by the employer (s51(3)(b) and (4)).

The amount of the compensation shall be such as the tribunal considers just and equitable in all the circumstances having regard to-

a) the employer's default in refusing to permit the employee to take time off; and

b) any loss sustained by the employee as a result.

Any maximum or minimum: There is no statutory limit to the compensation.

Mitigation: It is likely that the principle of mitigation would be applied in an appropriate case. However this would most likely operate to restrict the losses that would be compensated for where it would have been reasonable for the employee to have incurred a lower level of losses than were in fact incurred, for example where the expenses incurred in making alternative arrangements were unreasonably expensive and reasonably avoidable.

Tax: See EIM02550. To the extent that the sum awarded is compensation for lost earnings for work done, it is likely to be taxed under s62 ITEPA 2003 (*Tax and termination payments* and EIM02550).

Statutory authorities: ERA 1996 ss50 and 51

Time off for study or training

Section 63D ERA 1996 creates the right to make a request in relation to study or training where the purpose of the study or training is to improve the employee's effectiveness or performance in the employer's business. The procedure for making the application and for the employer's consideration of that application are set out at s63D to 63H ERA 1996.

An employee may bring a complaint to an employment tribunal that his or her employer has failed to follow the required procedure, reached its decision on impermissible basis or based its decision on incorrect facts (s63I(1) ERA 1996). There are various procedural hurdles to bringing such a claim (s63I(2) to (6) ERA 1996).

Remedy: If an employment tribunal finds the complaint well founded it must make a declaration to that effect and may make an order:

a) for reconsideration of the application; and/or

b) for an award of compensation.

The amount of any compensation will that which the tribunal considers just and equitable in all the circumstances, limited to 8 week's pay (see s63J ERA 1996 and EST(ECR) Regs 2010).

Gross or net: Gross. The definition of a week's pay as defined in ss220 to 229 ERA 1996 will apply (see *Week's pay*).

Limit on a week's pay: Currently £464 (see Table 1 for historical rates).

Limit on number of weeks: 8 (see the Employee Study and Training (Eligibility, Complaints and Remedies) Regulations 2010 SI No. 156)

Any maximum or minimum: Currently the maximum is £3,712

Adjustments: None

Mitigation: N/A

Tax: The tax treatment is not clear. To the extent that the sum awarded is compensation for lost earnings for work done, it is likely to be taxed under s62 ITEPA 2003 (*Tax and termination payments* and EIM02550).

Statutory authorities: ERA 1996 s63D to K, The Employee Study and Training (Eligibility, Complaints and Remedies) Regulations 2010 (SI 2010/156)

Time off for union duties, activities and union learning reps

An employee who is an official of an independent trade union recognised by his or her employer is entitled to take time off during working hours to carry out various official union duties (s168 TULR(C)A 1992)

An employee who is a member of a recognised trade union and a learning representative of that trade union is entitled to take time off during his working hours for a number of training related activities (s168A).

An employee who is a member of a recognised trade union is entitled to take time off during his working hours to take part in activities of the union, and activities in relation to which the employee is acting as a representative of the union (s170).

The amount of time off which must be permitted is that which is reasonable in all the circumstances having regard to any relevant provisions of a code of practice issued by ACAS (s168(3), s168A(8) and 170(3)).

The employee must be paid by his or her employer for the time taken off under section s168 or 168A, but not s170 (s169). Where the employee's remuneration would not have varied with the amount of work done during the period of absence, the employee should be paid as if he or she had worked for the whole of that time (s169(2)). However where the employee's remuneration would have varied with the amount of work done, he or she should be paid their average hourly earnings for the period (s169(3) and (4)).

Any contractual remuneration paid to an employee in respect of such a period of time off goes towards discharging the liability under s169 (see s169(4)).

An employee may bring a complaint to a tribunal that his employer has unreasonably refused to permit him to take time off (s168(4), s168A(9) and s170(4)). An employee may bring a complaint to a tribunal that his or her employer has failed to pay the employee during their time off under s169 (s169(5)).

Remedy: Where the tribunal upholds a complaint for failure to permit time off it will make a declaration to that effect and may also make an award of compensation to be paid by the employer (172(1) and (2) TULR(C)A 1992.

The amount of compensation will be that which it considers just and equitable in all the circumstances having regard to-

a) the employer's default in refusing to permit the employee to take time off; and

b) any loss sustained by the employee as a result.

Where a tribunal finds that an employer has failed to pay the employee during their time off, the tribunal will order that the employer pay the amount found to be due (s172(3)).

Gross or net: Net loss, or gross where taxable under s62ITEPA 2003.

Adjustments: None

Mitigation: It is likely that the principle of mitigation would be applied in an appropriate case. However this would most likely operate to restrict the losses that would be compensated for where it would have been reasonable for the employee to have incurred a lower level of losses than were in fact incurred, for example where the expenses incurred in making alternative arrangements were unreasonably expensive and reasonably avoidable.

Tax: The tax treatment is not clear. To the extent that the sum awarded is compensation for lost earnings for work done, it is likely to be taxed under s62 ITEPA 2003 (*Tax and termination payments* and EIM02550).

Recoupment: N/A

Statutory authorities: TULR(C)A 1992 ss168 to 173

Time off for young person for study or training

An employee who is aged 16 or 17, is not receiving full-time secondary or further education, and has not attained such standard of achievement as is prescribed by regulations made by the Secretary of State, is entitled to take time off during his or her working hours to undertake study or training leading to a relevant qualification (s63A(1) and (2) ERA 1996). The right extends to such employees who are supplied by their employer to another 'principal' (s63A(3)). The right also extends to employees who have begun their study or training but have turned 18 (s63A(4)).

The amount of time off permitted is that which is reasonable in all the circumstances having regard to the requirements of the employee's study or training and the effect of the employee's absence on the running of the employer's business (s63A(5) ERA 1996).

The employee is entitled to be paid at their "appropriate hourly rate" for their period of absence. Unless the employee works a varying number of working hours, the appropriate hourly rate is one week's pay divided by the normal working hours in a week when the time off was taken. For employees whose hours of work vary over a week or longer period, the appropriate hourly rate is obtained by dividing one week's pay by the average number of hours worked over the previous twelve weeks, or where the employee has not been employed for twelve weeks, a number which fairly represents the number of normal working hours in a week (see s63B(1) to (4)).

A week's pay will be calculated in accordance with s220 to s229 ERA 1996 (see *Week's pay*). Any contractual remuneration paid to an employee in respect of such a period of time off goes towards discharging the liability under S63B (see s63B(5) and (6)).

An employee may bring a complaint to a tribunal that his or her employer has unreasonably refused to permit him or her to take the time off under S63A, or has failed to pay the sums due under s63B (see s63C).

Remedy: Where a tribunal finds a complaint well founded, it will make a declaration to that effect (s65C(3)).

Further, if the tribunal has found that the employer has unreasonably refused to permit the employee to take time off, the tribunal will also order the employer to pay to the employee an amount equal to the remuneration to which he or she would have been entitled under s63B if the employer had not refused (s63C(4)).

Also, if the tribunal finds that the employer has failed to pay the employee the whole or part of any amount to which he or she is entitled under s63B, the tribunal will also order the employer to pay to the employee the amount he or she is owed (s63C(5)).

For employees working fixed number of hours per week

Sum to which the employee is entitled = (gross weekly pay) x 1/(number of normal working hours in a week) x (number of hours absent) (s63B(2) ERA 1996)

For employees with varying number of hours worked per week

Sum to which the employee is entitled = gross weekly pay x 12/(number of normal hours worked in the last 12 weeks ending with the last complete week before the day on which the time off is taken) x (number of hours absent) (s63B(3) ERA 1996

For employees with varying number of hours

worked per week and who have worked for less than 12 weeks

Sum to which the employee is entitled = (gross weekly pay) x 1/(number of normal hours which fairly represents the number of normal working hours in a week) x (number of hours absent) (s63B(3) and (4) ERA 1996)

Gross or net: Gross. The definition of a week's pay as defined in ss220 to 229 ERA 1996 will apply (see *Week's pay*).

Limit on a week's pay: None. The calculation is based on actual gross weekly pay.

Limit on number of weeks: None

Any maximum or minimum: None

Adjustments: None

Mitigation: N/A

Tax: The tax treatment is not clear. To the extent that the sum awarded is compensation for lost earnings for work done, it is likely to be taxed under s62 ITEPA 2003 (*Tax and termination payments* and EIM02550).

Recoupment: N/A

Statutory authorities: ERA 1996 s63A to 63C

Time off to look for work or arrange training after being made redundant

An employee who is given notice of dismissal by reason of redundancy and who has sufficient continuity of service to receive a statutory redundancy payment, is entitled to take reasonable time off during his or her working hours before the end of his notice in order to look for new employment, or make arrangements for training for future employment (s52 ERA 1996).

The employee is entitled to be paid at their "appropriate hourly rate" for their period of absence. Unless the employee works a varying number of working hours, the appropriate hourly rate is one week's pay divided by the normal working hours in a week when the time off was taken. For employees whose hours of work vary over a week or longer period, the appropriate hourly rate is obtained by dividing one week's pay by the average number of hours per week worked over the previous twelve weeks (s53(1) to (3)).

If an employer unreasonably refuses to permit an employee to take the time permitted by s52, the employee is entitled to be paid the amount of remuneration he would have been entitled to if he had been given the time off (s53(4)). A week's pay will be calculated in accordance with s220 to s229 ERA 1996 (see *Week's pay*). Any contractual remuneration paid to an employee in respect of such a period of time off goes towards discharging the liability under s53 (see s53(6) and (7)).

The total liability to pay remuneration for an employee's time off is limited to 40 per cent of a week's pay for that employee (s53(5) ERA 1996).

An employee may bring a complaint to a tribunal that his or her employer has unreasonably refused to permit him or her to take the time off under s52, or has failed to pay the sums due under s53 (see s54).

Remedy: Where a tribunal finds a complaint well founded, it will make a declaration to that effect (s54(3)(a)) and will order the employer to pay the employee the amount which it finds due to him (s54(3)(b)).

For employees working fixed number of hours per week
Sum to which the employee is entitled = (gross weekly pay) x 1/(number of normal working hours in a week) x (number of hours absent) (s53(2) ERA 1996)

For employees with varying number of hours worked per week
Sum to which the employee is entitled = gross weekly pay x 12/(number of normal hours worked in the last 12 weeks ending with the last complete week before the day on which the time off is taken) x (number of hours absent) (s53(3) ERA 1996)

Gross or net: Gross. The definition of a week's pay as defined in ss220 to 229 ERA 1996 will apply (see *Week's pay*).

Limit on a week's pay: None. The calculation is based on actual gross weekly pay.

Limit on number of weeks: None

Any maximum or minimum: Yes, the maximum payable is 40% of an actual week's gross pay (s53(5) ERA 1996).

Tax: The tax treatment is not clear. To the extent that the sum awarded is compensation for lost earnings for work done, it is likely to be taxed under s62 ITEPA 2003 (see EIM02550). The sum may also be paid in connection with termination and be taxable under s401 (see *Tax*).

Statutory authorities: ERA 1996 ss52 to 54

Trade unions: see Union activities or collective bargaining (inducements); Union member, Right not to suffer deduction of unauthorised or excessive subscriptions; Union member, Right not to suffer deduction of contributions to political fund; Union member, Right to compensation if declared to be unjustifiably disciplined; Union membership (refusal of employment); Union (member expelled or excluded)

TUPE consultation

The employer of any employees affected by a TUPE transfer must inform and consult their appropriate representatives before the transfer to enable consultation with any affected employees. The information must include: the fact that the transfer is to take place, the date or proposed date of the transfer and the reasons for it; the legal, economic and social implications of the transfer for any affected employees; the measures which he envisages he will take in relation to any affected employees; and if the employer is the transferor, the measures, in connection with the transfer, which he envisages the transferee will take in relation to any affected employees who will become employees of the transferee after the transfer by virtue of regulation 4. Consultation must be with a view to seeking the agreement of the representatives to the intended measures (Reg 13 TUPE 2006).

Appropriate employee representatives will be the representatives of a recognised trade union, or if that situation does not exist, representatives appointed or elected with the authority to be informed and consulted (Regs 13(3) and 14). There is an exception for employers with fewer than 10 employees who if certain conditions are met may inform and consult the affected employees directly (Reg 13A (in force for transfers occurring on or after 31 July 2014)).

Generally speaking, it is the representatives who may bring a claim to a tribunal for failure to consult (Reg 15(1)). Once a tribunal has made an award, an employee who falls within the description of employees covered by the award may bring a complaint to a tribunal that the particular award to which he is entitled has not been paid to him (Reg 15(10)).

Remedy: Where the tribunal finds a complaint under s15(1) well founded it will make a declaration to that effect and can award such compensation as the tribunal considers just and equitable having regard to the seriousness of the failure of the employer to comply with the duty, of up to 13 weeks pay. The compensation will be ordered to be paid to "such descriptions of affected employees as may be specified", which will reflect the employees in respect of whom there has been a failure (Reg 15(7) and (8)).

The purpose of the award is to provide a sanction for breach of the obligation to inform and consult, the tribunal has a wide discretion but it will focus on the seriousness of the default, which may vary from the technical to a complete failure to comply with the duties, and it may consider the deliberateness of the failure. The proper approach where there has been no consultation is to start at the maximum and reduce it if there are mitigating circumstances justifying a reduction (see *Susie Radin Ltd v GMB & Ors* [2004] ICR 893). The tribunal should not start at the maximum and reduce for mitigating circumstances where there has been some information given and/or some consultation (see *Todd v Strain & Ors* [2011] IRLR 11 and *London Borough of Barnet v Unison & Ors* UKEAT/0191/13).

Where a tribunal finds a complaint by a particular employee under Reg 15(10) well founded, the tribunal will order the transferor or transferee (as applicable) the amount of compensation due to him or her (Reg 15(11)).

Gross or net: Gross. A week's pay as defined in ss220 to 229 ERA 1996 applies (see *Week's pay*).

Limit on a week's pay: None. The calculation is based on actual gross weekly pay (see *Zaman & Ors v Kozee Sleep Products Ltd t/a Dorlux Beds* UK UKEAT/0312/10/CEA).

Limit on number of weeks: 13

Adjustments: None

Mitigation: N/A

Tax: The tax treatment is unclear but it is likely that HMRC would regard any payment made

under TUPE to fall under s401 ITEPA 2003 (see *Tax*).

Recoupment: N/A

Statutory authorities: TUPE 2006 Regs 13 to 16

Relevant case law: *Cable Realisations Ltd v GMB Northern* [2010] IRLR 42; *London Borough of Barnet v Unison & Ors* UKEAT/0191/13; *Susie Radin Ltd v GMB & Ors* [2004] ICR 893; *Sweeting v Coral Racing* [2006] IRLR 252; *Todd v Strain & Ors* [2011] IRLR 11; *Zaman & Ors v Kozee Sleep Products Ltd t/a Dorlux Beds UK* UKEAT/0312/10/CEA

TUPE (failure to notify employee liability information)

The transferor is obliged to provide specified employee liability information to the transferee for any employees who will be transferred, at least 14 days before the relevant transfer (reg 11 TUPE 2006). For any transfer occurring on or after 1 May 2014, the information must be provided at least 28 days before the relevant transfer (Reg 10 CRATU(PE) Regs 2014).

A transferee may present a complaint to a tribunal that the transferor has failed to comply with any provisions of Reg 11 (Reg 12(1)).

Remedy: Where a tribunal finds a complaint well founded it must make a declaration to that effect and may make an award of compensation to be paid by the transferor to the transferee (Reg 12(3)). The amount of compensation will be that which the tribunal considers just and equitable in all the circumstances having particular regard to the losses sustained by the transferee as a result of the failure to provide information, and any relevant terms of any contract between the transferor and transferee dealing with payment for such a failure (Reg 12(4)).

There are two further provisions that may influence the amount of any award. By Reg 12(5) the amount of compensation must be a minimum of £500 per employee whose liability information has not been provided, subject to the discretion of the tribunal to award a lesser sum if in all the circumstances it considers it just and equitable. By Reg 12(6) the tribunal must apply the common law rules as to mitigation in assessing the loss suffered by the transferee.

Gross or net: Loss will likely be calculated net of any tax that may be payable.

Any maximum or minimum: minimum is £500 per employee whose liability information has notbeen provided, unless the tribunal considers it is just and equitable to award a lesser sum.

Adjustments: N/A

Mitigation: The transferee is under a duty to mitigate their loss.

Tax: The tax treatment is unclear.

Statutory authorities: TUPE 2006 ss11 and 12; Reg 10 CRATU(PE) Regs 2014

Unauthorised deductions: see Unlawful deductions

Unfair dismissal

(see also Additional award; Adjustments; Basic award; Compensatory award; Mitigation; Wrongful dismissal)

The right not to be unfairly dismissed is established by s94 ERA 1996. The definition of a dismissal is set out at s95, and includes dismissal with or without notice, the termination of a fixed term contract and dismissal where the employer or employee has committed a repudiatory breach of contract entitling the other to terminate the contract immediately (for example constructive dismissal and dismissal for gross misconduct). Whether a dismissal is fair or unfair will be determined by a tribunal applying the tests set out in s98, which include that the employer's reason for the dismissal must be one of a number of specified reasons (including misconduct and redundancy), and require the tribunal to assess whether the employer acted reasonably or unreasonably in treating its reason as a sufficient reason for dismissing the employee.

Where the reason, or if more than one reason the principle reason for the dismissal is one of a number of protected reasons, the dismissal will be automatically unfair. The protected reasons are:

- Being summoned to attend for jury service or being absent for attending jury service (s98B ERA 1996);

- Exercising rights to family leave (s99 ERA 1996);

- Exercising various health and safety functions (s100 ERA 1996);

- Refusing to work on a Sunday (if a specified shop or betting worker) (s101 ERA 1996);

- Taking various actions under the Working Time Regulations 1998 (s101A ERA 1996);

- Exercising various rights to participate in education or training (s101B ERA 1996);

- Performing various functions of the trustee of an occupational pension scheme (s102 ERA 1996);

- Performing various functions related to being an employee representative (s103 ERA 1996);

- Making a protected disclosure (s103A ERA 1996);

- Asserting one of a number of statutory rights (s104 ERA 1996);

- Reasons related to action taken under the National Minimum Wage Act 1998 (s104A ERA 1996);

- Reasons related to actions taken under the Tax Credits Act 2002 (s104B ERA 1996);

- Exercising various rights to flexible working (s104C ERA 1996);

- Reasons related to actions taken relating to pension enrolment (s104D ERA 1996);

- Exercising various rights to study and training (s104E ERA 1996);

- Reasons related to the existence of trade union blacklist (s104F ERA 1996);

- Refusing to accept an offer of employee shareholder status (s104G ERA 1996);

- Reasons relating to actions taken related to trade union recognition (para 161 Sch A1 TULR(C)A 1992);

- Reasons related to trade union membership or activities (s152 TULR(C)A 1992); and

- Redundancy, but the reason or principal reason for selection for redundancy was one of a long list of protected reasons (s105(3) to (7N), s153 TULR(C)A 1992 and paragraph 162 Sch 1A TULR(C)A 1992.

The right to not be dismissed unfairly generally accrues to an employee after the completion of 2 years service (see s108(1) ERA 1996). However, where the dismissal relates to a number of protected reasons, the period of continuous service required is either reduced or removed entirely (s108(2) to (4)). Most of the automatically unfair dismissal provisions can be relied upon by a dismissed employee who has not completed two years continuous service.

Where the reason for a dismissal is related to industrial action, specific provisions apply, see s237 to 239 TULR(C)A 1992.

An individual may bring a complaint to a tribunal that he or she has been unfairly dismissed (s111 ERA 1996).

An individual may also bring a complaint to a tribunal that he or she has been unfairly dismissed and seek an order for continuation of the contract of employment under the interim relief provisions (s128 to 132 ERA 1996 and s161 to 167 TULR(C)A 1992). This remedy is limited to allegations of unfair dismissal where the alleged reason or principal reason for the dismissal falls within the automatically unfair dismissal provisions relating to representative roles, the existence of a blacklist, trade union membership and activities and making a protected disclosure.

Remedy: Where a tribunal has found a dismissal to be unfair the remedies available are reinstatement, re-engagement and compensation (see *Reinstatement, Re-engagement, Compensation for Unfair dismissal*) (s112 to 126 ERA 1996).

The tribunal must explain to a successful claimant the three orders available to it (s112(2) ERA 1996). Though the primary remedies are reinstatement or re-engagement, it is most often the case that claimants seek only an award of compensation.

Where an order for reinstatement or re-engagement is not fully complied with, the tribunal will award compensation under s117(2) (s117(1) ERA 1996).

Where the tribunal is not asked to order reinstatement or re-engagement, or where a claimant has not been reinstated or re-engaged, the tribunal will make an award of compensation under s118 to 126 ERA 1996 (s117(3) and (4) and s112(4) ERA 1996).

The award of compensation under s118 to 126 ERA 1996 consists of a basic award and compensatory award (see *Basic award, Compensatory award*).

The basic award is calculated on the basis of (capped) weekly pay and the number of years

continuous service (the longer the service the higher the award).

The compensatory award compensates the individual for the financial losses suffered as a result of the dismissal. Except where the dismissal is for one of a limited number of protected reasons, the compensatory award is capped at the lesser of one year's pay and currently £76,574 (see *Statutory cap* and Table 1). Compensation for non-pecuniary losses, such as injury to feelings, is not available within a compensatory award (see *Dunnachie v Kingston upon Hull City Council* [2005] 1 AC 226).

Awards of compensation for unfair dismissal may be adjusted for failure to comply with a relevant code of practice (see *Adjustments*).

The specific interim remedy of a continuation order is available in limited circumstances where a claimant has sought interim relief under s128 to s132 ERA 1996 and s161 to 167 TULR(C)A 1992 (see *Interim relief*).

Union activities or collective bargaining (inducements)

A worker has the right not to have an offer made to him by his employer to induce the worker: not to be or seek to become a member of a trade union; not to take part in the activities of a trade union; not to make use of trade union services; or to be or become a member of any trade union (s145A of TULR(C)A 1992.

A worker who is a member of a trade union which is recognised, or seeking to be recognised, by his employer has the right not to have an offer made to him by his employer if: acceptance of the offer, together with other workers' acceptance of offers which the employer also makes to them, would have 'the prohibited result', and the employer's sole or main purpose in making the offers is to achieve that result. The 'prohibited result' is that the workers' terms will not or will not continue to be determined by collective bargaining (s145B of TULR(C)A 1992).

A worker or former worker may bring a complaint to a tribunal that the employer has made an offer in contravention of s145A or 145B (s145A(5) and s145B(5)).

Remedy: Where a tribunal finds such a complaint well founded, it will make a declaration to that effect and will make an award of £3,715 (s145E(1) to (3) TULR(C)A 1992).

Section 145E prescribes certain other consequences where an unlawful offer has been made, which exist without a claim having been brought to a tribunal. By s145E(4) any agreement to vary the terms of employment between the worker and employer will not be enforceable by the employer, however if merely as a result of the acceptance (e.g. because collectively agreed terms would have been different in those circumstances) nothing in s145A or 145B makes the variation unenforceable by either party.

Adjustments: s38 EA 2002 adjustment for failure to give statement of employment particulars applies. ACAS uplift applies (Schedule A2 TULRCA).

Mitigation: N/A

Tax: The tax treatment of this award is unclear.

Recoupment: N/A

Statutory authorities: TULR(C)A 1992 ss145A, B and E

Union member (deduction of unauthorised or excessive subscriptions)

Where arrangements exist between an employer and a trade union for the deduction of membership subscriptions from an employee, the employer must ensure that no subscription deductions are made for any worker if he or she has not authorised the deduction or has withdrawn authorization (see s68 TULR(C)A 1992).

A worker may bring a complaint to a tribunal that that his employer has made such a deduction (s68A(1) TULR(C)A 1992).

Remedy: : Where a tribunal finds that the complaint is well founded, it will make a declaration to that effect and will order the employer to pay to the worker the amount of the deduction owing to the employee (s68A(3)). s68A(4) makes provision to ensure there is no double recovery where the sum deducted might also be claimed under another jurisdiction, such as s13 ERA 1996 (unlawful deductions from wages).

Gross or net: The actual amount of any deductions owing should be paid.

Any maximum or minimum: None

Statutory authorities: TULR(C)A 1992 ss68 and 68A

Union member (deduction of contributions to political fund)

Trade unions may maintain political funds, and seek contributions to that fund from members. A member may object to contribute to the political fund. If a member of a trade union which has a political fund informs his employer in writing that he is exempt from the obligation to contribute to the fund, or he has notified the union in writing of his objection to contributing to the fund, the employer is obliged to ensure that no amount representing a contribution to the political fund is deducted by him from emoluments payable to that individual (see s84 and s86 TULR(C)A 1992).

A member may bring a claim to the tribunal alleging that his employer has made a deduction contrary to s86 (s87(1)) TULR(C)A 1992.

A member may bring a further complaint in circumstances where an order granted under the first complaint to prevent a repetition of the failure has not been complied with (s87(5) TULR(C)A 1992).

Remedy: Where a tribunal finds a complaint under s87(1) well founded, it will make a declaration to that effect and may order the employer to pay to the complainant the amount deducted less any part of that amount already paid to him by the employer (s87(4)(a) TULR(C)A) The tribunal may also order the employer to take steps to prevent a repetition of the failure (s87(4)(b)).

A complainant may bring a complaint alleging that his or her employer has not complied with the order under s87(4)(b) (s87(5)). If the tribunal finds that the employer has without reasonable excuse failed to comply with the order, it will order the employer to pay the complainant two weeks pay (s87(7)).

Gross or net: Deductions under s87(4)(a): the actual amount of the deducted owing must be paid. Non-compliance with s87(4)(b): gross weekly pay according to s220 to s229 ERA 1996 (s87(8) TULR(C)A 1992).

Limit on a week's pay: None

Limit on number of weeks: For a complaint under s87(7) the limit is 2 weeks pay.

Any maximum or minimum: None

Adjustments: None

Mitigation: N/A

Tax: The actual deductions should be repaid, and there should be no impact on tax calculations. It is unclear whether the 2 weeks pay will be subject to tax.

Recoupment: N/A

Statutory authorities: TULR(C)A 1992 ss84 to 87

Union member (unjustifiably disciplined)

An individual who is or has been a member of a trade union has the right not to be unjustifiably disciplined by the union (s64(1) TULR(C)A 1992. Section 64(2) identifies what actions of the union amount to 'discipline', whilst s65 identifies those reasons for the discipline which render the discipline 'unjustified'.

This right gives rise to two circumstances in which a claim may be brought to a tribunal. First, a member may bring a claim alleging that he or she has been unjustifiably disciplined (s66(1)). Second, where such a claim has been declared well founded it is envisaged the parties may reach agreement to deal with the issue between them, but the individual may bring a claim under s67(1) to enforce such an agreement or seek compensation.

Remedy: The primary remedy, following a complaint under s66(1), is a declaration from the tribunal that the individual has been unjustifiably disciplined (s66(3)).

Where the individual has succeeded under a s66(1) claim, it is envisaged the parties may reach agreement to deal with the issue between them, but the individual may bring a claim under s67(1) to enforce such an agreement or seek compensation.

The amount of compensation awarded will be

that which the employment tribunal considers just and equitable in all the circumstances (s67(3)). The tribunal will apply the common law principles of mitigation (s67(4)) and may reduce any award for contributory fault (s67(5)).

The total award will not exceed the aggregate of the maximum basic award (£13,920) and the maximum compensatory award (£76,574) i.e. £90,494 (TULR(C)A 1992 s67(7) and ERA 1996 s227(1)(a) and s124(1)).

The amount of compensation will not be less than £8,400 where on the date the s67(1) application was made the union has not revoked the decision to discipline the member or taken all necessary steps to secure the reversal of anything done to give effect to the disciplinary sanction (TULR(C)A 1992 s67(8A) and s176(6A)).

Gross or net: It is likely that this will be paid gross

Any maximum or minimum:
Minimum: The amount of compensation will not be less than £8,400 where on the date the s67(1) application was made the union has not revoked the decision to discipline the member or taken all necessary steps to secure the reversal of anything done to give effect to the disciplinary sanction (TULR(C)A 1992 s67(8A) and s176(6A)).

Maximum: The total award will not exceed the aggregate of the maximum basic award (£13,920) and the maximum compensatory award (£76,574) i.e. £90,494 (TULR(C)A 1992 s67(5) to (8)).

Adjustments: Yes, for contributory conduct.

Cap: A cap applies (see above).

Mitigation: Yes, the member is under a duty to mitigate any losses.

Tax: It is likely that this will be treated as a punishment or fine, and not taxed.

Recoupment: N/A

Statutory authorities: ERA 1996 s227(1)(a) and s124(1); TULR(C)A 1992 ss64 to 67

Union membership (blacklists, unfair dismissal/redundancy); see Basic award, minimum; Unfair dismissal

Union member (refusal of employment)

It is unlawful to refuse a person employment because he or she is or is not a member of a trade union, or because he or she is unwilling to accept a requirement that he or she take steps to cease to be or to remain or to become a member of a trade union, or a requirement to make payments or suffer deductions in the event of him or her not being a member of a trade union (s137 TULR(C)A 1992).

An equivalent right applies where an employment agency refuses such a person any of its services (s138 TULR(C)A 1992).

An individual may bring a complaint to a tribunal that this right has been infringed (s137(2) and s138(2) TULR(C)A 1992).

Remedy: Where a tribunal finds such a complaint well founded, it will make a declaration to that effect and may make an order of compensation (s140(1)(a) and/or a recommendation (s140(1)(b)).

Compensation will be assessed on the same basis as damages for breach of statutory duty (as are discrimination claims) and may include compensation for injury to feelings (s140(1)(a) and s140(2) TULR(C)A). The total compensation is limited to the maximum sum available under a compensatory award (s140(4)).

Any recommendation will require the respondent to take action to obviate or reduce the adverse effect on the complainant of the conduct that forms the basis of the complaint (s140(1)(b)).

Where the respondent fails without reasonable justification to comply with a recommendation, the tribunal may make an award of compensation, or increase it if it has already made an award (s140(3)).

Gross or net: The award of compensation will be made on the basis of net loss.

Limit on a week's pay: None

Limit on number of weeks: None

Any maximum or minimum: The maximum award is that of the statutory cap on unfair dismissal in force at the date of the breach under s124(1) ERA 1996, currently £76,574. There is no minimum.

Adjustments: None

Compensation cap: See maximum above.

Mitigation: The usual rules as to mitigation in discrimination claims will apply.

Tax: The tax treatment of this award is unclear.

Recoupment: N/A

Statutory authorities: ERA 1996 s124(1); TULR(C)A 1992 ss137 to 143

Union membership or activities (detriment); see Detriment

Union member (expelled or excluded)

An individual is protected from being excluded or expelled from a trade union unless the exclusion or expulsion is permitted by s174(2) TULR(C)A. The legitimate reasons for exclusion or expulsion include that the individual no longer satisfies enforceable membership criteria or has committed misconduct.

This right gives rise to two circumstances in which a claim may be brought to a tribunal. First, a member may bring a claim alleging that he or she has been excluded or expelled from a trade union (s174(5)). Second, where such a claim has been declared well founded it is envisaged the parties may reach agreement to deal with the issue between them, but the individual is may bring a claim under s176(2) to enforce such an agreement or seek compensation.

Remedy: The primary remedy, following a complaint under s174(5), is a declaration from the tribunal that the claim is well founded (s176(1)). The tribunal must also make a declaration, stating that effect, where the exclusion or expulsion was mainly attributable to a reason relating to the individual being a member of a political party (s176(1A)) and (if it applies) that the exclusion or expulsion was otherwise wholly or mainly attributable to conduct of the individual contrary to a rule of the union or an objective of the union (s176(1B)).

Where the individual has succeeded under a s176(1) claim, the individual may bring a claim under s176(2) to seek compensation. The amount of compensation awarded will be that which the employment tribunal considers just and equitable in all the circumstances (s176(4)). The tribunal may reduce any award for contributory fault (s176(5)).

The total award will not exceed the aggregate of 30 times the limit on a week's pay under s227(1)(a) ERA 1996 (£13,920) and the maximum compensatory award (£76,574) i.e. £90,494 (TULR(C)A 1992 s176(7) and ERA 1996 s227(1)(a) and s124(1)).

The amount of compensation will not be less than £8,400 where on the date the s176(1) application was made the union has not admitted or readmitted the member (TULR(C)A 1992 s67(8A) and s176(6A)), unless the tribunal also made declarations under s176(1A) and (1B) (see s176(6B)).

Gross or net: It is likely that this will be paid gross.

Any maximum or minimum:
Minimum: The amount of compensation will not be less than £8,669 where on the date the s67(1) application was made the union has not revoked the decision to discipline the member or taken all necessary steps to secure the reversal of anything done to give effect to the disciplinary sanction (s67(8A) TULR(C)A and s176(6A).

Maximum: The total award will not exceed the aggregate of the maximum basic award (£13,920) and the maximum compensatory award (£76,574) i.e. £90,494 (TULR(C)A 1992 s67(7) and ERA 1996 s227(1)(a) and s124(1)).

Adjustments: Yes, for contributory conduct.

Cap: A cap applies (see above).

Mitigation: The member is likely to be under a duty to mitigate any losses for which he or she seeks compensation

Tax: It is likely that this will be treated as a punishment or fine, and not taxed.

Recoupment: N/A

Statutory authorities: ERA 1996 ss113, 124(1) and 227(1); TULR(C)A 1992 ss174 to 176

Unlawful deductions from wages

(see also Holiday pay; National Minimum Wage)

A worker has the right not to suffer deductions from wages except under prescribed circumstances, which are as follows:

- Deductions required or authorised by statute (such as PAYE) or by a provision in the worker's contract (s13(1)(a));

- Deductions previously agreed to and signified in writing by the worker (s13(1)(b));

- Deductions for reimbursement of an overpayment of wages or expenses (s14(1));

- Payment to third parties for which the individual has given written consent (s14(4));

- Deductions on account of the worker's participation in industrial action (s14(5));

- Deductions made in respect of an attachment of earnings order made by a court, where the individual has given written consent (s14(6));

- Deductions made to a public authority as required under statute (s14(3)).

Wages is broadly interpreted, including salaries, fees, bonuses, commissions and holiday pay (both contractual and under the WTR 1998 (see *HMRC v Stringer* [2009] IRLR 677). Wages does not usually include pay in lieu of notice (see *Delaney v Staples* [1992] ICR 483). Also, where the sum claimed is dependent on the exercise of a discretion by the employer that has yet to be determined, such as a discretionary bonus, no identifiable sum exists and the claim must be brought as a breach of contract claim in the tribunal or the civil courts, rather than as an unlawful deduction claim (see *Adcock v Coors Brewers Ltd* [2007] IRLR 440).

Workers in the retail industry have special protection, whereby deductions to compensate for cash or stock shortages within a period may not exceed 10 per cent of the worker's gross wages in that period (see s17 to 22).

A worker may bring a claim to a tribunal that his employer has made unlawful deductions from his wages (s23(1) ERA 1996).

Remedy: Where a tribunal finds a complaint under s23 well founded, it will make a declaration to that effect and will order the employer to pay the worker the sum found to have been deducted unlawfully (s24(1)). The tribunal may also make such award as it considers appropriate in all the circumstances to compensate the worker for any financial loss sustained by him which is attributable to the unlawful deduction (s24(2))

Gross or net: The sums awarded ought to be calculated on a gross basis, since they will be taxable under s62 ITEPA 2003.

Adjustments: The ACAS uplift applies (Schedule A2 TULR(C)A).

Cap: There is no statutory cap on the sums that may be awarded by the tribunal.

Mitigation: The usual principles of mitigation will likely apply to any award under s24(2), but the award for repayment of deductions does not need to be mitigated.

Tax: Taxable under s62 ITEPA 2003

Recoupment: N/A

Statutory authorities: ERA 1996 ss13 to 26

Unreasonable refusal to be reinstated; see Additional award

Variable hours: see Holiday pay; Week's pay

Varying pay with output: see Holiday pay; Week's pay

Victimisation: see Discrimination

Week's pay

The concept of a week's pay is defined by ss220 to 229 and s234 ERA 1996. It is used for calculating a remedy in each of the following employment rights (see Table 5 for a list of claims, the relevant calculation date and whether a limit on a week's pay applies).

- Additional award (s117(1) ERA 1996);

- Basic award/Redundancy pay (ss119(2), 121 and 162(2) ERA 1996);

- Guarantee pay (s30(2) ERA 1996);

- Payments on the insolvency of an employer;

- Protective award (s190(2) TULR(C)A 1992);

- Remuneration whilst suspended on medical or maternity grounds (s69(1) ERA 1996);

- Right for union member not to be unjustifiably disciplined/expelled and blacklisting claims (ss67(8)(a) and 176(6)(a) TULR(C)A 1992);

- Failure to inform and consult union on training for workers (s70C(4) TULR(C)A 1992);

- Time off to look for work or arrange training after being made redundant (s54(4) ERA 1996);

- Time off for antenatal care (s56(2) ERA 1996);

- Absence during statutory notice period (ss88(1) to 89(1) ERA 1996);

- Time off for employee representatives (including ICE and OPPS) (s62(2) ERA 1996, Reg 28(2) ICE Regs 2004, Sch para 3(2) OPPS Regs 2006);

- Time off for study or training (s63J(3) ERA 1996);

- Time off for young person for study or training (s63B(2) ERA 1996);

- Time off for members of a European Works Council (Reg 26(2) TICE 1999);

- Failure to inform and consult under TUPE (Reg 16(3) TUPE Regs 2006);

- Right to be accompanied at a disciplinary or grievance meeting (s11(3) ERelA 1999);

- Infringement of right to be accompanied at flexible working meeting (Reg 15(3) FW(PRR) Regs 2002);

- Rejection of flexible working application (Reg 7) FW(ECR) Regs 2002;

- Written reasons for dismissal (s93(2) ERA 1996);

- Written statement of particulars (s38 EA 2002);

- Paid annual leave under the Working Time Regulations (Reg 16(1) WTR 1998).

In essence a week's pay is the gross contractual remuneration an employee is entitled to be paid when working their normal hours each week. Difficulties emerge in the calculation where an individual typically receives pay in addition to their contractual salary (such as voluntary overtime), or where they do not have normal working hours each week, such as when working irregular shift patterns.

Since pay will vary over the period of employment of an individual, for each remedy that uses the definition of a week's pay, a calculation date is specified (see Table 5). For a number of remedies a week's pay is capped, currently at £464 (see Table 5).

An employee's normal working hours will often

be identified in their written particulars (s221(1)). Failing this, it may be clear from the hours actually worked.

Matters are complicated where a contract specifies a minimum number of hours to be worked each week and also provides for an increased overtime wage to be paid beyond a certain number of hours. By s234, in that situation the normal working hours will be the minimum number of hours specified, even if overtime is paid for a smaller number of hours, and even if the minimum number of hours can be reduced in certain circumstances.

• Where overtime is obligatory for the employee, but is not guaranteed by the employer, the normal working hours will not include those additional hours - they will only amount to normal working hours if the obligation to work and provide work for that period is mutual (see *Tarmac Roadstone Holdings Ltd v Peacock* [1973] ICR 273). Further, where employees are paid on the basis of a pre-estimate of the number of hours a task will take, though the time taken may vary, the pre-estimate will not amount to normal working hours (see *Sanderson v Exel Management Services Ltd* [2006] ICR 1337).

• Remuneration where an employee has normal working hours is calculated as the contractual payments made to the employee for the work they have done.

• Contractual bonuses are usually included, such as a regular shift bonus (see *Mole Mining Ltd v Jenkins* [1972] ICR 282). It may be possible to infer a contractual term that a regular bonus, such as a site bonus in the construction industry, will be paid unless certain conditions are met, such that it falls within remuneration (see *Donelan v Kerrby Constructions* [1983] ICR 237);

• Discretionary bonuses will not form part of the remuneration, unless deemed a contractual payment (see *Canadian Imperial Bank of Commerce v Beck* EAT/0141/10/RN and *Hoyland v Asda Stores Ltd* [2006] IRLR 468);

• Tips paid by the employer (but not by customers to the employee in cash) will count as remuneration (see *Palmanor Ltd v Cedron* [1978] ICR 1008 and *Nerva v RL&G Ltd* [1997] ICR 11). However, it may be that non-cash tips distributed through a tronc system set up by the employer do not count as remuneration, as they do not count towards the minimum

wage (see *Revenue and Customs Commissioners v Annabel's (Berkeley Square) Ltd* [2009] ICR 1123);

• Commission which is a regular part of an employee's earnings will amount to remuneration, and can be apportioned as the tribunal deems appropriate (see *Weevsmay Ltd v Kings* [1977] ICR 244 and *J and S Bickley Ltd v Washer* [1977] ICR 425);

• Benefits in kind, such as free lodging, will not count as remuneration.

• Where an individual has been paid less than the minimum wage, the calculation of a week's pay should be based on the pay the individual ought to have received, but at the rate applicable at the date of the hearing (see *Paggetti v Cobb* [2002] IRLR 861).

Where an employee has normal working hours
There are three alternative routes to calculating a week's pay:

• **'time workers'**, where the remuneration does not vary with the amount of work done, which includes work where commission is awarded for success achieved, as opposed to being awarded for the work actually done (see *Evans v Malley Organisation Ltd t/a First Business Support* [2003] ICR 432). A week's pay is the amount payable by the employer to the employee under the contract in force at the calculation date if the individual works the normal working hours in a week (s221(2));

• **'piece workers'**, where the remuneration varies according to the amount of work done during normal working hours but does not vary according to the times or days when the work is done. A week's pay is the average hourly rate for the normal working hours calculated over the previous 12 weeks (s221(3)). For these purposes remuneration will include commission which is awarded for success achieved, as opposed to being awarded for the work actually done (see *Evans v Malley Organisation Ltd t/a First Business Support* [2003] ICR 432

• **'shift workers'**, where normal working hours are worked at times of the day or days of the week that vary from week to week and where remuneration also varies from week to week. A week's pay is calculated over a period of 12 weeks by reference to the average hourly rate multiplied by the average number of normal weekly hours (s222).

Where an employee has no normal working hours

A week's pay is calculated by reference to average weekly remuneration over a 12 week period (s224). In this situation any overtime payments received will count towards remuneration, whether or not there is a mutual obligation to work and provide overtime (see above re normal working hours).

The 12 week period is based on complete weeks worked (s221(3) and (4) and s235(1)). Any week in which the individual was not working or was not paid remuneration will not count, and an earlier week will be brought in to make up the 12 weeks (s223(2) and s224(3)).

Is the calculation of a week's pay in compliance with EU law?

The concept of a week's pay is used in the working time regulations to calculate holiday pay entitlement. However, the particular means to calculate a week's pay frequently leads to individuals receiving less holiday pay than they would have received had they not taken the holiday, for example where regular overtime is required but there is no obligation on the employer to offer it. There are currently a number of cases progressing through tribunals in which it is being argued that this calculation fails fully to import the right to paid holiday from the Working Time Directive, relying on *BA v Williams* [2011] IRLR 948. If tribunals (and the appeal courts) can be persuaded that the provisions of s220 to 229 and s234 ERA can be read to comply with the directive, the routes to calculation described above may well be altered.

The following examples demonstrate the calculation of a week's pay.

Normal working hours

Straightforward number of hours and constant pay per hour/week/month

1. Weekly pay for hourly paid employees

Weekly pay for hourly paid employees = number of normal hours worked per week x (hourly rate + hourly commission/bonus if they are constant).

If the commission is not constant, this calculation does not apply (see below). If the period of commission does not coincide with the period of payment, the weekly pay should be calculated in a manner which is just, over the whole period (s229(2)).

2. Weekly pay for monthly, annual or other period paid employees

The tribunal must apportion the payment in the manner that is considers just (ERA 1996 s229(2)).

One way in which this could be done is as follows:

> Weekly pay = Monthly salary ÷ 4.3 (or alternatively, monthly salary x 12 ÷ 365 x 7 which produces a slightly different answer because of rounding errors)
>
> Weekly pay = Annual salary ÷ 52
>
> Weekly pay = Other period salary ÷ number of days in which it was earned x 7

3. Weekly pay with differing commission

Weekly pay with differing commission = Number of hours worked in a week x hourly rate + (total commission earned ÷ number of weeks in which *it was earned*)

Straightforward but pay and/or commission/bonus varying with output (piece workers)

Weekly pay = Average hourly rate x hours in a normal working week = (Total remuneration, including overtime, in the previous 12 week period ÷ total hours worked in the 12 week period) x hours in a normal working week

However, note that overtime hours are rated as basic hours - overtime premiums are ignored.

Variable hours (shift workers)

Weekly pay = Average hourly rate x average hours in a normal working week = (Total remuneration in previous 12 weeks ÷ Total hours worked in previous 12 weeks, including overtime hours if they form part of the normal working hours) x (number of hours worked in the 12 week period ÷12)

Note: the 12 weeks needs to be taken prior to the pay date or the calculation date, whichever is the earlier

Also, if in any week no remuneration or guaranteed pay was paid, those weeks are ignored and an earlier week is used in the calculation.

No normal working hours (casual workers)

Weekly pay = Total remuneration, including overtime and overtime rates, in 12 weeks immediately before calculation date (or the pay day immediately before the calculation date if calculation date is not the same as the pay date) ÷ 12

Statutory authorities: Chapter II ERA 1996

Relevant case law: *BA v Williams* [2011] IRLR 948; *Canadian Imperial Bank of Commerce v Beck* EAT

0141/10; *Donelan v Kerrby Constructions* [1983] ICR 237; *Evans v Malley Organisation Ltd t/a First Business Support* [2003] ICR 432; *Fox v C Wright (Farmers) Ltd* [1978] ICR 98; *Hoyland v Asda Stores Ltd* [2006] IRLR 468; *J and S Bickley Ltd v Washer* [1977] ICR 425; *Mole Mining Ltd v Jenkins* [1972] ICR 282; *Nerva v RL&G Ltd* [1997] ICR 11; *Paggetti v Cobb* [2002] IRLR 861; *Palmanor Ltd v Cedron* [1978] ICR 1008; *Revenue and Customs Commissioners v Annabel's (Berkeley Square) Ltd* [2009] ICR 1123; *Sanderson v Exel Management Services Ltd* [2006] ICR 1337; *Tarmac Roadstone Holdings Ltd v Peacock* [1973] ICR 273; *Toni & Guys (St Pauls) Ltd v Georgiou* UKEAT/0085/13/DM; *Weevsmay Ltd v Kings* [1977] ICR 244

Working Time Regulations

An adult worker is entitled to various periods of rest as detailed in the WTR 1998. A breach of these regulations could entitle the worker to bring a claim at the ET.

By Reg 30(1)(a) a worker may bring a claim to the tribunal that his employer has denied him the following rights:

- Sufficient daily rest under Reg 10(1) or (2);

- Sufficient weekly rest under Reg 11(1), (2) or (3);

- Sufficient rest breaks within a working day under Reg 12(1) or (4);

- Sufficient annual leave under Reg 13;

- Entitlement to additional annual leave under Reg 13A;

- Compensatory rest under Reg 24;

- Adequate rest (if a mobile worker) under Reg 24A;

- Compensatory rest (if a young worker in the armed forces) under Reg 25(3);

- Compensatory rest (during night work if a young worker) under Reg 27A(4)(b); or

- Compensatory rest (if a young worker and certain exceptional circumstances apply) under Reg 27(3).

By Reg 30(1)(b) a worker may bring a bring a claim to the tribunal that his employer has failed to pay him the whole or any part of his or her

entitlement to paid leave or payment in lieu of leave untaken at termination (Reg 30(1)(b)). Such a claim may also be brought as a deduction from wages claim under s13 ERA 1996 (see *Stringer v HM Revenue and Customs* [2009] IRLR 677).

Remedy: Where a tribunal finds a complaint under Reg 30(1)(a) well founded, it will make a declaration to that effect and may make an award compensation.

Compensation will be determined as that which the tribunal considers to be just and equitable in all the circumstances having regard to the employer's default in refusing to permit the worker to exercise his right and any loss sustained by the worker as a result.

Where a tribunal finds a complaint under Reg 30(1)(b) that certain pay for leave entitlement has not been paid, it will order the employer to pay the worker the sums owing (Reg 30(5)).

Gross or net: N/A for regs 10, 11, 12, 13, 24 or 24A; Gross for regs 14 and 16

Tax: The tax treatments is unclear for payments under regs 10, 11, 12, 13, 24 or 24A. However, tax should be paid under s62 ITEPA 2003 for payments under regs 14 and 16.

Written reasons for dismissal

An employee is entitled a written statement of reasons for dismissal from his or her employer where the dismissal arises from either: the employer giving notice, the employer terminating without notice, or if a limited term contract terminates by virtue of its limiting event (s92(1) ERA 1996). Generally, the employee must have made a request for the written reasons and must have been continuously employed for two years (s92(2) and (3)). The exception is where when someone is dismissed she is pregnant or on maternity leave until dismissed (s92(4)), or he or she is on adoption leave until dismissed (s92(4A)).

An employee may make a complaint to a tribunal that his or her employer has unreasonably failed to provide the statement or that the particulars of the statement given are inadequate or untrue (s93(1)).

Remedy: Where a tribunal finds such a complaint well founded, it may make a declaration as to what it finds the employer's reasons were for dismissing the employee and will make an award of two weeks pay.

Gross or net: Gross. A week's pay as defined in ss220 to 229 ERA 1996 applies (see *Week's pay*).

Limit on a week's pay: None

Limit on number of weeks: 2

Any maximum or minimum: The award is simply two weeks pay.

Adjustments: None

Cap: The award will form part of the compensatory award and the cap will apply in non-discriminatory unfair dismissal cases.

Mitigation: N/A

Tax: Any payment made in connection with the termination of employment will be taxed under s401 ITEPA 2003, of which this award will form a part.

Recoupment: The award should not form part of the prescribed element.

Statutory authorities: ERA 1996 ss92 and 93

Written statement of particulars

Employees have the right to be given written particulars of their terms of employment within 2 months of starting their employment (ss1 to 7B ERA 1996) and itemised pay statements (s8 and s9 ERA 1996).

An employee may bring a claim to a tribunal alleging that his or her employer has not complied with these obligations (s11(1)), and either party may bring a reference to a tribunal to determine what particulars ought to have been supplied (s11(2)).

Remedy (1): The tribunal has the power to determine the particulars of employment between the parties (s12(1) and (2)). Where an itemised pay statement has not been provided, or where deductions have been made which were not itemised on such a statement, the tribunal will make a declaration to that effect and may order the employer to pay the employee the value of the deductions (s12(3) and (4)).

Remedy (2): There is an additional right to a remedy from a tribunal where a claim has been brought within the list of jurisdictions in Sch 5 to EA 2002 (the list is extensive and includes many of the common, and not so common, claims).

Where under such a claim the tribunal finds for the employee, whether or not it makes an award in respect of that claim, and where when the proceedings were brought the employer was in breach of the duty to give written particulars, the tribunal will make an award of two weeks pay unless it would be unjust and inequitable to do so, and may if it considers it just and equitable in all the circumstances make an award of four weeks pay (see s38(1) to (5) ERA 1996).

Gross or net: Gross. A week's pay as defined in ss220 to 229 ERA 1996 applies (see *Week's pay*).

Limit on a week's pay: The current weekly limit is £464 (see Table 1 for historical rates).

Limit on number of weeks: Minimum is 2; Maximum is 4 (s38(4) EA 2002).

Any maximum or minimum: Minimum is two weeks pay, capped; Maximum is four weeks pay, capped.

Adjustments: Contributory conduct applies. See *Adjustments and order of adjustments* for information about the order in which they apply when this head of loss is being claimed.

Cap: The award or increase of any award will fall within any applicable statutory cap for that award.

Mitigation: The usual rules of mitigation apply to the compensatory award.

Tax: The tax rules applicable to the particular award that has been made or increased, will apply.

Recoupment: The award should not be included in the prescribed element.

Statutory authorities: EA 2002 s38, ERA 1996 ss1 to 12 and ss220 to 229

Wrongful dismissal: see Damages for wrongful dismissal

Tables

Caps and limits

Table 1: Statutory cap, maximum basic award and the limit on gross weekly pay

Date	Maximum Compensatory Award	Maximum Basic Award	Maximum Total	Gross Weekly Pay Limit
01/10/2009 to 31/01/2010	£66,200	£11,400	£77,600	£380
01/02/2010 to 31/01/2011	£65,300	£11,400	£76,700	£380
01/02/2011 to 31/01/2012	£68,400	£12,000	£80,400	£400
01/02/2012 to 31/01/2013	£72,300	£12,900	£85,200	£430
01/02/2013 to 28/07/2013	£74,200	£13,500	£87,700	£450
29/07/2013 to 05/04/2014	£74,200 or gross annual pay, whichever is the smaller	£13,500	£87,700	£450
06/04/2014 to 05/04/2015	£76,574 or gross annual pay, whichever is the smaller	£13,920	£90,494	£464

Notes
1. The cap on gross weekly pay is only applicable to claims of Statutory redundancy pay, Basic award; Right to written particulars of employment; Right to be accompanied at a disciplinary hearing; Right to request flexible working; Insolvency provisions; Additional award
2. The Employment Rights (Increase of Limits) Order 2014 increased the limits to take effect from 06/04/2014. Limits will be increased in line with inflation every 6th April (as opposed to 1st February).

Table 2: Limits on awards (other) (see Employment Rights (Increase of Limits) Orders)

		01/02/2011 to 31/01/2012	01/02/2012 to 31/01/2013	01/02/2013 to 05/04/2014	06/04/2014 to 05/04/2015
s145E(3) TULR(C)A 1992	Amount of award for unlawful inducement relating to trade union membership or activities, or for unlawful inducement relating to collective bargaining.	£3,300	£3,500	£3,600	£3,715
s156(1) TULR(C)A 1992	Minimum amount of basic award of compensation where dismissal is unfair by virtue of section 152(1) or 153 of the 1992 Act.	£5,000	£5,300	£5,500	£5,676
s176(6A) TULR(C)A 1992	Minimum amount of compensation where individual excluded or expelled from union in contravention of section 174 of the 1992 Act and not admitted or re-admitted by date of tribunal application.	£7,600	£8,100	£8,400	£8,669
s31(1) ERA 1996	Limit on amount of guarantee payment payable to an employee in respect of any day.	£22.20	£23.50	£24.20	£25.00
s120(1) ERA 1996	Minimum amount of basic award of compensation where dismissal is unfair by virtue of section 100(1)(a) and (b), 101A(d), 102(1) or 103 of the 1996 Act.	£5,000	£5,300	£5,500	£5,676

Table 3: Guarantee Payments

Date	Daily limit	Maximum amount in any 3 month period (5 days)
Up to 01/02/2011	£21.20	£106.00
01/02/2011 to 31/01/2012	£22.20	£111.00
01/02/2012 to 31/01/2013	£23.50	£117.50
01/02/2013 to 05/04/2014	£24.20	£121.00
06/04/2014 to 05/04/2015	£25.00	£125.00

Table 4: Time limits for appeals

Review of ET decision	14 days
Appeal to EAT from ET	42 days
Review of EAT decision	14 days
Appeal to Court of Appeal from EAT	14 days

Table 5: Gross weekly pay: claims for which gross weekly pay is used in the calculation and the related calculation dates

Claim	Calculation date	Limit on a week's pay
Additional award	Date on which employee is given notice or the EDT	£464
Basic award	If the employee is summarily dismissed or dismissed with less than the statutory notice, the calculation date is the date on which the employment ended. If the employee was dismissed with notice equal to or more than the statutory notice, the calculation date is found by subtracting the statutory notice period from the actual notice given. This means that if statutory notice is given, the calculation date is the date that notice was given. If statutory notice is 3 weeks and actual notice given is 4 weeks, the calculation date is the day after the end of the first week of notice.	£464
Guarantee pay	The day when the guarantee pay is due	See separate limits
Insolvency	For arrears of pay and holiday, the date on which the employer became insolvent. For the Basic award the latest of (i) the date on which the employer became insolvent, (ii) the date of the termination of the employee's employment, and (iii) the date on which the award was made. In relation to any other debt whichever is the later of (i) the date on which the employer became insolvent, and (ii) the date of the termination of the employee's employment.	£464
Protective award	The date on which the protective award was made or, in the case of an employee who was dismissed before the date on which the protective award was made, the calculation date for the purpose of computing the amount of a redundancy payment	Unlimited
Remuneration whilst suspended on medical grounds	The day before suspension began	Unlimited
Right for union member not to be unjustifiably disciplined/expelled and blacklisting claims	N/A	£464 for the Basic award element

Table 5: Gross weekly pay: claims for which gross weekly pay is used in the calculation and the related calculation dates

Claim	Calculation date	Limit on a week's pay
Time off to look for work or arrange training after being made redundant	The day on which the employer's notice was given	Actual gross weekly pay is used but limited to 40% of a week's pay
Time off for antenatal care	The day of ante-natal appointment.	Unlimited
Time off for employee representatives (including ICE and OPPS); pension trustees; union duties, activities and union learning reps; study or training; young person for study or training; members of a European Works Council	Date on which time off was taken or should have been permitted	No limit apart from for Study or training (not Young person study or training) where the limit is £450
TUPE claims	In the case of an employee who is dismissed by reason of redundancy the date which is the calculation date for the purposes of any entitlement of his to a redundancy payment. In the case of an employee who is dismissed for any other reason, the effective date of termination. In any other case, the date of the relevant transfer.	Unlimited
Right to be accompanied at a disciplinary or grievance meeting	Date of dismissal/EDT or if no dismissal the date of the hearing	£464
Right to request flexible working	Date on which the application was made	£464
Written reasons for dismissal	Date notice was given or if no notice the EDT	Unlimited
Written statement of particulars	If the employee was employed by the employer on the date the proceedings were begun, that date. If he was not, the effective date of termination	£464
Paid annual leave under the Working Time Regulations	Payment based on a normal week's pay on the first day of the period of leave in question	Unlimited
Redundancy payments	Depends on the circumstances	£464

Fees

(see Employment Tribunals and the Employment Appeal Tribunal Fees Order 2013 SI 2013/1893)

Table 6: Fees for individual claimants

Fee type	Type A claim	Type B claim
Issue fee	£160	£250
Hearing fee	£230	£950

Table 7: Fees for multiple claimants - Type A claims

	Number of claimants/ amount of fee		
Type of fee	2 to 10	11 to 200	Over 200
Issue fee	£320	£640	£960
Hearing fee	£460	£920	£1380

Table 8: Fees for multiple claimants - Type B claims

	Number of claimants/fee amount		
Type of fee	2 to 10	11 to 200	Over 200
Issue fee	£500	£1,000	£1,500
Hearing fee	£1,900	£3,800	£5,700

Table 9: Specific Fees

Type of application	Type A Claim	Type B Claim	EAT fees
Reconsideration of a default judgment	£100	£100	N/A
Reconsideration of a judgment following a final hearing	£100	£350	N/A
Dismissal following withdrawal	£60	£60	N/A
An employer's contract claim made by way of application as part of the response to the employee's contract claim	£160	N/A	N/A
Appeal Fee	N/A	N/A	£400
Hearing Fee	N/A	N/A	£1,200
Fee for Judicial Mediation (payable by the respondent)	N/A	£600	N/A

Table 10: Remission 1 Disposable capital test (under 61 years old)

Court or tribunal fee	Disposable capital threshold
Up to £1,000	£3,000
£1,001 - £1,335	£4,000
£1,336 - £1,665	£5,000
£1,666 - £2,000	£6,000
£2,001 - £2,330	£7,000
£2,331 - £4,000	£8,000
£4,001 - £5,000	£10,000

Table 10: Remission 1 Disposable capital test (under 61 years old)

Court or tribunal fee	Disposable capital threshold
£5,001 - £6,000	£12,000
£6,001 - £7,000	£14,000
£7001 or more	£16,000

For applicants 61 years old or older there is a single disposable capital threshold of £16,000 whatever the Tribunal fee.

Table 11: Remission 2 - Gross monthly income thresholds – full remissions

Gross monthly income with:	Single	Couple
No children	£1,085	£1,245
One Child	£1,330	£1,490
Two Children	£1,575	£1,735

£245 for each additional child

For every £10 of income over the threshold set out in the table above, parties will be required to pay £5 towards the court or tribunal fee up until the thresholds below, in which case no remission will be given.

Table 12: Remission 2 - Gross monthly income cap thresholds – partial remissions

Gross monthly income with:	Single	Couple
No children	£5,085	£5,245
One Child	£5,330	£5,490
Two Children	£5,575	£5,735

£245 for each additional child

Table 13: Type A Claims (Type B claims are any claims not listed in this table) (Schedule 2, Table 2 Employment Tribunals and the Employment Appeal Tribunal Fees Order 2013)

Description of claim	Provision identifying the rights of the claimant	Provision conferring jurisdiction on tribunal
Application by the Secretary of State to prohibit a person from running an Employment Agency	Sections 3A EAA	Sections 3A EAA
Application by a person subject to a prohibition order to vary or set it aside	Section 3C EAA	Section 3C EAA
Appeal against improvement or prohibition notice	Section 24 HSWA	Section 24 HSWA
Appeal against assessment of training levy	Section 12 ITA	Section 12 ITA
Complaint of deduction of unauthorised subscriptions	Section 68 TULR(C)A	Section 68A TULR(C)A
Complaint relating to failure to deduct or refuse to deduct an amount to a political fund	Section 86 TULR(C)A	Section 87 TULR(C)A
Complaint that an employer has failed to permit time off for carrying out trade union duties	Section 168 TULR(C)A	Section 168 TULR(C)A
Complaint that an employer has failed to permit time off for union learning representatives	Section 168A TULR(C)A	Section 168A TULR(C)A
Complaint that an employer has failed to pay for time off for union learning representatives	Section 169 TULR(C)A	Section 169 TULR(C)A

Table 13: Type A Claims (Type B claims are any claims not listed in this table) (Schedule 2, Table 2 Employment Tribunals and the Employment Appeal Tribunal Fees Order 2013)

Description of claim	Provision identifying the rights of the claimant	Provision conferring jurisdiction on tribunal
Complaint that an employer has failed to permit time off for trade union activities	Section 170 TULR(C)A	Section 170 TULR(C)A
Complaint that employer has failed, wholly or in part, to pay remuneration under a protective award	Section 190 TULR(C)A	Section 192 TULR(C)A
Complaint that the Secretary of State has not paid, or has paid less than, the amount of relevant contributions which should have been paid into a pension scheme	Section 124 PSA	Section 126 PSA
Breach of contract, except where the employer's contract claim is made by way of application as part of the employer's response to the employee's contract claim (as to which, see instead article 4 and Schedule 1 to this Order)		Section 3 ETA; Articles 3 and 4 of each of the EJOs
Reference to determine what particulars ought to be included in a statement of employment particulars or changes to particulars	Sections 1 and 4 ERA	Section 11 ERA
Reference to determine what particulars ought to be included in an itemised pay statement	Section 8 ERA	Section 11 ERA
Complaint of unauthorised deductions from wages	Section 13 ERA	Section 23 ERA
Complaint that employer has received unauthorised payments	Section 15 ERA	Section 23 ERA
Complaint that employer has failed to pay guaranteed payment	Section 28 ERA	Section 34 ERA
Complaint that employer has failed to permit time off for public duties	Section 50 ERA	Section 51 ERA
Complaint that employer has refused to permit, or has failed to pay for, time off to look for work or arrange training	Sections 52 and 53 ERA	Section 54 ERA
Complaint that employer has refused to allow, or has failed to pay for, time off for ante-natal care	Sections 55, 56, 57ZA and 57ZB ERA	Sections 57 and 57ZC ERA
Complaint that employer has refused to allow time off for dependants	Section 57A ERA	Section 57B ERA
Complaint that employer has failed to allow, or to pay for, time off for trustee of pension scheme	Sections 58 and 59 ERA	Section 60 ERA
Complaint that employer has failed to allow, or to pay for, time off for employee representative	Sections 61 and 62 ERA	Section 63 ERA
Complaint that employer has failed to allow, or to pay for, time off for young people in Wales and Scotland	Section 63A and 63B ERA	Section 63C ERA
Complaint that employer has failed to pay for time off on medical or maternity grounds	Sections 64, 68 and 68C ERA	Sections 70 and 70A ERA
Complaint that employer has failed to deal with an application in relation to study or training in accordance with regulations or refused the application on the basis of incorrect facts	Sections 63D to 63H ERA	Section 63I ERA

Table 13: Type A Claims (Type B claims are any claims not listed in this table) (Schedule 2, Table 2 Employment Tribunals and the Employment Appeal Tribunal Fees Order 2013)		
Description of claim	Provision identifying the rights of the claimant	Provision conferring jurisdiction on tribunal
Complaint that employer has unreasonably failed to provide a written statement of reasons for dismissal or the particulars are inadequate or untrue	Section 92 ERA	Section 93 ERA
Reference in respect of a right to redundancy payment	Section 135 ERA	Sections 163 and 177 ERA
Reference related to payment out of National Insurance Fund	Section 166 ERA	Section 170 ERA
References related to payments equivalent to redundancy payments	Sections 167, 168 and 177 ERA	Section 177 ERA
Complaint that the Secretary of State has failed to make any, or insufficient, payment of out the National Insurance Fund	Section 182 ERA	Section 188 ERA
Appeal against a notice of underpayment	Section 19C NMWA	Section 19C NMWA
Appeal against a notice issued by the Commission for Equality and Human Rights where the notice relates to an unlawful act	Section 21 EA 2006	Section 21 EA 2006
Complaint that prospective employer made enquiries about disability or health	Section 60 EA 2010	Section 120 EA 2010
Application in relation to the effect of a non-discrimination rule in an occupational pension scheme	Section 61 EA 2010	Section 120 EA 2010
Complaint in relation to a breach of a maternity equality clause	Section 73 EA 2010	Section 127 EA 2010
Complaint in relation to a breach of, or application in relation to the effect of, a maternity equality rule in an occupational pension scheme	Section 75 EA 2010	Section 127 EA 2010
Complaint in relation to terms prohibiting discussions about pay	Section 77 EA 2010	Section 120 EA 2010
Complaint that a term in a collective agreement is void or unenforceable	Section 145 EA 2010	Section 146 EA 2010
Appeal of decision of compensating authority	Regulation 42 CEC	Regulation 42 CEC
Complaint that employer has failed to pay for remunerated time off for safety representative	Regulation 4(2) of, and Schedule 2 to, the SRSC	Regulation 11 SRSC
Reference that there has been a failure to consult with employee representatives about contracting out of pension scheme	Regulation 4 OPS(CO)R and regulation 9 of OPS(DI)R	Regulation 4 OPS(CO)R and regulation 9 of OPS(DI)R
Complaint that employer has failed to pay for time off to carry out Safety Representative duties or undertake training	Regulation 7 of, and Schedule 1 to, the HSCE	Schedule 2 to the HSCE
Complaint that employer has refused to allow annual leave or make payment in respect of annual leave	Regulations 13, 13A,14 and 16 WTR	Regulation 30 WTR
Appeal against improvement or prohibition notice	Paragraph 6 of Schedule 3 to WTR	Paragraph 6 of Schedule 3 to WTR
Appeal against improvement or prohibition notice	Regulation 18 COMAH	Regulation 18 COMAH
Complaint in relation to refusal of annual leave or to make payment	Regulation 11 MSR	Regulation 18 MSR
Complaint in relation to refusal to provide paid annual leave	Regulation 4 CAR	Regulation 18 CAR

Table 13: Type A Claims (Type B claims are any claims not listed in this table) (Schedule 2, Table 2 Employment Tribunals and the Employment Appeal Tribunal Fees Order 2013)

Description of claim	Provision identifying the rights of the claimant	Provision conferring jurisdiction on tribunal
Complaint in relation to failure to provide free health assessments	Regulation 5 CAR	Regulation 18 CAR
Complaint in relation to refusal of annual leave or to make payment	Regulation 11 FVR	Regulation 19 FVR
Complaint that employer has refused to allow or failed to pay for time off for information and consultation or negotiating representatives	Regulations 27 and 28 ICR	Regulation 29 ICR
Appeal against improvement notice	Paragraph 6(2) of Schedule 2 to the RTR	Paragraph 6(2) of Schedule 2 to the RTR
Complaint in relation to failure to pay compensation in pursuance of tribunal order	Regulation 15(7) and 15(8) TUPE	Regulation 15(10) TUPE
Complaint that employer has failed to allow, or pay for, time off for functions as employee representative	Paragraphs 2 and 3 of the Schedule to OPR	Paragraph 4 of the Schedule to OPR
Complaint that employer has failed to allow, or pay for, time off for members of special negotiating body	Regulations 28 and 29 ECSR	Regulation 30 ECSR
Complaint that employer has failed to allow, or pay for, time off for members of special negotiating body	Regulations 43 and 44 CCBR	Regulation 45 CCBR
Appeal against notice from Health and Safety Executive or a local authority	Regulation 21 and Part 2 of Schedule 8 to REACHER	Regulation 21 and Part 2 of Schedule 8 to REACHER
Reference to determine what particulars ought to be included in an itemised statement of stipend	Regulation 6 EOR	Regulation 9 EOR
Reference to determine what particulars ought to be included in a statement of particulars or changes to particulars	Regulations 3 and 6 EOR	Regulation 9 EOR
Complaint that employer has failed to allow, or pay for, time off for members of special negotiating body	Regulations 26 and 27 ELLR	Regulation 28 ELLR

Holiday

Table 14: Holiday Pay crib sheet (Holidays and holiday pay leaflet – ACAS)

Working Pattern	Before 1 April 2009	After 1 April 2009
Full-time (5 day week)	4.8 weeks (24 days)	5.6 weeks (28 days)
Part-time (4 day week)	4.8 weeks (19.2 days)	5.6 weeks (22.4 days)
Part-time (3 day week)	4.8 weeks (14.4 days)	5.6 weeks (16.8 days)
6 day week	4.8 weeks (28 days – the maximum statutory entitlement)	5.6 weeks (28 days – the maximum statutory entitlement)
Compressed hours e.g. 36 hours in 4 days	36 hours x 4.8 weeks = 172.8 hours per year	36 hours x 5.6 weeks = 201.6 hours per year
Annualised hours e.g. 1,600 hours at an average of 33.5 hours week	33.5 hours x 4.8 weeks = 160.8 hours per year	33.5 hours x 5.6 weeks = 187.6 hours per year
Bank Holidays	Can be included in the 4.8 weeks leave – check the contract	Can be included in the 5.6 weeks leave – check the contract

Income Tax and National Insurance

Table 15: Income Tax Rates and Taxable Bands

Rate	2012-2013	2013-2014	2014-2015
Starting rate for savings: 10%*	£0 - £2,710	£0 - £2,790	£0 - £2,880
Basic rate: 20%	£0 - £34,370	£0 - £32,010	£0 - £31,865
Higher rate: 40%	£34,371 - £150,000	£32,011 - £150,000	£31,866 - £150,000
Additional rate: 50%	Over £150,000	N/A	N/A
Additional rate: 45% from 6 April 2013	N/A	Over £150,000	Over £150,000

* The 10% starting rate applies to savings income only. If, after deducting the Personal Allowance from the total income liable to Income Tax, the non-savings income is above this limit then the 10% starting rate for savings will not apply. Non-savings income includes income from employment, profits from self-employment, pensions, income from property and taxable benefits. The rates available for dividends are the 10% ordinary rate, the 32.5% dividend upper rate and the dividend additional rate of 42.5% (the dividend additional rate is 37.5% from 2013-14).

Table 16: Income Tax Allowances

Income Tax allowances	2012-2013	2013-2014	2014-2015
Personal Allowance for people aged under 65 [1]	£8,105	£9,440	£10,000
Personal Allowance for people aged 65-74 [1][2]	£10,500	£10,500	£10,500
Personal Allowance for people aged 75 and over [1][2]	£10,660	£10,660	£10,660
Income limit for Personal Allowance	£100,000	£100,000	£100,000
Income limit for age- related allowances	£25,400	£26,100	£27,000
Married Couple's Allowance (born before 6th April 1935 (maximum) [2][3]	£7,705	£7,915	£8,165
Minimum amount of Married Couple's Allowance	£2,960	£3,040	£3,140
Blind Person's Allowance	£2,100	£2,160	£2,230

[1] The Personal Allowance reduces, where the income is above £100,000, by £1 for every £2 of income above the £100,000 limit. This reduction applies irrespective of age.

[2] These allowances reduce where the income is above the income limit by £1 for every £2 of income above the limit. The Personal Allowance for people aged 65 and over (up to and including 2012-13) and born before 6 April 1948 (from 2013-14) can be reduced below the basic Personal Allowance where the income is above £100,000.

[3] Tax relief for the Married Couple's Allowance is given at the rate of 10%.

Table 17: National Insurance Contributions - Rates and Allowances

	2012-2013	2013-2014	2014-2015
Lower earnings limit, primary Class 1	£107	£109	£111
Upper earnings limit, primary Class 1	£817	£797	£805
Upper accrual point	£770	£770	£770
Primary threshold (employee contribution)	£146	£149	£153
Secondary threshold (employer contribution)	£144	£148	£153
Employees' primary Class 1 rate between primary threshold and upper earnings limit (not contracted out)	12%	12%	12%
Employees' primary Class 1 rate between primary threshold and upper earnings limit (contracted out)	10.60%	10.60%	10.60%
Employees' primary Class 1 rate above upper earnings limit	2%	2%	2%

Table 17: National Insurance Contributions - Rates and Allowances

	2012-2013	2013-2014	2014-2015
Class 1A rate on employer provided benefits [1]	13.80%	13.80%	13.80%
Employers' secondary Class 1 rate above secondary threshold – no limit (not contracted out)	13.80%	13.80%	13.80%
Employers' contracted-out rebate, salary-related schemes	3.40%	3.40%	3.40%
Class 2 Rate	£2.65 per week	£2.70 per week	£2.75 per week
Class 2 small earnings exception	£5,595 per year	£5,725 per year	£5,885 per year
Special Class 2 rate for share fishermen	£3.30 per week	£3.35 per week	£3.40 per week
Special Class 2 rate for volunteer development workers	£5.35 per week	£5.45 per week	£5.55 per week
Class 3 rate	£13.25 per week	£13.55 per week	£13.90 per week
Class 4 lower profits limit	£7,605 per year	£7,755 per year	£7,956 per year
Class 4 upper profits limit	£42,475 per year	£41,450 per year	£41,865 per year
Class 4 rate between lower profits limit and upper profits limit	9%	9%	9%
Class 4 rate above upper profits limit	2%	2%	2%

[1] Class 1A NICs are payable in July and are calculated on the value of taxable benefits provided in the previous tax year, using the secondary Class 1 percentage rate appropriate to that tax year.

Table 18: Class 1 NICs: Rates for employee (primary) contributions 2014-2015

Category letter	£111 to £153 a week	£153.01 to £770 a week	£770.01 to £805 a week	Balance over £805 a week	Rebate on earnings above £111 up to and including £153 a week
A	0%	12%	12%	2%	N/A
B	0%	5.85%	5.85%	2%	N/A
C	NIL	NIL	NIL	NIL	N/A
D	0%	10.60%	12%	2%	1.40%
E	0%	5.85%	5.85%	2%	NIL
J	0%	2%	2%	2%	N/A
L	0%	2%	2%	2%	1.40%

Table 19: Class 1 NICs: Rates for employer (secondary) contributions 2014-2015

Category letter	£111 to £153 a week	£153.01 to £770 a week	£770.01 to £805 a week	Balance over £805 a week	Rebate on earnings above £111 up to and including £153 a week
A	0%	13.80%	13.80%	13.80%	N/A
B	0%	13.80%	13.80%	13.80%	N/A
C	0%	13.80%	13.80%	13.80%	N/A
D	0%	10.40%	13.80%	13.80%	3.40%
E	0%	10.40%	13.80%	13.80%	3.40%
J	0%	13.80%	13.80%	13.80%	N/A
L	0%	10.40%	13.80%	13.80%	3.40%

Table 20: Class 3 NI Weekly Rates

Date	Weekly Rate
Up to and including 05/04/2010	£12.05
06/04/2010 to 05/04/2011	£12.05
06/04/2011 to 05/04/2012	£12.60
06/04/2012 to 05/04 /2013	£13.25
06/04/2013 to 05/04/2014	£13.55
06/04/2014 to 05/04/2015	£13.90

Table 21: Income tax and NI - Gross to Net Salaries 2013 - 2014 - Not contracted out of S2P for Class 1 NIC

Gross (Annual)	Tax	NI	Net (Annual)
Up to 7,605	0.00	0.00	7,605.00
8,000	0.00	29.40	7,970.60
9,000	0.00	149.40	8,850.60
10,000	111.00	269.40	9,619.60
11,000	311.00	389.40	10,299.60
12,000	511.00	509.40	10,979.60
13,000	711.00	629.40	11,659.60
14,000	911.00	749.40	12,339.60
15,000	1,111.00	869.40	13,019.60
16,000	1,311.00	989.40	13,699.60
17,000	1,511.00	1,109.40	14,379.60
18,000	1,711.00	1,229.40	15,059.60
19,000	1,911.00	1,349.40	15,739.60
20,000	2,111.00	1,469.40	16,419.60
21,000	2,311.00	1,589.40	17,099.60
22,000	2,511.00	1,709.40	17,779.60
23,000	2,711.00	1,829.40	18,459.60
24,000	2,911.00	1,949.40	19,139.60
25,000	3,111.00	2,069.40	19,819.60
26,000	3,311.00	2,189.40	20,499.60
27,000	3,511.00	2,309.40	21,179.60
28,000	3,711.00	2,429.40	21,859.60
29,000	3,911.00	2,549.40	22,539.60
30,000	4,111.00	2,669.40	23,219.60
35,000	5,111.00	3,269.40	26,619.60
40,000	6,111.00	3,869.40	30,019.60
45,000	7,820.00	4,114.40	33,065.60
50,000	9,820.00	4,214.40	35,965.60
55,000	11,820.00	4,314.40	38,865.60
60,000	13,820.00	4,414.40	41,765.60
65,000	15,820.00	4,514.40	44,665.60
70,000	17,820.00	4,614.10	47,565.90
75,000	19,820.00	4,714.40	50,465.60
80,000	21,820.00	4,814.40	53,365.60

Table 21: Income tax and NI - Gross to Net Salaries 2013 - 2014 - Not contracted out of S2P for Class 1 NIC

Gross (Annual)	Tax	NI	Net (Annual)
85,000	23,820.00	4,914.40	56,265.60
90,000	25,820.00	5,014.40	59,165.60
95,000	27,820.00	5,114.40	62,065.60
100,000	29,820.00	5,214.40	64,965.60
150,000	49,820.00	6,214.40	93,965.60
200,000	71,847.75	7,214.40	120,937.85

Assumption: the above figures are based on a tax code of 944L

Table 22: Income tax and NI - Gross to Net Salaries 2013 - 2014 - Contracted out of S2P for Class 1 NIC and pension contribution of 3%

Gross (Annual)	Tax	NI	Pension contribution	Net (Annual)
Up to 7,605	0.00	0.00		7605.00
8,000	0.00	0.00	240	7,760.00
9,000	0.00	102.75	270	8,627.25
10,000	51.00	208.75	300	9,440.25
11,000	245.00	314.75	330	10,110.25
12,000	439.00	420.75	360	10,780.25
13,000	633.00	526.75	390	11,450.25
14,000	827.00	632.75	420	12,120.25
15,000	1,021.00	738.75	450	12,790.25
16,000	1,215.00	844.75	480	13,460.25
17,000	1,409.00	950.75	510	14,130.25
18,000	1,603.00	1,056.75	540	14,800.25
19,000	1,797.00	1,162.75	570	15,470.25
20,000	1,991.00	1,268.75	600	16,140.25
21,000	2,185.00	1,374.75	630	16,810.25
22,000	2,379.00	1,480.75	660	17,480.25
23,000	2,573.00	1,586.75	690	18,150.25
24,000	2,767.00	1,692.75	720	18,820.25
25,000	2,961.00	1,798.75	750	19,490.25
26,000	3,155.00	1,904.75	780	20,160.25
27,000	3,349.00	2,010.75	810	20,830.25
28,000	3,543.00	2,116.75	840	21,500.25
29,000	3,737.00	2,222.75	870	22,170.25
30,000	3,931.00	2,328.75	900	22,840.25
35,000	4,901.00	2,858.75	1,050	26,190.25
40,000	5,871.00	3,388.75	1,200	29,540.25
45,000	7,281.00	3,633.19	1,350	32,735.81
50,000	9,221.00	3,733.19	1,500	35,545.81
55,000	11,160.00	3,833.19	1,650	38,356.81
60,000	13,100.00	3,933.19	1,800	41,166.81
65,000	15,042.00	4,033.19	1,950	43,974.81
70,000	16,980.00	4,133.19	2,100	46,786.81
75,000	18,920.00	4,233.19	2,250	49,596.81

Table 22: Income tax and NI - Gross to Net Salaries 2013 - 2014 - Contracted out of S2P for Class 1 NIC and pension contribution of 3%

Gross (Annual)	Tax	NI	Pension contribution	Net (Annual)
80,000	20,860.00	4,333.19	2,400	52,406.81
85,000	22,800.00	4,433.19	2,550	55,216.81
90,000	24,740.00	4,533.19	2,700	58,026.81
95,000	26,680.00	4,633.19	2,850	60,836.81
100,000	28,620.00	4,733.19	3,000	63,646.81
150,000	48,020.00	5,733.19	4,500	91,746.81
200,000	69,147.75	6,733.19	6,000	118,119.06

Assumption: the above figures are based on a tax code of 944L

Interest

Table 23: Interest Rates

Until 29 July 2013 the interest rate to be applied in England and Wales was that prescribed for the special investment account under rule 27(1) of the Court Funds Rules 1987. The interest rate until 29 July 2013 was 0.5%. For claims presented on or after 29 July 2013 the relevant interest rate is that specified in s17 of the Judgments Act 1838. The interest rate now to be applied is 8% which is in line with Scotland.

From 01/08/1999	7%
From 01/02/2002	6%
From 01/02/2009	3%
From 01/06/2009	1.5%
From 01/07/2009	0.5%
From 29/07/2013	8%

Table 24: Ogden Table 27 - Factors to be applied for calculating deduction for accelerated payment

Term	−2.0%	−1.5%	−1.0%	−0.5%	0.00%	0.50%	1.00%	1.50%	2.00%	2.50%	3.00%	Term
1	1.0204	1.0152	1.0101	1.005	1	0.995	0.9901	0.9852	0.9804	0.9756	0.9709	1
2	1.0412	1.0307	1.0203	1.0101	1	0.9901	0.9803	0.9707	0.9612	0.9518	0.9426	2
3	1.0625	1.0464	1.0306	1.0152	1	0.9851	0.9706	0.9563	0.9423	0.9286	0.9151	3
4	1.0842	1.0623	1.041	1.0203	1	0.9802	0.961	0.9422	0.9238	0.906	0.8885	4
5	1.1063	1.0785	1.0515	1.0254	1	0.9754	0.9515	0.9283	0.9057	0.8839	0.8626	5
6	1.1289	1.0949	1.0622	1.0305	1	0.9705	0.942	0.9145	0.888	0.8623	0.8375	6
7	1.1519	1.1116	1.0729	1.0357	1	0.9657	0.9327	0.901	0.8706	0.8413	0.8131	7
8	1.1754	1.1285	1.0837	1.0409	1	0.9609	0.9235	0.8877	0.8535	0.8207	0.7894	8
9	1.1994	1.1457	1.0947	1.0461	1	0.9561	0.9143	0.8746	0.8368	0.8007	0.7664	9
10	1.2239	1.1632	1.1057	1.0514	1	0.9513	0.9053	0.8617	0.8203	0.7812	0.7441	10
11	1.2489	1.1809	1.1169	1.0567	1	0.9466	0.8963	0.8489	0.8043	0.7621	0.7224	11
12	1.2743	1.1989	1.1282	1.062	1	0.9419	0.8874	0.8364	0.7885	0.7436	0.7014	12
13	1.3004	1.2171	1.1396	1.0673	1	0.9372	0.8787	0.824	0.773	0.7254	0.681	13
14	1.3269	1.2356	1.1511	1.0727	1	0.9326	0.87	0.8118	0.7579	0.7077	0.6611	14

Table 24: Ogden Table 27 - Factors to be applied for calculating deduction for accelerated payment

Term	−2.0%	−1.5%	−1.0%	−0.5%	0.00%	0.50%	1.00%	1.50%	2.00%	2.50%	3.00%	Term
15	1.354	1.2545	1.1627	1.0781	1	0.9279	0.8613	0.7999	0.743	0.6905	0.6419	15
16	1.3816	1.2736	1.1745	1.0835	1	0.9233	0.8528	0.788	0.7284	0.6736	0.6232	16
17	1.4098	1.293	1.1863	1.0889	1	0.9187	0.8444	0.7764	0.7142	0.6572	0.605	17
18	1.4386	1.3126	1.1983	1.0944	1	0.9141	0.836	0.7649	0.7002	0.6412	0.5874	18
19	1.4679	1.3326	1.2104	1.0999	1	0.9096	0.8277	0.7536	0.6864	0.6255	0.5703	19
20	1.4979	1.3529	1.2226	1.1054	1	0.9051	0.8195	0.7425	0.673	0.6103	0.5537	20
21	1.5285	1.3735	1.235	1.111	1	0.9006	0.8114	0.7315	0.6598	0.5954	0.5375	21
22	1.5596	1.3944	1.2475	1.1166	1	0.8961	0.8034	0.7207	0.6468	0.5809	0.5219	22
23	1.5915	1.4157	1.2601	1.1222	1	0.8916	0.7954	0.71	0.6342	0.5667	0.5067	23
24	1.624	1.4372	1.2728	1.1278	1	0.8872	0.7876	0.6995	0.6217	0.5529	0.4919	24
25	1.6571	1.4591	1.2856	1.1335	1	0.8828	0.7798	0.6892	0.6095	0.5394	0.4776	25
26	1.6909	1.4814	1.2986	1.1392	1	0.8784	0.772	0.679	0.5976	0.5262	0.4637	26
27	1.7254	1.5039	1.3117	1.1449	1	0.874	0.7644	0.669	0.5859	0.5134	0.4502	27
28	1.7606	1.5268	1.325	1.1507	1	0.8697	0.7568	0.6591	0.5744	0.5009	0.4371	28
29	1.7966	1.5501	1.3384	1.1565	1	0.8653	0.7493	0.6494	0.5631	0.4887	0.4243	29
30	1.8332	1.5737	1.3519	1.1623	1	0.861	0.7419	0.6398	0.5521	0.4767	0.412	30
31	1.8706	1.5976	1.3656	1.1681	1	0.8567	0.7346	0.6303	0.5412	0.4651	0.4	31
32	1.9088	1.622	1.3793	1.174	1	0.8525	0.7273	0.621	0.5306	0.4538	0.3883	32
33	1.9478	1.6467	1.3933	1.1799	1	0.8482	0.7201	0.6118	0.5202	0.4427	0.377	33
34	1.9875	1.6717	1.4074	1.1858	1	0.844	0.713	0.6028	0.51	0.4319	0.366	34
35	2.0281	1.6972	1.4216	1.1918	1	0.8398	0.7059	0.5939	0.5	0.4214	0.3554	35
36	2.0695	1.723	1.4359	1.1978	1	0.8356	0.6989	0.5851	0.4902	0.4111	0.345	36
37	2.1117	1.7493	1.4504	1.2038	1	0.8315	0.692	0.5764	0.4806	0.4011	0.335	37
38	2.1548	1.7759	1.4651	1.2098	1	0.8274	0.6852	0.5679	0.4712	0.3913	0.3252	38
39	2.1988	1.803	1.4799	1.2159	1	0.8232	0.6784	0.5595	0.4619	0.3817	0.3158	39
40	2.2437	1.8304	1.4948	1.222	1	0.8191	0.6717	0.5513	0.4529	0.3724	0.3066	40
41	2.2894	1.8583	1.5099	1.2282	1	0.8151	0.665	0.5431	0.444	0.3633	0.2976	41
42	2.3362	1.8866	1.5252	1.2343	1	0.811	0.6584	0.5351	0.4353	0.3545	0.289	42
43	2.3838	1.9153	1.5406	1.2405	1	0.807	0.6519	0.5272	0.4268	0.3458	0.2805	43
44	2.4325	1.9445	1.5561	1.2468	1	0.803	0.6454	0.5194	0.4184	0.3374	0.2724	44
45	2.4821	1.9741	1.5719	1.253	1	0.799	0.6391	0.5117	0.4102	0.3292	0.2644	45
46	2.5328	2.0042	1.5877	1.2593	1	0.795	0.6327	0.5042	0.4022	0.3211	0.2567	46
47	2.5845	2.0347	1.6038	1.2657	1	0.791	0.6265	0.4967	0.3943	0.3133	0.2493	47
48	2.6372	2.0657	1.62	1.272	1	0.7871	0.6203	0.4894	0.3865	0.3057	0.242	48
49	2.6911	2.0971	1.6363	1.2784	1	0.7832	0.6141	0.4821	0.379	0.2982	0.235	49
50	2.746	2.1291	1.6529	1.2848	1	0.7793	0.608	0.475	0.3715	0.2909	0.2281	50
51	2.802	2.1615	1.6696	1.2913	1	0.7754	0.602	0.468	0.3642	0.2838	0.2215	51

Table 24: Ogden Table 27 - Factors to be applied for calculating deduction for accelerated payment

Term	−2.0%	−1.5%	−1.0%	−0.5%	0.00%	0.50%	1.00%	1.50%	2.00%	2.50%	3.00%	Term
52	2.8592	2.1944	1.6864	1.2978	1	0.7716	0.5961	0.4611	0.3571	0.2769	0.215	52
53	2.9175	2.2278	1.7035	1.3043	1	0.7677	0.5902	0.4543	0.3501	0.2702	0.2088	53
54	2.9771	2.2617	1.7207	1.3109	1	0.7639	0.5843	0.4475	0.3432	0.2636	0.2027	54
55	3.0378	2.2962	1.7381	1.3174	1	0.7601	0.5785	0.4409	0.3365	0.2572	0.1968	55
56	3.0998	2.3312	1.7556	1.3241	1	0.7563	0.5728	0.4344	0.3299	0.2509	0.191	56
57	3.1631	2.3667	1.7733	1.3307	1	0.7525	0.5671	0.428	0.3234	0.2448	0.1855	57
58	3.2277	2.4027	1.7913	1.3374	1	0.7488	0.5615	0.4217	0.3171	0.2388	0.1801	58
59	3.2935	2.4393	1.8094	1.3441	1	0.7451	0.556	0.4154	0.3109	0.233	0.1748	59
60	3.3607	2.4764	1.8276	1.3509	1	0.7414	0.5504	0.4093	0.3048	0.2273	0.1697	60
61	3.4293	2.5141	1.8461	1.3577	1	0.7377	0.545	0.4032	0.2988	0.2217	0.1648	61
62	3.4993	2.5524	1.8647	1.3645	1	0.734	0.5396	0.3973	0.2929	0.2163	0.16	62
63	3.5707	2.5913	1.8836	1.3713	1	0.7304	0.5343	0.3914	0.2872	0.2111	0.1553	63
64	3.6436	2.6308	1.9026	1.3782	1	0.7267	0.529	0.3856	0.2816	0.2059	0.1508	64
65	3.718	2.6708	1.9218	1.3852	1	0.7231	0.5237	0.3799	0.2761	0.2009	0.1464	65
66	3.7938	2.7115	1.9412	1.3921	1	0.7195	0.5185	0.3743	0.2706	0.196	0.1421	66
67	3.8713	2.7528	1.9608	1.3991	1	0.7159	0.5134	0.3688	0.2653	0.1912	0.138	67
68	3.9503	2.7947	1.9806	1.4061	1	0.7124	0.5083	0.3633	0.2601	0.1865	0.134	68
69	4.0309	2.8373	2.0007	1.4132	1	0.7088	0.5033	0.358	0.255	0.182	0.1301	69
70	4.1132	2.8805	2.0209	1.4203	1	0.7053	0.4983	0.3527	0.25	0.1776	0.1263	70
71	4.1971	2.9243	2.0413	1.4275	1	0.7018	0.4934	0.3475	0.2451	0.1732	0.1226	71
72	4.2827	2.9689	2.0619	1.4346	1	0.6983	0.4885	0.3423	0.2403	0.169	0.119	72
73	4.3702	3.0141	2.0827	1.4418	1	0.6948	0.4837	0.3373	0.2356	0.1649	0.1156	73
74	4.4593	3.06	2.1038	1.4491	1	0.6914	0.4789	0.3323	0.231	0.1609	0.1122	74
75	4.5503	3.1066	2.125	1.4564	1	0.6879	0.4741	0.3274	0.2265	0.1569	0.1089	75
76	4.6432	3.1539	2.1465	1.4637	1	0.6845	0.4694	0.3225	0.222	0.1531	0.1058	76
77	4.738	3.2019	2.1682	1.471	1	0.6811	0.4648	0.3178	0.2177	0.1494	0.1027	77
78	4.8347	3.2507	2.1901	1.4784	1	0.6777	0.4602	0.3131	0.2134	0.1457	0.0997	78
79	4.9333	3.3002	2.2122	1.4859	1	0.6743	0.4556	0.3084	0.2092	0.1422	0.0968	79
80	5.034	3.3504	2.2345	1.4933	1	0.671	0.4511	0.3039	0.2051	0.1387	0.094	80

Legislation

Table 25: List of abbreviated statutes and statutory instruments	
CAR 2004	Civil Aviation (Working Time) Regulations 2004
CCBR 2007	Companies (Cross-Border Mergers) Regulations 2007
CEC 1975	Colleges of Education (Compensation) Regulations 1975
COMAH 1999	Control of Major Accident Hazards Regulations 1999
CRA(TU)PE 2014	Collective Redundancies and Transfer of Undertakings (Protection of Employment) (Amendment) Regulations 2014
EA 2002	Employment Act 2002
EA 2010	Equality Act 2010
EAA 1973	Employment Agencies Act 1973
ECSR 2006	European Cooperative Society (Involvement of Employees) Regulations 2006
EJOs 1994	Employment Tribunals Extension of Jurisdiction (England and Wales) Order 1994(13); and Employment Tribunals Extension of Jurisdiction (Scotland) Order 1994
EOR 2009	Ecclesiastical Offices (Terms of Service) Regulations 2009
ELLR 2009	European Public Limited-Liability Company (Employee Involvement) (Great Britain) Regulations 2009
EP(RJAIS) Regs 1996	Employment Protection (Recoupment of Jobseeker's Allowance and Income Support) Regulations 1996
ERA 1996	Employment Rights Act 1996
ERelA 1999	Employment Relations Act 1999
EST (PR) Regs 2010	Employee Study and Training (Procedural Requirements) Regulations 2010
EST (ECR) Regulations 2010	Employee Study and Training (Eligibility, Complaints and Remedies) Regulations 2010
ETA 1996	Employment Tribunals Act 1996
ET(I) Order 2013	Employment Tribunals (Interest) Order (Amendment) Order 2013
ET(IADC) Regs 2013	Employment Tribunals (Interest on Awards in Discrimination Cases)(Amendment) Regulations 2013
FTE(PLFT) Regs 2002	Fixed Term Employees (Prevention of less favourable treatment) Regulations 2002
FVR 2004	Fishing Vessels (Working Time: Sea-fishermen) Regulations 2004
FW(PR) Regs 2002	Flexible Working (Procedural Requirements) Regulations 2002
FW(ECR) Regs 2002	Flexible Working (Eligibility, Complaints and Remedies) Regulations 2002
HSCE 1996	Health and Safety (Consultation with Employees) Regulations 1996
HSWA	Health and Safety at Work etc Act 1974
ICE Regs 2004	Information and Consultation of Employees Regulations 2004
ICR 2004	Information and Consultation of Employees Regulations 2004
ITA 1982	Industrial Training Act 1982
IT(IADC) Regs 1996	Industrial Tribunals (Interest on Awards in Discrimination Cases) Regulations 1996
MSR 2003	Merchant Shipping (Working Time: Inland Waterways) Regulations 2003
NMWA 1998	National Minimum Wage Act 1998
OPPS Regs 2006	The Occupational and Personal Pension Schemes (Consultation by Employers and Miscellaneous Amendment) Regulations 2006
OPS(CO)R 1996	Occupational Pension Schemes (Contracting-Out) Regulations 1996
OPS(DI)R 1996	Occupational Pensions Schemes (Disclosure of Information) Regulations 199
PSA 1993	Pension Schemes Act 1993
PTW(PLFT) Regs 2000	Part Time Workers (Prevention of less favourable treatment) Regulations 2000
REACHER 2008	REACH Enforcement Regulations 2008
RTR 2005	Road Transport (Working Time) Regulations 2005
TICE 1999	Transnational Information and Consultation of Employees Regulations 1999
TULR(C)A 1992	Trade Union and Labour Relations (Consolidation) Act 1992

Table 25: List of abbreviated statutes and statutory instruments	
TUPE Regs 2006	The Transfer of Undertakings (Protection of Employment) Regulations 2006
WTR 1998	Working Time Regulations 1998

Table 26: Limitation periods and requisite minimum qualifying periods for claims

Claim	Limitation period (maximum length of time that can elapse for claim to be brought to ET)	Length of service required before a claim can be brought to ET
Discrimination (ss13, 15, 16, 18, 19, 21, 26, 27 EA 2010)	3 months (or 6 months if relating to armed forces service) (s123 EA 2010)	None
Right of union member not to be unjustifiably disciplined (s64 TULR(C)A)	3 months (s66 TULR(C)A)	None
Right of union member to compensation if declared to be unjustifiably disciplined (s67 TULR(C)A)	6 months, but not before 4 weeks (s67(3) TULR(C)A)	None
Right of union member not to suffer deduction of unauthorised or excessive subscriptions (s68 TULR(C)A)	3 months (s68A(1) TULR(C)A)	None
Right of union member not to suffer deduction of contributions to a political fund (s86 TULR(C)A)	3 months (s87(2) TULR(C)A)	None
Right of union member if employer has failed to comply with their right not to suffer deduction of contributions to a political fund (s87(5) TULR(C)A)	6 months but not before 4 weeks (s87(6) TULR(C)A)	None
Refusal of employment on grounds related to trade union membership (s137 TULR(C)A)	3 months (s139(1) TULR(C)A)	None
Right not to be offered inducements relating to union membership or activities (s145A TULR(C)A)	3 months (s145C TULR(C)A)	None
Right not to be offered inducements relating to collective bargaining (s145B TULR(C)A)	3 months (s145C TULR(C)A)	None
Protection from detriment (not dismissal) relating to union membership or activities (s146 TULR(C)A)	3 months (s147(1) TULR(C)A)	None
Time off for union duties (s168 TULR(C)A)	3 months (s171 TULR(C)A)	None
Time off for union learning representatives (s168A TULR(C)A)	3 months (s171 TULR(C)A)	None
Payment for time off for union duties and union learning reps (s169 TULR(C)A)	3 months (s171 TULR(C)A)	None
Time off for union activities (s170 TULR(C)A)	3 months (s171 TULR(C)A)	None
Right not to be excluded or expelled from union (s174 TULR(C)A)	6 months (s175 TULR(C)A)	None
Right to compensation if excluded or expelled from union (s176(2) TULR(C)A)	6 months (but not before 4 weeks) (s176(3) TULR(C)A)	None
Redundancy - right to be consulted (s188 TULR(C)A)	3 months (s189(5) TULR(C)A)	None
Redundancy - right to election of employee reps (s188A TULR(C)A)	3 months (s189(5) TULR(C)A)	None
Redundancy - right to be paid during protected period (s190 TULR(C)A)	3 months (s192(3) TULR(C)A)	None
Right to written statement of particulars (s1(1) ERA), or change in particulars (s4(1) ERA), or itemised pay statement (s8(1) ERA)	During employment or within 3 months of termination (s11(4) ERA)	1 month (s198 ERA) (none in the case of itemised statement)
Right not to suffer unauthorised deductions (normal) (s13(1) ERA), (retail) (s18(1)), not to	3 months (s23 ERA)	None

Table 26: Limitation periods and requisite minimum qualifying periods for claims

Claim	Limitation period (maximum length of time that can elapse for claim to be brought to ET)	Length of service required before a claim can be brought to ET
make payments to employer (normal) (s15(1)), (retail) (s21(1))		
Right to guarantee payments (s28(1) ERA)	3 months (s34(2) ERA)	1 month (s29 ERA)
Right not to suffer detriment (ss43M, 44, 45, 45A, 46, 47, 47A, 47B, 47C, 47D, 47E, 47F ERA	3 months (s48(3) ERA)	None, except: 26 weeks in the case of Ordinary Adoption Leave, Additional Adoption Leave, Ordinary Paternity Leave (birth), Additional Paternity Leave (birth), Paternity Leave (adoption); 1 year in the case of Parental Leave (reg 13 Maternity and Parental Leave etc Regs 1999)
Time off for public duties (s50(1) ERA)	3 months (s51(2) ERA)	None
Time off on redundancy to look for work or arrange training (s52(1) ERA) and payment for time off on redundancy to look for work or arrange training (ss53(1) and 53(4) ERA)	3 months (s54(2) ERA)	2 years (s52(2) ERA)
Time off for ante-natal care (s55(1) ERA) and payment for this time off (s56(1) ERA)	3 months (s57(2) ERA)	None
Time off for dependants (s57A ERA)	3 months (s57B(2) ERA)	None
Time off for pension scheme trustees (s58(1) ERA) and payment for this time off (s59(1) ERA)	3 months (s60(2) ERA)	None
Time off for employee representatives (s61(1) ERA) and payment for this time off (s62(1) ERA)	3 months (s63(2) ERA)	None
Time off for young person for study or training (s63A ERA) and payment for this time off (s63B ERA)	3 months (s63C(2) ERA)	None
Time off for study or training (s63D ERA)	3 months (s63I(5) ERA)	26 weeks (s63D(a) ERA)
Payment for suspension on medical grounds (s64(1) ERA) or maternity grounds (s68 ERA)	3 months (s70(2) ERA)	1 month (s65(1) ERA)
Offer of alternative work when suspended on maternity grounds (s67 ERA)	3 months (s70(5) ERA)	None
Right to request flexible working (s80F ERA)	3 months (s80H(5) ERA)	26 weeks (reg 13 Flexible Working (Eligibility etc) Regs 2002
Right of employee to minimum notice period (s86 ERA)	6 years under contract	1 month (s86 ERA 1996)
Right to written reasons for dismissal (s92(1) ERA)	3 months (s93(3) ERA)	1 year (s92(3) ERA)
Unfair dismissal (s94(1) ERA)	3 months (s111(2) ERA)	1 year where period of continuous service started prior to 6 April 2012; 2 years where period of continuous service started on or after 6 April 2012 There is no qualifying period if the principal reasons for dismissal relates to: ERA ss98B; 99; 100 (1); 101; 101A(1); 102; 103; 103A; 104; s104A; 104B; 104C; 104E; 104F; 105; TULR(C)A Sch A1 para 161; ss238A; 152-153; ICE Reg 30 TICE Reg 28; OPPS 2006; Reg 7 PRW Regs; Reg 6 FTE Regs; s12 ERelA 1999; Sch 6 para

Table 26: Limitation periods and requisite minimum qualifying periods for claims

Claim	Limitation period (maximum length of time that can elapse for claim to be brought to ET)	Length of service required before a claim can be brought to ET
		13(5)
Right to redundancy payment (s135(1) ERA)	6 months (s164 ERA)	2 years (s155) ERA)
Insolvency claim to Secretary of State (s182 ERA)	3 months (s188(2) ERA)	None
Time off for health and safety reps 1996 and payment for time off (reg7 HSC Regs)	3 months (sch 2 HSC Regs 1996)	None
Claims under the Working Time Regulations (Regs 10, 11, 12, 13, 14, 16, 24, 24A, 25, 27, 27A WTR)	3 months (reg 30(2) WTR)	None
Right to National Minimum Wage (s1(1) NMWA 1998)	3 months (s23(2) ERA) or 6 years under contract	None
Right to access to records in relation to (s10 NMWA)	3 months (s11 NMWA)	None
Right not to suffer detriment for asserting rights in connection with (s23 NMW A)	3months (s24(2) NMWA)	None
Right to be accompanied at a grievance or disciplinary meeting (s10 ERelA 1999) and right not to suffer detriment in connection with this right (s12 ERelA)	3 months (s11(2) and s12(2) ERelA)	None
Time off for works body member and right to payment during this time off (regs 25 and 26 TICE 1999)	3 months (Reg 27(2) TICE)	None
Part-time worker discrimination(regs 5 and 7(2) PTW Regs 2000)	3 months (Reg 8(2) PTW Regs)	None
Fixed term worker discrimination (Regs 3 and 6(2) FTE Regs 2002)	3 months (Reg 7(2) FTE)	None
Right to be accompanied at, or postponement of, flexible working meeting (Reg 14(2) and 14(4) FW(PR) Regs 2002)	3 months (Reg 15(2) FW(PR) Regs)	None
Time off for employee reps (reg 27 ICE Regs 2004) and payment for time off (Reg 28 ICE)	3 months (reg 29(2) ICE)	None
Right to be informed and /or consulted over TUPE (reg 13 TUPE 2006) and right to election of employee reps (reg 14 TUPE)	3 months (reg 15(12) TUPE)	None
Time off for employee reps (Sch paragraph 2 OPPS Regs 2006) and payment for time off (Sch paragraph 3 OPPS)	3 months (Schedule paragraph 4(2) OPPS)	None
Right not to suffer detriment in connection with employee reps (schedule paragraph 7 OPPS)	3 months (schedule paragraph 8(2) OPPS)	None
Breach of Sex Equality Clause (s66 EA 2010) or Maternity Equality Clause (s73 EA 2010)	6 months (or 9 months if relating to armed forces service (s129 EA 2010)	None
Right to be accompanied to a meeting concerning study and training (reg 16 EST (PR) Regs 2010)	3 months (reg 17(2) EST (PR) Regs)	None

Table 27: Matters to which the prescribed element is attributable (Schedule to Employment Protection (Recoupment of Jobseeker's Allowance and Income Support) Regulations 1996)

Payment	Proceedings	Matter to which prescribed element is attributable
Guarantee payments under section 28	Complaint under section 34.	Any amount found to be due to the employee and ordered to be paid under section 34(3) for a period before the conclusion of the tribunal proceedings.
Payments under any collective agreement having regard to which the appropriate Minister has made an exemption order under section 35.	Complaint under section 35(4).	Any amount found to be due to the employee and ordered to be paid under section 34(3), as applied by section 35(4), for a period before the conclusion of the tribunal proceedings.
Payments of remuneration in respect of a period of suspension on medical grounds under section 64 and section 108(2).	Complaint under section 70.	Any amount found to be due to the employee and ordered to be paid under section 70(3) for a period before the conclusion of the tribunal proceedings.
Payments of remuneration in respect of a period of suspension on maternity grounds under section 68.	Complaint under section 70.	Any amount found to be due to the employee and ordered to be paid under section 70(3) for a period before the conclusion of the tribunal proceedings
Payments under an order for reinstatement under section 114(1).	Complaint of unfair dismissal under section 111(1).	Any amount ordered to be paid under section 114(2)(a) in respect of arrears of pay for a period before the conclusion of the tribunal proceedings.
Payments under an order for re-engagement under section 117(8).	Complaint of unfair dismissal under section 111(1).	Any amount ordered to be paid under section 115(2)(d) in respect of arrears of pay for a period before the conclusion of the tribunal proceedings.
Payments under an award of compensation for unfair dismissal in cases falling under section 112(4) (cases where no order for reinstatement or re-engagement has been made).	Complaint of unfair dismissal under section 111(1).	Any amount ordered to be paid and calculated under section 123 in respect of compensation for loss of wages for a period before the conclusion of the tribunal proceedings.
Payments under an award of compensation for unfair dismissal under section 117(3) where reinstatement order not complied with.	Proceedings in respect of non-compliance with order.	Any amount ordered to be paid and calculated under section 123 in respect of compensation for loss of wages for a period before the conclusion of the tribunal proceedings.
Payments under an award of compensation for unfair dismissal under section 117(3) where re-engagement order not complied with.	Proceedings in respect of non-compliance with order	Any amount ordered to be paid and calculated under section 123 in respect of compensation for loss of wages for a period before the conclusion of the tribunal proceedings.
Payments under an interim order for reinstatement under section 163(4) of the 1992 Act.	Proceedings on an application for an order for interim relief under section 161(1) of the 1992 Act.	Any amount found to be due to the complainant and ordered to be paid in respect of arrears of pay for the period between the date of termination of employment and the conclusion of the tribunal proceedings.
Payments under an interim order for re-engagement under section 163(5)(a) of the 1992 Act.	Proceedings on an application for an order for interim relief under section 161(1) of the 1992 Act.	Any amount found to be due to the complainant and ordered to be paid in respect of arrears of pay for the period between the date of termination of employment and the conclusion of the tribunal proceedings.
Payments under an order for the continuation of a contract of employment under section 163(5)(b) of the 1992 Act where employee reasonably refuses re-engagement.	Proceedings on an application for an order for interim relief under section 161(1) of the 1992 Act.	Any amount found to be due to the complainant and ordered to be paid in respect of arrears of pay for the period between the date of termination of employment and the conclusion of the tribunal proceedings.

Table 27: Matters to which the prescribed element is attributable (Schedule to Employment Protection (Recoupment of Jobseeker's Allowance and Income Support) Regulations 1996)

Payment	Proceedings	Matter to which prescribed element is attributable
Payments under an order for the continuation of a contract of employment under section 163(6) of the 1992 Act where employer fails to attend or is unwilling to reinstate or re-engage.	Proceedings on an application for an order for interim relief under section 161(1) of the 1992 Act.	Any amount found to be due to the complainant and ordered to be paid in respect of arrears of pay for the period between the date of termination of employment and the conclusion of the tribunal proceedings.
Payments under an order for the continuation of a contract of employment under sections 166(1) and (2) of the 1992 Act where reinstatement or re-engagement order not complied with.	Proceedings in respect of non-compliance with order.	Any amount ordered to be paid to the employee by way of compensation under section 166(1)(b) of the 1992 Act for loss of wages for the period between the date of termination of employment and the conclusion of the tribunal proceedings.
Payments under an order for compensation under sections 166(3)–(5) of the 1992 Act where order for the continuation of contract of employment not complied with.	Proceedings in respect of non-compliance with order	Any amount ordered to be paid to the employee by way of compensation under section 166(3)–(4) of the 1992 Act for loss of wages for the period between the date of termination of employment and the conclusion of the tribunal proceedings.
Payments under an order under section 192(3) of the 1992 Act on employer's default in respect of remuneration due to employee under protective award.	Complaint under section 192(1) of the 1992 Act.	Any amount ordered to be paid to the employee in respect of so much of the relevant protected period as falls before the date of the conclusion of the tribunal proceedings.

Pensions

(Tables 28 to 34 have been reproduced from 'Compensation for Loss of Pension Rights - Employment Tribunals' published by the Government Actuary Department)

Table 28: Tables of multipliers to be applied to the deferred annual pension to assess compensation for loss of enhancement of accrued pension rights

GAD Table 4.1 Men in private sector schemes				GAD Table 4.2 Men in public sector schemes			
Age last birthday at dismissal	Normal Retirement Age - Men			Age last birthday at dismissal	Normal Retirement Age - Men		
	55	60	65		55	60	65
20 and under	5.62	5.22	4.63	20 and under	6.26	5.91	5.33
21	5.55	5.18	4.6	21	6.19	5.85	5.3
22	5.49	5.13	4.57	22	6.1	5.8	5.26
23	5.41	5.09	4.55	23	6.02	5.74	5.22
24	5.34	5.03	4.51	24	5.92	5.68	5.18
25	5.25	4.98	4.48	25	5.83	5.61	5.14
26	5.17	4.92	4.44	26	5.73	5.54	5.09
27	5.08	4.86	4.41	27	5.62	5.47	5.05
28	4.98	4.8	4.37	28	5.51	5.39	4.99
29	4.88	4.73	4.32	29	5.39	5.31	4.94
30	4.78	4.66	4.28	30	5.27	5.22	4.88
31	4.67	4.58	4.23	31	5.14	5.13	4.82
32	4.55	4.5	4.18	32	5.01	5.04	4.76
33	4.43	4.42	4.12	33	4.87	4.94	4.69
34	4.3	4.33	4.06	34	4.72	4.83	4.62
35	4.17	4.24	4	35	4.57	4.72	4.54
36	4.03	4.14	3.94	36	4.41	4.61	4.47
37	3.88	4.03	3.87	37	4.25	4.49	4.38
38	3.73	3.93	3.79	38	4.08	4.36	4.3
39	3.57	3.81	3.72	39	3.9	4.23	4.21
40	3.4	3.7	3.64	40	3.71	4.1	4.11
41	3.22	3.57	3.55	41	3.51	3.96	4.01
42	3.04	3.44	3.47	42	3.31	3.81	3.91
43	2.85	3.31	3.37	43	3.1	3.65	3.8
44	2.65	3.16	3.28	44	2.88	3.49	3.69
45	2.45	3.02	3.17	45	2.66	3.33	3.57
46	2.23	2.86	3.07	46	2.42	3.15	3.45
47	2.01	2.7	2.96	47	2.17	2.97	3.32
48	1.77	2.53	2.84	48	1.92	2.78	3.18
49	1.53	2.36	2.72	49	1.65	2.59	3.05
50	1.28	2.18	2.59	50	1.38	2.39	2.9
51	1.01	1.99	2.46	51	1.09	2.18	2.75
52	0.74	1.79	2.32	52	0.79	1.96	2.59
53	0.45	1.58	2.18	53	0.49	1.73	2.43

Table 28: Tables of multipliers to be applied to the deferred annual pension to assess compensation for loss of enhancement of accrued pension rights

GAD Table 4.1 Men in private sector schemes				GAD Table 4.2 Men in public sector schemes			
Age last birthday at dismissal	Normal Retirement Age - Men			Age last birthday at dismissal	Normal Retirement Age - Men		
	55	60	65		55	60	65
54	0.15	1.37	2.03	54	0.16	1.49	2.26
55		1.14	1.87	55		1.24	2.09
56		0.91	1.71	56		0.99	1.9
57		0.66	1.54	57		0.72	1.71
58		0.4	1.37	58		0.44	1.52
59		0.14	1.18	59		0.15	1.31
60			0.99	60			1.1
61			0.79	61			0.87
62			0.57	62			0.64
63			0.35	63			0.39
64			0.12	64			0.13

Table 29: Tables of multipliers to be applied to the deferred annual pension to assess compensation for loss of enhancement of accrued pension rights

GAD Table 4.3 Women in private sector schemes				GAD Table 4.4 Women in public sector schemes			
Age last birthday at dismissal	Normal Retirement Age - Women			Age last birthday at dismissal	Normal Retirement Age - Women		
	55	60	65		55	60	65
20 and under	5.89	5.54	4.96	20 and under	6.53	6.22	5.68
21	5.83	5.49	4.94	21	6.45	6.17	5.65
22	5.75	5.44	4.91	22	6.36	6.11	5.61
23	5.68	5.39	4.88	23	6.27	6.04	5.57
24	5.59	5.34	4.84	24	6.18	5.98	5.52
25	5.51	5.28	4.81	25	6.08	5.91	5.48
26	5.42	5.22	4.77	26	5.97	5.83	5.43
27	5.32	5.15	4.73	27	5.86	5.75	5.38
28	5.22	5.09	4.68	28	5.74	5.67	5.32
29	5.12	5.01	4.63	29	5.62	5.59	5.26
30	5	4.94	4.58	30	5.49	5.49	5.2
31	4.89	4.85	4.53	31	5.36	5.4	5.14
32	4.77	4.77	4.47	32	5.22	5.3	5.07
33	4.64	4.68	4.42	33	5.07	5.19	4.99
34	4.5	4.58	4.35	34	4.92	5.08	4.92
35	4.36	4.48	4.28	35	4.76	4.97	4.84
36	4.21	4.38	4.21	36	4.59	4.85	4.75
37	4.06	4.27	4.14	37	4.42	4.72	4.66
38	3.9	4.16	4.06	38	4.24	4.59	4.57
39	3.73	4.03	3.98	39	4.05	4.45	4.48

Table 29: Tables of multipliers to be applied to the deferred annual pension to assess compensation for loss of enhancement of accrued pension rights							
GAD Table 4.3 Women in private sector schemes				GAD Table 4.4 Women in public sector schemes			
Age last birthday at dismissal	Normal Retirement Age - Women			Age last birthday at dismissal	Normal Retirement Age - Women		
	55	60	65		55	60	65
40	3.55	3.91	3.89	40	3.86	4.31	4.37
41	3.37	3.78	3.8	41	3.66	4.16	4.27
42	3.18	3.64	3.71	42	3.44	4	4.16
43	2.98	3.5	3.61	43	3.23	3.84	4.04
44	2.77	3.35	3.5	44	3	3.67	3.92
45	2.56	3.19	3.39	45	2.76	3.49	3.79
46	2.33	3.02	3.28	46	2.51	3.31	3.66
47	2.1	2.85	3.16	47	2.26	3.12	3.53
48	1.85	2.68	3.04	48	1.99	2.92	3.38
49	1.6	2.49	2.91	49	1.72	2.72	3.24
50	1.33	2.3	2.77	50	1.43	2.5	3.08
51	1.06	2.09	2.63	51	1.13	2.28	2.92
52	0.77	1.88	2.48	52	0.82	2.05	2.75
53	0.47	1.67	2.33	53	0.5	1.81	2.58
54	0.16	1.44	2.17	54	0.17	1.56	2.4
55		1.2	2	55		1.3	2.21
56		0.95	1.83	56		1.03	2.02
57		0.69	1.64	57		0.75	1.81
58		0.42	1.46	58		0.46	1.6
59		0.14	1.26	59		0.15	1.38
60			1.05	60			1.16
61			0.84	61			0.92
62			0.61	62			0.67
63			0.37	63			0.41
64			0.13	64			0.14

Table 30: Tables of multipliers to be applied to the estimated final annual pension to assess value of pension arising from service to Normal Retirement Age

GAD Table 5.1 Men in private sector schemes				GAD Table 5.2 Men in Public Sector Schemes			
Age last birthday at dismissal	Normal Retirement Age - Men			Age last birthday at dismissal	Normal Retirement Age - Men		
	55	60	65		55	60	65
20 and under	12.79	10.83	8.91	20 and under	15.97	13.65	11.36
21	12.92	10.94	9	21	16.13	13.79	11.47
22	13.05	11.05	9.09	22	16.3	13.93	11.59
23	13.19	11.16	9.18	23	16.46	14.07	11.71
24	13.32	11.28	9.27	24	16.63	14.21	11.82
25	13.46	11.39	9.36	25	16.8	14.36	11.95
26	13.6	11.51	9.46	26	16.98	14.51	12.07
27	13.74	11.63	9.56	27	17.15	14.66	12.19
28	13.88	11.75	9.66	28	17.33	14.81	12.32
29	14.02	11.87	9.76	29	17.51	14.96	12.44
30	14.17	11.99	9.86	30	17.69	15.12	12.57
31	14.32	12.12	9.96	31	17.87	15.27	12.7
32	14.47	12.25	10.07	32	18.06	15.43	12.84
33	14.62	12.37	10.17	33	18.25	15.59	12.97
34	14.77	12.5	10.28	34	18.44	15.75	13.11
35	14.93	12.64	10.39	35	18.63	15.92	13.24
36	15.08	12.77	10.5	36	18.82	16.08	13.38
37	15.24	12.9	10.61	37	19.02	16.25	13.52
38	15.4	13.04	10.72	38	19.22	16.42	13.66
39	15.57	13.18	10.83	39	19.42	16.6	13.8
40	15.73	13.32	10.95	40	19.63	16.77	13.95
41	15.9	13.46	11.06	41	19.83	16.95	14.1
42	16.07	13.6	11.18	42	20.05	17.13	14.24
43	16.24	13.75	11.29	43	20.26	17.31	14.4
44	16.42	13.89	11.41	44	20.48	17.5	14.55
45	16.6	14.04	11.53	45	20.7	17.68	14.7
46	16.78	14.2	11.66	46	20.93	17.88	14.86
47	16.97	14.35	11.78	47	21.16	18.07	15.02
48	17.16	14.51	11.91	48	21.4	18.27	15.18
49	17.35	14.67	12.04	49	21.64	18.48	15.35
50	17.55	14.84	12.17	50	21.89	18.69	15.52
51	17.76	15.01	12.3	51	22.15	18.9	15.69
52	17.97	15.18	12.44	52	22.41	19.12	15.87
53	18.19	15.36	12.58	53	22.69	19.35	16.05
54	18.42	15.55	12.72	54	22.97	19.59	16.24
55		15.74	12.87	55		19.83	16.44
56		15.95	13.03	56		20.09	16.64
57		16.16	13.19	57		20.35	16.85

Table 30: Tables of multipliers to be applied to the estimated final annual pension to assess value of pension arising from service to Normal Retirement Age

GAD Table 5.1 Men in private sector schemes				GAD Table 5.2 Men in Public Sector Schemes			
Age last birthday at dismissal	Normal Retirement Age - Men			Age last birthday at dismissal	Normal Retirement Age - Men		
	55	60	65		55	60	65
58		16.38	13.36	58		20.63	17.07
59		16.61	13.54	59		20.92	17.3
60			13.73	60			17.55
61			13.93	61			17.81
62			14.14	62			18.08
63			14.37	63			18.38
64			14.62	64			18.7

Table 31: Tables of multipliers to be applied to the estimated final annual pension to assess value of pension arising from service to Normal Retirement Age

GAD Table 5.3 Women in private sector schemes				GAD Table 5.4 Women in public sector schemes			
Age last birthday at dismissal	Normal Retirement Age - Women			Age last birthday at dismissal	Normal Retirement Age - Women		
	55	60	65		55	60	65
20 and under	13.26	11.32	9.37	20 and under	16.48	14.19	11.91
21	13.39	11.43	9.47	21	16.64	14.33	12.02
22	13.53	11.55	9.56	22	16.81	14.48	12.15
23	13.67	11.67	9.66	23	16.98	14.62	12.27
24	13.8	11.78	9.75	24	17.15	14.77	12.39
25	13.94	11.9	9.85	25	17.32	14.92	12.51
26	14.08	12.02	9.95	26	17.5	15.07	12.64
27	14.23	12.14	10.05	27	17.68	15.22	12.77
28	14.37	12.27	10.15	28	17.86	15.37	12.9
29	14.52	12.39	10.26	29	18.04	15.53	13.03
30	14.66	12.51	10.36	30	18.22	15.69	13.16
31	14.81	12.64	10.46	31	18.4	15.85	13.29
32	14.96	12.77	10.57	32	18.59	16.01	13.43
33	15.11	12.9	10.67	33	18.78	16.17	13.56
34	15.27	13.03	10.78	34	18.97	16.33	13.7
35	15.42	13.16	10.89	35	19.16	16.5	13.84
36	15.58	13.3	11	36	19.36	16.67	13.98
37	15.74	13.43	11.11	37	19.56	16.84	14.12
38	15.9	13.57	11.22	38	19.76	17.01	14.26
39	16.07	13.71	11.34	39	19.96	17.18	14.41
40	16.23	13.85	11.45	40	20.17	17.36	14.56
41	16.4	13.99	11.57	41	20.38	17.54	14.7
42	16.57	14.13	11.69	42	20.59	17.72	14.86
43	16.74	14.28	11.81	43	20.81	17.91	15.01

Table 31: Tables of multipliers to be applied to the estimated final annual pension to assess value of pension arising from service to Normal Retirement Age

GAD Table 5.3 Women in private sector schemes				GAD Table 5.4 Women in public sector schemes			
Age last birthday at dismissal	Normal Retirement Age - Women			Age last birthday at dismissal	Normal Retirement Age - Women		
	55	60	65		55	60	65
44	16.92	14.43	11.93	44	21.02	18.09	15.16
45	17.1	14.58	12.05	45	21.25	18.28	15.32
46	17.28	14.73	12.18	46	21.47	18.48	15.48
47	17.47	14.89	12.3	47	21.7	18.67	15.64
48	17.66	15.05	12.43	48	21.94	18.87	15.81
49	17.85	15.21	12.56	49	22.18	19.08	15.98
50	18.05	15.38	12.7	50	22.42	19.28	16.15
51	18.25	15.55	12.84	51	22.67	19.5	16.33
52	18.46	15.72	12.98	52	22.93	19.72	16.51
53	18.67	15.9	13.12	53	23.19	19.94	16.69
54	18.89	16.08	13.27	54	23.46	20.17	16.88
55		16.27	13.42	55		20.41	17.08
56		16.47	13.58	56		20.65	17.28
57		16.67	13.74	57		20.9	17.48
58		16.88	13.91	58		21.16	17.7
59		17.1	14.09	59		21.43	17.92
60			14.27	60			18.15
61			14.46	61			18.4
62			14.66	62			18.65
63			14.88	63			18.92
64			15.10	64			19.21

Table 32: Tables of multipliers to be applied to the deferred annual pension to assess value of deferred pension

GAD Table 6.1 Men in private sector schemes				GAD Table 6.2 Men in public sector schemes			
Age last birthday at dismissal	Retirement Age - Men			Age last birthday at dismissal	Retirement Age - Men		
	55	60	65		55	60	65
20 and under	7.17	5.61	4.28	20 and under	9.71	7.74	6.03
21	7.37	5.76	4.4	21	9.95	7.93	6.18
22	7.57	5.92	4.51	22	10.19	8.13	6.33
23	7.77	6.08	4.63	23	10.45	8.33	6.48
24	7.98	6.24	4.76	24	10.71	8.54	6.64
25	8.2	6.41	4.88	25	10.97	8.75	6.81
26	8.43	6.59	5.02	26	11.25	8.97	6.97
27	B.66	6.77	5.15	27	11.53	9.19	7.15
28	8.9	6.95	5.29	28	11.82	9.42	7.32
29	9.14	7.14	5.43	29	12.11	9.65	7.5
30	9.39	7.34	5.58	30	12.42	9.89	7.69

Table 32: Tables of multipliers to be applied to the deferred annual pension to assess value of deferred pension

GAD Table 6.1 Men in private sector schemes				GAD Table 6.2 Men in public sector schemes			
Age last birthday at dismissal	Retirement Age - Men			Age last birthday at dismissal	Retirement Age - Men		
	55	60	65		55	60	65
31	9.65	7.54	5.73	31	12.73	10.14	7.88
32	9.92	7.74	5.89	32	13.05	10.4	8.08
33	10.19	7.96	6.05	33	13.37	10.66	8.28
34	10.47	8.18	6.22	34	13.71	10.92	8.49
35	10.76	8.4	6.39	35	14.05	11.2	8.7
36	11.06	8.63	6.56	36	14.41	11.48	8.91
37	11.36	8.87	6.74	37	14.77	11.76	9.14
38	11.68	9.11	6.92	38	15.14	12.06	9.36
39	12	9.36	7.11	39	15.53	12.36	9.6
40	12.33	9.62	7.31	40	15.92	12.67	9.84
41	12.67	9.89	7.51	41	16.32	12.99	10.08
42	13.03	10.16	7.71	42	16.73	13.32	10.34
43	13.39	10.44	7.92	43	17.16	13.66	10.59
44	13.76	10.73	8.14	44	17.6	14	10.86
45	14.15	11.03	8.36	45	18.05	14.36	11.13
46	14.55	11.33	8.59	46	18.51	14.72	11.41
47	14.96	11.65	8.83	47	18.99	15.1	11.7
48	15.38	11.98	9.07	48	19.48	15.49	12
49	15.82	12.31	9.32	49	19.99	15.89	12.3
50	16.28	12.66	9.57	50	20.51	16.3	12.62
51	16.75	13.02	9.84	51	21.06	16.73	12.94
52	17.24	13.4	10.12	52	21.62	17.17	13.27
53	17.74	13.78	10.4	53	22.2	17.62	13.62
54	18.27	14.19	10.69	54	22.81	18.1	13.98
55		14.6	11	55		18.59	14.35
56		15.04	11.32	56		19.1	14.74
57		15.5	11.65	57		19.63	15.14
58		15.97	12	58		20.19	15.56
59		16.47	12.36	59		20.78	15.99
60			12.74	60			16.45
61			13.14	61			16.94
62			13.56	62			17.45
63			14.02	63			17.99
64			14.5	64			18.57

Table 33: Tables of multipliers to be applied to the deferred annual pension to assess value of deferred pension

GAD Table 6.3 Women in private sector schemes				GAD Table 6.4 Women in public sector schemes			
Age last birthday at dismissal	Normal Retirement Age - Women			Age last birthday at dismissal	Normal Retirement Age - Women		
	55	60	65		55	60	65
20 and under	7.37	5.79	4.41	20 and under	9.94	7.97	6.22
21	7.57	5.94	4.53	21	10.19	8.17	6.38
22	7.78	6.11	4.66	22	10.45	8.37	6.54
23	7.99	6.27	4.78	23	10.71	8.58	6.7
24	8.21	6.44	4.91	24	10.97	8.79	6.87
25	8.43	6.62	5.05	25	11.25	9.01	7.04
26	8.67	6.8	5.18	26	11.53	9.24	7.21
27	8.9	6.99	5.33	27	11.82	9.47	7.39
28	9.15	7.18	5.47	28	12.11	9.7	7.58
29	9.4	7.38	5.62	29	12.42	9.94	7.76
30	9.66	7.58	5.77	30	12.73	10.19	7.96
31	9.92	7.79	5.93	31	13.05	10.45	8.16
32	10.2	8	6.09	32	13.37	10.71	8.36
33	10.48	8.22	6.26	33	13.71	10.98	8.57
34	10.77	8.45	6.43	34	14.05	11.25	8.78
35	11.06	8.68	6.61	35	14.4	11.53	9
36	11.37	8.92	6.79	36	14.77	11.82	9.22
37	11.68	9.16	6.97	37	15.14	12.12	9.45
38	12	9.41	7.16	38	15.52	12.42	9.69
39	12.34	9.67	7.36	39	15.91	12.73	9.93
40	12.68	9.94	7.56	40	16.31	13.05	10.18
41	13.03	10.21	7.77	41	16.72	13.38	10.44
42	13.39	10.49	7.98	42	17.15	13.72	10.7
43	13.76	10.79	8.2	43	17.58	14.07	10.97
44	14.15	11.08	8.42	44	18.03	14.42	11.24
45	14.54	11.39	8.66	45	18.49	14.79	11.53
46	14.95	11.71	8.9	46	18.96	15.16	11.82
47	15.37	12.04	9.14	47	19.45	15.55	12.12
48	15.8	12.37	9.4	48	19.95	15.95	12.43
49	16.25	12.72	9.66	49	20.46	16.36	12.74
50	16.71	13.08	9.93	50	20.99	16.78	13.07
51	17.19	13.45	10.21	51	21.54	17.22	13.41
52	17.69	13.84	10.49	52	22.11	17.67	13.75
53	18.2	14.23	10.79	53	22.69	18.13	14.11
54	18.73	14.65	11.1	54	23.29	18.61	14.48
55		15.07	11.42	55		19.11	14.86
56		15.52	11.75	56		19.62	15.26
57		15.98	12.1	57		20.15	15.67

Table 33: Tables of multipliers to be applied to the deferred annual pension to assess value of deferred pension

GAD Table 6.3 Women in private sector schemes				GAD Table 6.4 Women in public sector schemes			
Age last birthday at dismissal	Normal Retirement Age - Women			Age last birthday at dismissal	Normal Retirement Age - Women		
	55	60	65		55	60	65
58		16.46	12.45	58		20.7	16.1
59		16.96	12.83	59		21.28	16.54
60			13.22	60			17
61			13.63	61			17.48
62			14.05	62			17.98
63			14.5	63			18.51
64			14.98	64			19.07

Table 34: Tables of factors to be applied to the standard contribution rate to assess the age specific contribution rate

GAD Table 7.1 Men				GAD Table 7.2 Women			
Age last birthday at dismissal	Normal Retirement Age - Men			Age last birthday at dismissal	Normal Retirement Age - Women		
	55	60	65		55	60	65
20 and	0.77	0.74	0.71	20 and	0.77	0.74	0.7
21	0.78	0.75	0.72	21	0.78	0.75	0.71
22	0.79	0.76	0.73	22	0.79	0.76	0.72
23	0.8	0.77	0.74	23	0.81	0.77	0.73
24	0.82	0.78	0.75	24	0.82	0.78	0.75
25	0.83	0.79	0.76	25	0.83	0.8	0.76
26	0.84	0.81	0.77	26	0.84	0.81	0.77
27	0.85	0.82	0.78	27	0.86	0.82	0.78
28	0.87	0.83	0.8	28	0.87	0.83	0.79
29	0.88	0.84	0.81	29	0.88	0.85	0.8
30	0.89	0.86	0.82	30	0.9	0.86	0.81
31	0.91	0.87	0.83	31	0.91	0.87	0.83
32	0.92	0.88	0.84	32	0.92	0.88	0.84
33	0.93	0.9	0.86	33	0.94	0.9	0.85
34	0.95	0.91	0.87	34	0.95	0.91	0.86
35	0.96	0.92	0.88	35	0.96	0.92	0.88
36	0.98	0.94	0.9	36	0.98	0.94	0.89
37	0.99	0.95	0.91	37	0.99	0.95	0.9
38	1.01	0.97	0.93	38	1.01	0.97	0.92
39	1.02	0.98	0.94	39	1.02	0.98	0.93
40	1.04	1	0.95	40	1.04	1	0.95
41	1.06	1.01	0.97	41	1.06	1.01	0.96
42	1.07	1.03	0.98	42	1.07	1.03	0.97
43	1.09	1.04	1	43	1.09	1.04	0.99

Table 34: Tables of factors to be applied to the standard contribution rate to assess the age specific contribution rate

GAD Table 7.1 Men				GAD Table 7.2 Women			
Age last birthday at dismissal	Normal Retirement Age - Men			Age last birthday at dismissal	Normal Retirement Age - Women		
	55	60	65		55	60	65
44	1.11	1.06	1.01	44	1.11	1.06	1
45	1.12	1.08	1.03	45	1.12	1.08	1.02
46	1.14	1.09	1.05	46	1.14	1.09	1.03
47	1.16	1.11	1.06	47	1.16	1.11	1.05
48	1.18	1.13	1.08	48	1.18	1.13	1.07
49	1.2	1.15	1.09	49	1.2	1.14	1.08
50	1.22	1.16	1.11	50	1.21	1.16	1.1
51	1.24	1.18	1.13	51	1.23	1.18	1.12
52	1.26	1.2	1.15	52	1.25	1.2	1.14
53	1.28	1.22	1.17	53	1.28	1.22	1.15
54	1.3	1.24	1.18	54	1.3	1.24	1.17
55		1.27	1.2	55		1.26	1.19
56		1.29	1.22	56		1.28	1.21
57		1.31	1.24	57		1.3	1.23
58		1.33	1.27	58		1.33	1.25
59		1.36	1.29	59		1.35	1.27
60			1.31	60			1.3
61			1.34	61			1.32
62			1.37	62			1.35
63			1.39	63			1.37
64			1.42	64			1.4

Table 35: State pension age for women born on or before 5 December 1953

For WOMEN born	State Pension Date
On or before 5 April 1950	Age 60
6 April 1950 to 5 May 1950	6 May 2010
6 May 1950 to 5 June 1950	6 July 2010
6 June 1950 to 5 July 1950	6 September 2010
6 July 1950 to 5 August 1950	6 November 2010
6 August 1950 to 5 September 1950	6 January 2011
6 September 1950 to 5 October 1950	6 March 2011
6 October 1950 to 5 November 1950	6 May 2011
6 November 1950 to 5 December 1950	6 July 2011
6 December 1950 to 5 January 1951	6 September 2011
6 January 1951 to 5 February 1951	6 November 2011
6 February 1951 to 5 March 1951	6 January 2012
6 March 1951 to 5 April 1951	6 March 2012

Table 35: State pension age for women born on or before 5 December 1953

For WOMEN born	State Pension Date
6 April 1951 to 5 May 1951	6 May 2012
6 May 1951 to 5 June 1951	6 July 2012
6 June 1951 to 5 July 1951	6 September 2012
6 July 1951 to 5 August 1951	6 November 2012
6 August 1951 to 5 September 1951	6 January 2013
6 September 1951 to 5 October 1951	6 March 2013
6 October 1951 to 5 November 1951	6 May 2013
6 November 1951 to 5 December 1951	6 July 2013
6 December 1951 to 5 January 1952	6 September 2013
6 January 1952 to 5 February 1952	6 November 2013
6 February 1952 to 5 March 1952	6 January 2014
6 March 1952 to 5 April 1952	6 March 2014
6 April 1952 to 5 May 1952	6 May 2014
6 May 1952 to 5 June 1952	6 July 2014
6 June 1952 to 5 July 1952	6 September 2014
6 July 1952 to 5 August 1952	6 November 2014
6 August 1952 to 5 September 1952	6 January 2015
6 September 1952 to 5 October 1952	6 March 2015
6 October 1952 to 5 November 1952	6 May 2015
6 November 1952 to 5 December 1952	6 July 2015
6 December 1952 to 5 January 1953	6 September 2015
6 January 1953 to 5 February 1953	6 November 2015
6 February 1953 to 5 March 1953	6 January 2016
6 March 1953 to 5 April 1953	6 March 2016
6 April 1953 to 5 May 1953	6 July 2016
6 May 1953 to 5 June 1953	6 November 2016
6 June 1953 to 5 July 1953	6 March 2017
6 July 1953 to 5 August 1953	6 July 2017
6 August 1953 to 5 September 1953	6 November 2017
6 September 1953 to 5 October 1953	6 March 2018
6 October 1953 to 5 November 1953	6 July 2018
6 November 1953 to 5 December 1953	6 November 2018

Table 36: State pension age for men and women born after 5 December 1953	
For MEN born	**State Pension Date**
On or before 5 December 1953	Age 65
For MEN and WOMEN born	**State Pension Date**
6 December 1953 to 5 January 1954	6 March 2019
6 January 1954 to 5 February 1954	6 May 2019
6 February 1954 to 5 March 1954	6 July 2019
6 March 1954 to 5 April 1954	6 September 2019
6 April 1954 to 5 May 1954	6 November 2019
6 May 1954 to 5 June 1954	6 January 2020
6 June 1954 to 5 July 1954	6 March 2020
6 July 1954 to 5 August 1954	6 May 2020
6 August 1954 to 5 September 1954	6 July 2020
6 September 1954 to 5 October 1954	6 September 2020
6 October 1954 to 5 April 1968	66th birthday
6 April 1968 to 5 May 1968	6 May 2034
6 May 1968 to 5 June 1968	6 July 2034
6 June 1968 to 5 July 1968	6 September 2034
6 July 1968 to 5 August 1968	6 November 2034
6 August 1968 to 5 September 1968	6 January 2035
6 September 1968 to 5 October 1968	6 March 2035
6 October 1968 to 5 November 1968	6 May 2035
6 November 1968 to 5 December 1968	6 July 2035
6 December 1968 to 5 January 1969	6 September 2035
6 January 1969 to 5 February 1969	6 November 2035
6 February 1969 to 5 March 1969	6 January 2036
6 March 1969 to 5 April 1969	6 March 2036
6 April 1969 to 5 April 1977	67th birthday ⯑
6 April 1977 to 5 May 1977	6 May 2044
6 May 1977 to 5 June 1977	6 July 2044
6 June 1977 to 5 July 1977	6 September 2044
6 July 1977 to 5 August 1977	6 November 2044
6 August 1977 to 5 September 1977	6 January 2045
6 September 1977 to 5 October 1977	6 March 2045
6 October 1977 to 5 November 1977	6 May 2045
6 November 1977 to 5 December 1977	6 July 2045
6 December 1977 to 5 January 1978	6 September 2045
6 January 1978 to 5 February 1978	6 November 2045
6 February 1978 to 5 March 1978	6 January 2046
6 March 1978 to 5 April 1978	6 March 2046

Redundancy and statutory notice

Table 37: Statutory Redundancy

Age	| 2	3	4	5	6	7	8	9	10	11	12	13	14	15	16	17	18	19	20
							Number of years continuous service												
17	1	-	-	-	-	-	-	-	-	-	-	-	-	-	-	-	-	-	-
18	1	1½	-	-	-	-	-	-	-	-	-	-	-	-	-	-	-	-	-
19	1	1½	2	-	-	-	-	-	-	-	-	-	-	-	-	-	-	-	-
20	1	1½	2	2½	-	-	-	-	-	-	-	-	-	-	-	-	-	-	-
21	1	1½	2	2½	3	-	-	-	-	-	-	-	-	-	-	-	-	-	-
22	1	1½	2	2½	3	3½	-	-	-	-	-	-	-	-	-	-	-	-	-
23	1½	2	2½	3	3½	4	4½	-	-	-	-	-	-	-	-	-	-	-	-
24	2	2½	3	3½	4	4½	5	5½	-	-	-	-	-	-	-	-	-	-	-
25	2	3	3½	4	4½	5	5½	6	6½	-	-	-	-	-	-	-	-	-	-
26	2	3	4	4½	5	5½	6	6½	7	7½	-	-	-	-	-	-	-	-	-
27	2	3	4	5	5½	6	6½	7	7½	8	8½	-	-	-	-	-	-	-	-
28	2	3	4	5	6	6½	7	7½	8	8½	9	9½	-	-	-	-	-	-	-
29	2	3	4	5	6	7	7½	8	8½	9	9½	10	10½	-	-	-	-	-	-
30	2	3	4	5	6	7	8	8½	9	9½	10	10½	11	11½	-	-	-	-	-
31	2	3	4	5	6	7	8	9	9½	10	10½	11	11½	12	12½	-	-	-	-
32	2	3	4	5	6	7	8	9	10	10½	11	11½	12	12½	13	13½	-	-	-
33	2	3	4	5	6	7	8	9	10	11	11½	12	12½	13	13½	14	14½	-	-
34	2	3	4	5	6	7	8	9	10	11	12	12½	13	13½	14	14½	15	15½	-
35	2	3	4	5	6	7	8	9	10	11	12	13	13½	14	14½	15	15½	16	16½
36	2	3	4	5	6	7	8	9	10	11	12	13	14	14½	15	15½	16	16½	17
37	2	3	4	5	6	7	8	9	10	11	12	13	14	15	15½	16	16½	17	17½
38	2	3	4	5	6	7	8	9	10	11	12	13	14	15	16	16½	17	17½	18
39	2	3	4	5	6	7	8	9	10	11	12	13	14	15	16	17	17½	18	18½
40	2	3	4	5	6	7	8	9	10	11	12	13	14	15	16	17	18	18½	19
41	2	3	4	5	6	7	8	9	10	11	12	13	14	15	16	17	18	19	19½
42	2½	3½	4½	5½	6½	7½	8½	9½	10½	11½	12½	13½	14½	15½	16½	17½	18½	19½	20½
43	3	4	5	6	7	8	9	10	11	12	13	14	15	16	17	18	19	20	21
44	3	4½	5½	6½	7½	8½	9½	10½	11½	12½	13½	14½	15½	16½	17½	18½	19½	20½	21½
45	3	4½	6	7	8	9	10	11	12	13	14	15	16	17	18	19	20	21	22
46	3	4½	6	7½	8½	9½	10½	11½	12½	13½	14½	15½	16½	17½	18½	19½	20½	21½	22½
47	3	4½	6	7½	9	10	11	12	13	14	15	16	17	18	19	20	21	22	23
48	3	4½	6	7½	9	10½	11½	12½	13½	14½	15½	16½	17½	18½	19½	20½	21½	22½	23½
49	3	4½	6	7½	9	10½	12	13	14	15	16	17	18	19	20	21	22	23	24
50	3	4½	6	7½	9	10½	12	13½	14½	15½	16½	17½	18½	19½	20½	21½	22½	23½	24½
51	3	4½	6	7½	9	10½	12	13½	15	16	17	18	19	20	21	22	23	24	25
52	3	4½	6	7½	9	10½	12	13½	15	16½	17½	18½	19½	20½	21½	22½	23½	24½	25½
53	3	4½	6	7½	9	10½	12	13½	15	16½	18	19	20	21	22	23	24	25	26
54	3	4½	6	7½	9	10½	12	13½	15	16½	18	19½	20½	21½	22½	23½	24½	25½	26½

Table 37: Statutory Redundancy

	Number of years continuous service																		
	2	3	4	5	6	7	8	9	10	11	12	13	14	15	16	17	18	19	20
55	3	4½	6	7½	9	10½	12	13½	15	16½	18	19½	21	22	23	24	25	26	27
56	3	4½	6	7½	9	10½	12	13½	15	16½	18	19½	21	22½	23½	24½	25½	26½	27½
57	3	4½	6	7½	9	10½	12	13½	15	16½	18	19½	21	22½	24	25	26	27	28
58	3	4½	6	7½	9	10½	12	13½	15	16½	18	19½	21	22½	24	25½	26½	27½	28½
59	3	4½	6	7½	9	10½	12	13½	15	16½	18	19½	21	22½	24	25½	27	28	29
60	3	4½	6	7½	9	10½	12	13½	15	16½	18	19½	21	22½	24	25½	27	28½	29½
61+	3	4½	6	7½	9	10½	1 2	13½	15	16½	18	19½	21	22½	24	25½	27	28½	30

Table 38: Statutory Notice Periods

Period of continuous employment (years)	Minimum period of notice (weeks)
Less than 2 years (but more than 1 month)	1
At least 2 but less than 3	2
At least 3 but less than 4	3
At least 4 but less than 5	4
At least 5 but less than 6	5
At least 6 but less than 7	6
At least 7 but less than 8	7
At least 8 but less than 9	8
At least 9 but less than 10	9
At least 10 but less than 11	10
At least 11 but less than 12	11
More than 12	12

Statutory rates

Table 39: National Minimum Wage Rates

Year	Adult Rate (for workers aged 22+ until 2010 when this rate applied to those aged 21+) (for workers aged 18-21)	Development Rate (for 18 to 20 year olds)	16-17 year olds rate	Apprentice rate*
01/10/2009 to 30/09/2010	£5.80	£4.83	£3.57	
01/10/2010 to 30/09/2011	£5.93	£4.92	£3.64	£2.50
01/10/2011 to 30/09/2012	£6.08	£4.98	£3.68	£2.60
01/10/2012 to 30/09/2013	£6.19	£4.98	£3.68	£2.65
01/10/2013 to 30/09/2014	£6.31	£5.03	£3.72	£2.68
01/10/2014 to 30/09/2015	£6.50	£5.13	£3.79	£2.73

* This rate is for apprentices under 19 or those in their first year. For anyone over the age of 19, and past their first year, the rate is applicable to the age

Table 40: Statutory maternity, paternity, adoption and sick pay rates

	Statutory Maternity Pay (SMP)	Ordinary Statutory Paternity Pay (OSPP) (payable for up to 2 weeks) and Additional Statutory Paternity Pay (ASOO) (remaining weeks up to 39)	Statutory Adoption Pay (SAP) (payable for up to 39 weeks)	Statutory Sick Pay (SSP)
01/04/2012 - 06/04/2013	90% of average weekly gross pay for first 6 weeks; and then £135.45 or 90% of average gross weekly earnings (whichever is lower) for the next 33 weeks	£135.45 or 90% of average gross weekly earnings (whichever is lower)	£135.45 or 90% of average gross weekly earnings (whichever is lower)	£85.85 per week
07/04/2013- 05/04/2014*	90% of average weekly gross pay for first 6 weeks; and then £136.78 or 90% of average gross weekly earnings (whichever is lower) for the next 33 weeks	£136.78 or 90% of average gross weekly earnings (whichever is lower)	£136.78 or 90% of average gross weekly earnings (whichever is lower)	£86.70 per week (*for sick days between 06/04/2013 to 05/04/2014
From 06/04/2014	90% of average weekly gross pay for first 6 weeks; and then £138.18 or 90% of average gross weekly earnings (whichever is lower) for the next 33 weeks	£138.18 or 90% of average gross weekly earnings (whichever is lower)	£138.18 or 90% of average gross weekly earnings (whichever is lower)	£87.55 per week

APPENDIX 1:
Presidential Guidance – General Case Management (published 14 March 2014)

REMEDY

What is remedy?

1) After a tribunal has decided whether the claimant's claim succeeds it will consider how a successful party should be compensated. This part of the judgment is called "Remedy". Sometimes it is done immediately after the merits judgment, but in long or complex cases it may be adjourned to another day.

2) The tribunal has different powers for each different type of claim. It must calculate loss and order an appropriate remedy for each part of a successful claim. Accurate and often detailed information from both parties is needed to make correct calculations and issue a judgment which is fair to all, but sometimes the tribunal can only estimate the loss, for example for how long a party may be out of work.

Different types of remedy

3) For some claims the only remedy is to order the employer to pay a sum of money – for example wages due, holiday and notice pay.

4) For unfair dismissal the tribunal may:

• order the employer to "reinstate" the dismissed employee, which is to put them back in their old job, as if they had not been dismissed; or to "re-engage" them, which is to employ them in a suitable different job. In each case the tribunal may order payment of lost earnings etc.

• If those orders are not sought by the claimant or are not practicable, it may order the employer to pay compensation, calculated in two parts: a "Basic Award", which is calculated in a similar way to a redundancy payment, and a "Compensatory Award", which is intended to compensate the employee for the financial loss suffered.

5) In claims of unlawful discrimination, the tribunal may;

• make a declaration setting out the parties' rights; and/or

• order compensation to be paid by the employer and/or fellow workers who have committed discriminatory acts, but if the employer can show that it has taken all reasonable steps to prevent employees from committing such acts (called the "Statutory Defence") the only award which can be made is against the fellow worker, not the employer; and/or

• make a recommendation, such as for the claimant's colleagues or managers to be given training to ensure that discrimination does not happen again.

Mitigation

6) All persons who have been subjected to wrongdoing are expected to do their best, within reasonable bounds, to limit the effects on them. If the tribunal concludes that a claimant has not done so, it must reduce the compensation so that a fair sum is payable. The tribunal will expect evidence to be provided by claimants about their attempts to obtain suitable alternative work; and by respondents who consider that the claimant has not tried hard enough, about other jobs which the claimant could have applied for. (See "Information needed for the tribunal to calculate remedy" below).

Statement of Remedy

7) The tribunal will usually order the claimant to make a calculation showing how each amount claimed has been worked out (eg. x weeks pay at £y per week). Sometimes this is called a "Schedule of Loss". As tribunals are expected to calculate remedy for each different type of loss - sometimes called "Heads of Loss" or "Heads of Damage"- the statement should show how much is claimed under each head. If the claimant has received state benefits it should also specify the type of benefit, the dates of receipt, the amount received and the claimant's national insurance number (see also "Recoupment" below).

8) Typical heads of loss include;

• wages due

• pay in lieu of notice, where no, or inadequate, notice was given

• outstanding holiday pay

- a basic award or redundancy payment

- past loss of earnings

- future loss of earnings

- loss of future pension entitlements

- in discrimination cases:

  - injury to feelings

  - aggravated or exemplary damages, (which are rare)

  - damages for personal injury- but only when the act of discrimination is the cause of the claimant becoming ill

- any tribunal fee paid

9) The tribunal will usually order the statement to be produced early in the proceedings, as it can help in settlement negotiations and when considering mediation, and when assessing the length of the hearing. It should however be updated near to the hearing date.

Submissions on *Polkey* and Contributory Fault

10) If an employee has been dismissed but the employer has not followed a proper procedure (such as the ACAS Code), tribunals will follow the guidance in Polkey v AE Dayton Services Limited and subsequent cases and consider whether, if a fair procedure had been followed, the claimant might still have been fairly dismissed, either at all, or at some later time. This question is often shortened to "Polkey". There are also cases where the dismissal may be procedurally unfair but the employee's own conduct has contributed to the position they now find themselves in. This is called "contributory conduct".

11) Where either or both of these are relevant, the tribunal will reduce the compensation awarded by an appropriate percentage in each case. This means that there may be two reductions, which, where there has been really serious misconduct, could be as high as 100%, so that nothing would be payable.

12) Generally the tribunal will decide these issues at the same time as it reaches its decision on the merits of the claim, and sometimes at a separate remedy hearing. It should explain at the start of the hearing which of those options it will follow, but if it does not, then the parties should ask for clarification of when they are expected to give evidence and make submissions (see separate guidance on "Timetabling") on these matters.

Injury to Feelings

13) In discrimination cases and some other detriment claims, tribunals may award a sum of money to compensate for injury to feelings. When they do so they must fix fair, reasonable and just compensation in the particular circumstances of the case, bearing in mind that compensation is designed to compensate the injured party not to punish the guilty one, and that awards should bear some relationship to those made by the courts for personal injury.

14) They follow guidelines first given in *Vento v Chief Constable of West Yorkshire Police*, which have since been updated by *Da Bell v NSPCC* and *Simmons v Castle*, but are still referred to as the "*Vento*" Guidelines. They identify three broad bands of compensation for injury to feelings as distinct from psychiatric or personal injury:

- The lower band is for less serious acts of discrimination. Awards in this band are currently between £660 and £6,600.

- The middle band is for cases which are more serious but do not come into the top band. These awards tend to be from £6,600 to £19,800.

- The top band is for the most serious cases such as where there has been a lengthy campaign of harassment. These awards are between £19,800 and £33,000, but are relatively rare. A case would have to be highly exceptional for any sum higher than this to be awarded.

15) Tribunals will expect claimants to explain in their statement of remedy which Vento band they consider their case falls in, and will also expect both parties to make submissions on this during the hearing.

Information needed for the tribunal to calculate remedy

16) This varies in each case dependant on what is being claimed. Each party should look for, provide to the other, and include in the bundle, copies of any of these which could help the tribunal with any necessary calculations in their case:

- Copy contract of employment or statement of terms & conditions with the old employer, including the date the claimant started work, and details of any pension scheme

• Copy pay slips for the last 13 weeks in the old employment or any other document showing the claimant's gross and net pay

• Proof of any payments actually made by the employer, such as a redundancy payment or pay in lieu of notice

• Any document recording the day s/he last actually worked

• Any document explaining how many days/hours per week the claimant worked

• Any document explaining how overtime is paid

• Any document recording when the holiday year starts,

• Any document recording when holiday has been taken in that year and what has been paid for those days

• Any documents setting out the terms of the former employer's pension scheme

• Any document showing the claimant's attempts to find other work

• Copy contract of employment and payslips for any new job

• Documents such as bank statements if losses for bank charges are claimed.

• Medical reports or "Fit" notes if unable to work since dismissal

• Any document showing that jobs were/are available in the locality for which the claimant could have applied.

17) The witness statements should tell the tribunal which parts of these documents are important and why. Providing enough information to the tribunal at an early stage could help to promote a settlement and so avoid a hearing.

Is all loss awarded?

18) For claims such as unpaid wages, holiday and notice pay the tribunal will order the difference between what should have been paid and what has actually been paid. Wages and holiday pay are usually calculated gross, but pay in lieu of notice is usually calculated net of tax and national insurance. The judgment should specify whether each

payment ordered has been calculated gross or net.

19) In the case of unfair dismissal there are several limits (called statutory caps) on what can be awarded:

• For the basic award there is a maximum sum for a week's pay, which, for dismissals on or after 1 February 2013, is£450 per week. It is usually increased each year.

• For the compensatory award there are two separate limits. The first is an overall maximum, which for dismissals on or after 1 February 2013 is £74,200 and usually increases each year. However under the Unfair Dismissal (Variation of the Limit of Compensatory Award) Order 2013, where the dismissal took effect on or after 29 July 2013 (subject to rules about the minimum notice having been given) the maximum which can be awarded to any individual is one year's salary.

• There is no limit to the maximum compensatory award where the reason for the dismissal was that the claimant made a Public Interest Disclosure, or complained of certain Health and Safety related matters, and no limit to an award for discrimination, as long as it genuinely compensates for loss actually incurred as a result of the discrimination.

Grossing up

20) The rules on when tax is payable on awards made by tribunals are too complex for inclusion here. When it is clear that the claimant will have to pay tax on the sum awarded, the tribunal will award a higher figure, calculated so that tax can be paid and the claimant will receive the net sum which properly represents the loss. This calculation is called "grossing up".

Interest

21) There are two separate situations where interest is relevant.

22) Firstly, when a tribunal calculates compensation for discrimination, it is obliged to consider awarding interest. If it decides to do so, it calculates interest from the date of the act of discrimination up to the date of the calculation, except for interest on lost wages, where the calculation is done from the middle of that period (as that is simpler than calculating interest separately on each missing wage but leads to a roughly similar result). The tribunal will then include that

interest in the award made. For claims presented on or after 29 July 2013 the rate of interest is 8%. For claims presented before that date, it is 0.5%.

23) In addition, interest of 8% is payable on awards for all claims if they are not paid when due. In respect of all claims presented on or after 29 July 2013 interest is calculated from the day after the day upon which the written judgment was sent to the parties, unless payment is actually made within the first 14 days, in which case no interest is payable. For claims presented before 29 July, interest is payable 42 days after the day upon which the written judgment was sent to the parties.

24) Employment Tribunals play no part in enforcing payment of the awards they make. That is done by the civil courts, who issue separate guidance on how to enforce payments.

Recoupment

25) For some claims, such as unfair dismissal, if the claimant has received certain state benefits the tribunal is obliged to ensure that the employer responsible for causing the loss of earnings reimburses the State for the benefits paid. In those cases the tribunal will order only part of the award to be paid to the claimant straight away, with the rest set aside until the respondent is told by the State how much the benefits were. The respondent then pays that money to the State and anything left over to the claimant. This is called "recoupment". The judge should set out in the judgment whether or not recoupment applies, and if it does, how much of the award is set aside for recoupment purposes. If either party is in any doubt about recoupment, they should ask the Judge to explain how it affects them.

APPENDIX 2: Sample schedule of loss

Claimant's schedule of loss – Green v XYZ Ltd

Background

Mrs Green, who was born on 14/02/1981, started work with XYZ Ltd on 24/10/2008. Her gross weekly salary was £1,600.00 and her net weekly salary, after the deduction of tax and employee national insurance, was £1,200.00. She was a member of the employer's defined benefit pension scheme, the details of which are added below. On 05/04/2012, she was dismissed summarily for gross misconduct and was given £1,000 as payment in lieu of notice. Her contractual notice period was 8 weeks. Mrs Green found part time work from 23/07/2012 until the date of the Tribunal hearing, earning a net amount of £15,523 up until the date of the hearing. This arrangement was expected to continue for the next few months at least. Mrs Green was not eligible to join the pension scheme in her new job until she had worked for them for 2 years.

The date of the remedies hearing was set to be 03/01/2013.

Mrs Green's claims

- On 28/06/2012 Mrs Green brought claims of unfair and wrongful dismissal and sex discrimination at the ET.

- She maintained it would take a year to find another equivalent permanent job and therefore was claiming future loss of earnings until 05/04/2013.

- She was entitled to a sum representing loss of statutory rights.

- Any award should be increased by 25% for the failure of the employer to comply with the Code of Practice.

- She was entitled to a sum of £850 representing untaken accrued holiday which the respondent had not paid on termination.

- She claimed a sum of £18,000 for injury to feelings and interest on this figure, from 01/01/2010 until 01/01/2012.

- Mrs Green argued that as it would take 2 years for her to become eligible to join the pension scheme in her new job she wants to be compensated for loss of pension for that time.

Pension information

- Mrs Green's normal retirement date is 14/02/2046 (i.e. at age 65).

- Her pensionable pay at the date of dismissal was £1,200.

- Her employer contributed 12% of its wage bill to the private pension scheme.

- The scheme administrator valued Mrs Green's deferred pension at EDT as £3,000.

Respondent's Counter Schedule of Loss – Green v XYZ Ltd

Counter arguments

- The claimant's schedule of loss does not include her expected earnings, which are estimated to be £3,000 from the date of the hearing to the date when the employer's liability ends. This needs to be recorded.

- The respondent disputes the 25% uplift for failing to follow the Code of Practice for unfair dismissal, submitting that the figure should be closer to 10%.

- The respondent also submits that the claimant was also partly responsible for her own dismissal to the extent of 10% (for both the basic and compensatory awards).

- There is a 10% chance that the claimant would not have remained in the pension scheme until normal retirement so this needs to be reflected in the pension calculation.

- A deduction of 2% should also be made for accelerated payment of future sums of compensation.

- The sum of £18,000 for injury to feelings is disputed – there was no discriminatory conduct on the part of the respondent.

- The compensation cap should be applied to the final figure since the dismissal of the claimant was not discriminatory.

IN THE EMPLOYMENT TRIBUNALS
CASE NO: 3452/87

BETWEEN

Green
AND
XYZ

CLAIMANT'S SCHEDULE OF LOSS

1. Details

Date of birth	14/02/1981
Date started employment	24/10/2008
Effective Date of Termination	05/04/2012
Period of continuous service (years)	3
Age at Effective Date of Termination	31
Remedy hearing date	03/01/2013
Cut-off date for future loss of earnings	05/04/2013
Contractual notice period (weeks)	8
Statutory notice period (weeks)	3
Net weekly pay at EDT	£1,200.00
Gross weekly pay at EDT	£1,600.00

2. Basic award

Number of qualifying weeks (3) x Gross weekly pay (£430.00[1])	£1,290.00
Total basic award	**£1,290.00**

3. Damages for wrongful dismissal

Loss of earnings: Damages period (8) x Net weekly pay (£1,200)	£9,600.00
Plus failure by employer to follow statutory procedures @ 25%[2]	2,400.00[3]
Total damages	**£12,000.00**

---

[1] £430 was the limit on a week's pay at an EDT of 05/04/2012

[2] The ACAS uplift can also apply to damages for wrongful dismissal – see *Adjustments and order of adjustments* and Schedule A2 of TULR(C)A

[3] £9,600 x 0.25

4. Compensatory award (immediate loss)

Loss of net earnings: Number of weeks (31[4]) x Net weekly pay (£1,200)	£37,200.00
Plus loss of statutory rights	£350.00
Plus accrued holiday pay	£850.00
Less payment in lieu	-£1,000.00
Less earnings: (23/07/2012 to 03/01/2013)	-£15,523.00
Pension loss	
Gross weekly pensionable pay (£1,200.00) x % of pensionable pay paid (12) x Multiplying factor (0.83[5]) x Number of weeks (31)	£3,705.12
Loss of enhancement of accrued pension rights: Deferred pension (3,000.00) x Multiplying factor (4.53[6])	£13,590.00
Total compensation (immediate loss)	**£39,172.12**

5. Compensatory award (future loss)

Loss of future earnings: Number of weeks (13.1) x Net Weekly pay (£1,200.00)	£15,720.00
Future loss of pension	£7,768.80
Number of weeks (65) x Gross weekly pensionable pay (£1,200.00) x % contributed by employer (12 x Multiplying factor (0.83)	
Total compensation (future loss)	**£ 23,488.80**

6. Adjustments to total compensatory award

Failure by employer to follow statutory procedures @ 25%	£15,665.23[7]
Compensatory award before adjustments	**£62,660.92**
Total adjustments to the compensatory award	**£15,665.23**
Compensatory award after adjustments	**£78,326.15**

---

[4] 31 weeks has been calculated by subtracting the damages period of 8 weeks from the total number of weeks between EDT and the hearing date

[5] This multiplier has been taken from Table 7.2 Appendix 7 of the Employment Tribunal Guidelines: Compensation for Loss of Pension Rights (Age last birthday is 31, Normal Retirement Age is 65)

[6] This multiplier has been taken from Table 4.3 Appendix 3 of the Employment Tribunal Guidelines: Compensation for Loss of Pension Rights (Private Sector Scheme, Age last birthday is 31, Normal Retirement Age is 65)

[7] (£39,172.12 + £23,488.80) x 0.25. Remember that accrued holiday pay which has not been paid can be classed as unlawful deductions and thus uplifted according to Schedule A2 of TULR(C)A

7. Discrimination

Injury to feelings	£18,000.00
Plus interest @ 0.5% for 730 days	£180.00[8]
Discrimination award	**£18,180.00**

8. Summary totals

Basic award	£1,290.00
Wrongful dismissal	£12,000.00
Compensation award	£78,326.15
Discrimination	£18,180.00
TOTAL	**£109,796.15**
TOTAL AFTER GROSSING UP AT 40%	**£150,306.92[9]**

---

[8] £18,000 x 0.005 x 730 ÷ 365

[9] (£1,290.00 + £12,000.00 + £78,326.15 - £850.00) - £30,000.00 = £90,766.15 - £30,000.00 = £60,766.15. Remember that the £850 holiday pay should not be grossed up since it should be paid gross by the employer. Nor should the injury to feelings figure because it is thought this will not be taxable.

Grossed up at 40% = £60,766.15 ÷ 0.6 = £101,276.92

Add back £18,180.00 + £30,000.00 + £850 = £150,306.92

The statutory cap does not apply since the claimant is claiming that the dismissal was for discriminatory reasons (see Respondent's counter schedule).

IN THE EMPLOYMENT TRIBUNALS
CASE NO: 3452/87

BETWEEN

Green
AND
XYZ

RESPONDENT'S COUNTER SCHEDULE OF LOSS

1. Details

Date of birth	14/02/1981
Date started employment	24/10/2008
Effective Date of Termination	05/04/2012
Period of continuous service (years)	3
Age at Effective Date of Termination	31
Remedy hearing date	03/01/2013
Cut-off date for future loss of earnings	05/04/2013
Contractual notice period (weeks)	8
Statutory notice period (weeks)	3
Net weekly pay at EDT	£1,200
Gross weekly pay at EDT	£1,600

2. Basic award

Number of qualifying weeks (3) x Gross weekly pay (£430.00)	£1,290.00
Less contributory fault @ 10%	-£129.00
Total basic award	**£1,161.00**

3. Damages for wrongful dismissal

Loss of earnings: Damages period (8) x Net weekly pay (£1,200)	£9,600.00
Plus failure by employer to follow statutory procedures @ 10%	£960.00
Total damages	**£10,560.00**

4. Compensatory award (immediate loss)

Loss of net earnings: Number of weeks (31) x Net weekly pay (£1,200)	£37,200.00
Plus loss of statutory rights	£350.00
Plus accrued holiday pay	£850.00
Less payment in lieu	-£1,000.00
Less earnings: (23/07/2012 to 03/01/2013)	-£15,523.00

Pension loss

Gross weekly pensionable pay (£1,200.00) x % of pensionable pay paid (12) x Multiplying factor (0.83) x Number of weeks (31)	£3,705.12
Loss of enhancement of accrued pension rights Deferred pension (£3,000.00) x Multiplier (4.53) x % for chance of withdrawal (10)	£12,231.00[10]
Total compensation (immediate loss)	**£37,813.12**

5. Compensatory award (future loss)

Loss of future earnings: Number of weeks (13.1) x Net Weekly pay (£1,200)	£15,720.00
Less expected future earnings (04/01/2013 to 05/04/2013)	-£3,000.00
Future loss of pension Number of weeks (65) x Gross weekly pensionable pay (£1,200.00) x % contributed by employer (12) x Multiplying factor (0.83)	£7,768.80
Total compensation (future loss)	**£20,488.80**

---

[10] £3,000 x 4.53 x 0.9

6. Adjustments to total compensatory award

Less accelerated payment	-£409.78[11]
Plus failure by employer to follow statutory procedures (ACAS uplift) @ 10%	£5,789.21[12]
Less contributory fault (compensation award) @ 10%	-£6,283.13[13]
Compensatory award before adjustments	**£58,301.92**
Total adjustments to the compensatory award	**-£903.70[14]**
Compensatory award after adjustments	**£57,398.22**

7. Summary totals

Basic award	£1,161.00
Wrongful dismissal	£10,560.00
Compensatory award	£57,398.22
TOTAL	**£69,119.22**
GROSSING UP AT 40%	**£94,632.03[15]**
AFTER STATUTORY CAP OF £72,300.00[16]	**£84,871.00[17]**

---

[11] Accelerated payment only applies to future loss. The future loss figure is £20,488.80 and 2% of this figure is £20,488.80 x 0.02 = £409.78

[12] Immediate loss + future loss – accelerated receipt = £37,813.12 + £20,488.80 - £409.78 = £57,892.14. The ACAS adjustment should now be applied to this figure = £57,892.14 x 0.1 = £5,789.21

[13] This has been calculated by first adding together the immediate loss, future loss and ACAS uplift, and deducting the sums for accelerated receipt to get £37,813.12 + £20,488.80 + £5,789.21 - £409.78 = £63,681.35

Next, the contributory fault deduction needs to be applied to this new figure but LESS the £850 holiday pay sum because contributory fault does not apply to holiday pay. This now becomes: (£63,681.35 - £850) x 0.1 = £6,283.13

[14] £409.78 + £5,789.21 - £6,283.13

[15] (£1,161.00 + £10,560.00 + £57,398.22 - £850) - £30,000 = £68,269.22 - £30,000 = £38,269.22. Remember that the £850 holiday pay should not be grossed up since it should be paid gross by the employer.

Grossed up at 40% = £38,269.22 ÷ 0.6 = £63,782.03

Add back £30,000 + £850 = £94,632.03

[16] This was the statutory cap applicable at an EDT of 05/04/2012 (see Table 1)

[17] First, we need to find out what the compensatory award is after the grossing up has been done. £18,279 was tax free (because £30,000 - £1,161.00 - £10,560.00 = £18,279). The balance i.e. £38,269.22 was grossed up to get £63,782.03.

Thus the total compensatory award = £18,279 + £63,782.03 (excluding the holiday pay) = £82,061.03 which exceeds the statutory cap. Therefore the total award is: £1,161 + £10,560 + £72,300 + £850 = £84,871. Remember that the £850 holiday pay does not count towards the compensation cap.